GALLUS

GALLUS

SCOTLAND, ENGLAND AND THE 1967 WORLD CUP FINAL

MICHAEL McEWAN

POLARIS
PUBLISHING

POLARIS PUBLISHING LTD
c/o Aberdein Considine
2nd Floor, Elder House
Multrees Walk
Edinburgh
EH1 3DX

www.polarispublishing.com

Text copyright © Michael McEwan, 2023

ISBN: 9781913538972
eBook ISBN: 9781913538989

The right of Michael McEwan to be identified as the authors of this work has been asserted by him in accordance with the Copyright, Designs and Patents Act 1988.

Interviews have been edited and condensed for clarity.

All rights reserved. No part of this publication may be reproduced, stored or transmitted in any form, or by any means electronic, mechanical, photocopying, recording or otherwise, without the express written permission of the publisher.

The views expressed in this book do not necessarily reflect the views, opinions or policies of Polaris Publishing Ltd (Company No. SC401508) (Polaris), nor those of any persons, organisations or commercial partners connected with the same (Connected Persons). Any opinions, advice, statements, services, offers, or other information or content expressed by third parties are not those of Polaris or any Connected Persons but those of the third parties. For the avoidance of doubt, neither Polaris nor any Connected Persons assume any responsibility or duty of care whether contractual, delictual or on any other basis towards any person in respect of any such matter and accept no liability for any loss or damage caused by any such matter in this book.

Every effort has been made to trace copyright holders and obtain their permission for the use of copyright material. The publisher apologises for any errors or omissions and would be grateful if notified of any corrections that should be incorporated in future reprints or editions of this book.

British Library Cataloguing-in-Publication Data
A catalogue record for this book is available on request from the British Library.

Designed and typeset by Polaris Publishing, Edinburgh
Printed in Great Britain by CPI Group (UK) Ltd, Croydon, CR0 4YY

For Juliet and Sadie.

CONTENTS

FOREWORD — xi
PROLOGUE — xvii
1: SO MUCH BICKERING — 1
2: THE WINTER GAME — 12
3: BROWN AMATEURISM — 18
4: EURO VISION — 27
5: WEAK, PUNY AND BESPECTACLED — 33
6: AN IMMOVABLE OBJECT, AN UNSTOPPABLE FORCE — 45
7: THE KNIGHT ACROSS THE TABLE — 55
8: HAVIN' A HAFFEY — 73
9: SEND FOR A SAINT — 83
10: QUIVERING FAULT LINES — 91
11: THE PROMISED LAND — 105
12: RUNNERS & RIDERS — 116
13: THE BIRDS OF THE COWDENBEATH PALAIS — 125
14: MR BROWN'S BOYS — 137
15: FAITHER — 145
16: A BOY AND THE DOC — 153
17: ORIGINAL WIZARDS — 168
18: 'WE CAN DO IT!' — 175
19: AND SO IT BEGINS — 182

20: WILLIAM WALLACE	187
21: SMOKED SALMON & ROAST BEEF	194
22: JIMMY CLITHEROE'S SON	203
23: THE RESURRECTION OF HARRY LAUDER	212
24: SOME PEOPLE ARE ON THE PITCH	228
25: THE OLD JOCK AND HAGGIS BIT	233
26: A CAT CALLED WEMBLEY	240
27: GLORIOUS FAILURE	247
28: STOP THE WORLD	257
29: WHERE THE GREEN GRASS GROWS	272
30: WHAT HAPPENED NEXT?	277
EPILOGUE	291
APPENDIX A	296
APPENDIX B	300
APPENDIX C	303
NOTES	307
SELECTED BIBLIOGRAPHY	309
ACKNOWLEDGEMENTS	312
ABOUT THE AUTHOR	315
INDEX	316

'Such seems to be the disposition of man, that whatever makes a distinction produces rivalry.'
Samuel Johnson

'The reason birds can fly and we can't is simply because they have perfect faith, for to have faith is to have wings.'
J.M. Barrie

FOREWORD

IN SEPTEMBER 2016, exactly two years after a referendum on Scottish independence came down narrowly on the side of the Union, a YouGov poll attempted to define – at once, if not for all – what it is that makes a person 'Scottish'.

According to the Scottish Government, all British citizens born in Scotland as well as all British citizens habitually resident in Scotland would, at a stroke, be considered Scottish in the event of independence. Beyond that, anybody with a Scottish parent or grandparent, or who had lived in Scotland for ten years and had established an ongoing connection to the country, would be eligible to apply for citizenship.

The study discovered that most Scots believe 'being Scottish' is a birth right and not something that can be applied for. Just over a quarter (28%) added they consider themselves to be Scottish, not British, as compared to only 6% who *feel* more British than Scottish.

Whilst broadly interesting, the study failed to account for some of the more abstract ideas of national identity. The intangibles, if you will. Identity, many believe, is a combination of who you are and who you feel you are – and it is a concept that varies from country to country. The UK is an object example of this.

'United' in a legislative sense if nothing else, the country is split into four nations, each with its own sense of identity, and often multiple different interpretations thereof. It is clear that these differences have intensified in the post-war era. A shrinking empire, combined with a struggling economy and a dwindling status in world affairs – not to mention greater scrutiny of a political structure which, as an example, has seen Scotland governed by multiple Tory governments, despite not voting for one since 1955 – has weakened the historic conceptualisation of 'Britishness'.

Regardless of your viewpoint, the consensus is that, by the mid to late 20th century, Britishness had declined in tandem with the advent or rebirth of 'historic' nationalism.

Whilst there were multiple social, economic and political factors that contributed to this, as we will come to, football played an irrefutably significant role in this pivot. The union was on fire and football was a jerrycan of petrol.

You see, unlike many other sports – and, for that matter, the Olympics – football in the United Kingdom was contested by teams representing the constituent parts of the country. The very first international match (more of which later) was contested by England and Scotland in November 1872. A decade later, the British Home Championship was established. As Matthew Taylor acknowledged in his book *The Association Game*, football fostered a series of singular national identities at the expense of the all-encompassing state.

This rang particularly true north of Hadrian's Wall. In *Sport and National Identity in the Post-War World*, Adrian Smith and Dilwyn Porter argued that Scotland's political evolution 'has been refracted through the prism of sport'. Bert Moorhouse, a sociologist at the University of Glasgow, went even further, arguing that sport had 'nurtured a continuing sense of national resentment against England', with parallels drawn between victories on the pitch and, say, the Battle of Bannockburn in 1314. As the great sportswriter Hugh McIlvanney once put it: 'There's only one thing better than beating England, and that's having to sit with nine Englishmen at the post-match dinner.'

Call it whatever you like – Anglophobia, xenophobia, bigotry, nativism, jingoism, prejudice, patriotism or harmless banter – there is no doubt that rivalry is one of the bedrocks of national identity.

Bobby Charlton and Denis Law, two men central to this book, illustrate the point perfectly. Close friends and teammates in Sir Matt Busby's all-conquering Manchester United side of the 1960s, they were fierce opponents – strangers, almost – whenever Scotland played England.

'If I had to pick a single, dominating aspect of [Denis's] character, apart from the tremendous commitment which marked his play, and which set him apart as much as his dramatic talent, it would be his sheer Scottishness,' wrote Charlton in his autobiography.

'Whenever we [Charlton and his brother Jack] played Scotland, Denis made sure to kick us both and call us English bastards within the first minute or so. It was as though he had been obliged to make a statement and having done so, he could then get on with the game.'

'I know all Scots aren't the same,' he added, 'but I do love the way so many of them see a love of their country as something at the heart of their existence and how it has always been so passionately expressed on the football field. Often, there is a show of toughness and quite a bit of bluster but you have to be so perceptive to see that at its core is deep pride in their people and a tough view of the world.

'I believe that it is part of the Scottish education in life, if not officially in the schoolroom agenda, to compete with most determination against England.'

That much is certainly true. The Scottish school history syllabus covers everything from the Battle of Bannockburn to the Jacobite uprising and the defeat at Culloden. The English school history syllabus does not.

Charlton recounts a story of his first time travelling to Scotland to represent England. 'I remember the bus journey from Troon up to Glasgow. It seemed that there was scarcely a house where someone wasn't hanging out of a window shouting the Scottish equivalent of, "You'll get nowt today." Sometimes we did, sometimes we didn't, but there was always one certainty: if there was ever a Scottish deficit, it would never be one of the heart.'

In his own memoir, Law acknowledged the importance of beating the 'Auld Enemy'. Due to his career coinciding with the aforementioned British Home Championship, Law faced England on a regular basis. Nine of his fifty-five Scotland caps, indeed, came against the 'Three Lions'.

'Those games were the be all and end all for many Scots,' he wrote. 'Some would save up for two years in order to attend the Wembley game. When I was a kid, the fixture was the highlight of the season. We were brought up on tales of the "Wee Blue Devils".' Those stories of the legendary Scotland team of 1928 that beat England 5–1 at Wembley 'were embedded in your brain,' said Law.

He added: 'If there was one thing any young Scot dreamed about, it was to watch Scotland beat England at Wembley; when you became a player, you dreamed of playing in one of those games and scoring the winning goal. It might not have meant as much to the English but to us it was everything. For me, as a player, it lived up to everything I had dreamed of.'

Of course, something else happened that intensified the enmity between the two nations. In 1966, England won the World Cup. It was as seminal a moment in the history of Scottish football as English football. It intensified a colonial inferiority complex that has long been recognised as an identifying feature of so-called 'submerged nations'. At club level, FC Barcelona is another prime example, their successes routinely hailed as victories for Catalonia.

England's rise to world champions bruised the pride of most Scots. Knocking them off their perch became a mission. As Ian Archer wrote in *The Herald* in 1974, beating England became a Scottish 'virility symbol' that 'brought hope and stature to a nation so often insecure and concealing of its own insecurity'. It's a mentality that Neal Ascherson identified as the 'St Andrews Fault' in his excellent book *Stone Voices: The Search for Scotland*.

Which brings us back to the central question of national identity. What does it mean to be 'Scottish'? For some, it seems the answer is quite simple.

Scottish = Not English.

It was this sentiment that, depending on your perspective, added a layer of small-minded triviality or critical importance to the April 1967 clash between the two sides. It may have been just any other game for an English side with nothing left to prove and in possession of the Jules Rimet Trophy but, for many Scots, it was a perfect and timely platform upon which to right a wrong, to settle a score, to prove a point, to stand against them, to be a nation again.

To rise now.

A matter of life and death? No, no. It was much, much more important than that.

PROLOGUE

AS THE RAIN HAMMERED AGAINST THE WINDOW, Britain's most expensive footballer picked up his phone and dialled the number. It was a little after 10 a.m. on the morning of 30 July 1966 and Denis Law wanted revenge. Distraction, too. But mainly revenge.

A few weeks earlier, one of the Manchester United forward's best friends, a local businessman called John Hogan, had beaten Law over eighteen holes at a local golf course. This, despite the fact that Law was the better player of the two (and by some distance).

Oh, how Hogan had revelled in what was a rare win over his old pal. 'Any time you want a return game,' he had crowed, 'just give me a shout.'

The words rang in Law's ears as Hogan answered.

'Remember how you said "a return match any day, you name it,"' Law reminded him. 'Well, I will name it now – today.'

Hogan was as incredulous as he was crestfallen, and it had nothing to do with being a fair-weather player.

'But Denis . . . today's the World Cup final.'

Not just any old World Cup final but the first World Cup final to feature England. A 2–1 win over a Eusébio-led Portugal in the semi-finals had earned the Three Lions a shot at the title, and on home soil, too. Ninety minutes. Ninety measly minutes were all that stood between Alf Ramsey's men and the right to hear their names echo in sporting perpetuity. The country had ground to a halt, intoxicated by an irresistible cocktail of anticipation and expectation. Shops closed early, alternative plans were cancelled, street parties were convened, and Hogan had been looking forward to joining in the fun.

Law had other ideas. A £25 wager managed to persuade Hogan and, in short order, a tee time at Chorlton-cum-Hardy Golf Club, just a few miles to the south of Manchester city centre, was booked.

Law was grateful for the diversion. Two years earlier, he had received the Ballon d'Or, the gilded trophy awarded to Europe's 'Footballer of the Year'. He was the first Scot and only the second Brit – following the great Stanley Matthews in 1956 – to land the prestigious honour.

Since then, though, his form and fortunes had taken a dip. The season just ended had finished in abject disappointment on all fronts for Law and his United teammates. Partizan Belgrade had beaten them 2–1 on aggregate in the semi-finals of the European Cup. Three days later, Everton denied them a place in the FA Cup final, a late goal from Colin Harvey settling a scrappy contest at Bolton's Burnden Park. Their league title defence finished on a note every bit as meek. Having won the old First Division for a sixth time twelve months earlier, the 'Red Devils' could do no better than fourth in 1965/66. Worse, they had to watch as fierce rivals Liverpool took the title – for a record seventh time. All of which is to say nothing of United's other major adversary, Manchester City, winning the Second Division to seal promotion back to the top flight after a three-year absence.

And yet that wasn't even the worst of it. At the end of the season, Law found himself transfer-listed by the Old Trafford club after asking for a pay rise. In a letter to manager Matt Busby, he outlined his desire for an extra £10 per week, explaining that he would look for a transfer if his demands weren't met. Busby, a shrewd operator, was less than impressed with his fellow Scot. 'Law has issued an ultimatum by letter that unless he receives certain terms and conditions, he wants a transfer,' he told the press. 'The club is certainly not prepared to consider it and has decided to put him on the transfer list.'

The news caught up with Law on a golf course in Aberdeen. He was in his hometown awaiting the birth of his second child when a reporter from the local *Evening Express* newspaper found him on the links and relayed Busby's bombshell.

The frenzied reaction forced Law to go into hiding for a couple of days to, as he would later put it, 'avoid the glare of publicity' but before the week was out, he flew to Manchester for showdown talks with the boss. It took them around an hour to thrash it all out. Busby privately agreed to Law's terms and took him off the transfer list. In return, he wanted to make an example of his star man, lest anyone else in the squad suddenly start feeling brave about his own situation. Busby opened a drawer and pulled out a pre-prepared written apology that was almost ready to be shared with the press and the public. All it needed was Law's signature. Busby handed him a pen and his comeuppance.

It was a humiliating end to a miserable year in which Law had nursed a bothersome knee injury that restricted him to only fifteen goals in thirty-five league appearances.

So, sit at home and watch England play in the World Cup final, potentially even win the bloody thing? Not today, thank you very much. The thought alone made Law's insides boil. It would be much more fun, he decided, to put Hogan back in his box.

At least, that was the plan.

* * *

AROUND THE SAME TIME, in the Hendon House Hotel in North London, Law's Manchester United teammate Nobby Stiles was making a phone call of his own. His need was different but no less urgent.

The night before, England boss Alf Ramsey had taken Stiles and his teammates to the cinema to see *Those Magnificent Men in Their Flying Machines*, a film about an air race set in 1910. Stiles, though, had accidentally left a cardigan behind and he wanted – no, *needed* – to get it back. This wasn't just any cardigan. It was his lucky cardigan. He had worn it before every big game he had ever played, and it had never let him down. The prospect of going into the World Cup final without it was precisely the kind of cosmic drama the twenty-two-year-old didn't need.

After what seemed like an eternity, somebody at the Hendon Odeon finally answered Stiles' desperate call. He waited as the person on the other end of the line rummaged through the lost property, but to no avail. Nothing had been handed in. Superstitious Stiles would need to tackle this one without his beloved knitwear.

Elsewhere in the same hotel, another Manchester United star was sizing up wardrobe issues of his own. Bobby Charlton had become accustomed to big games and occasions since making his debut for Matt Busby's Red Devils a decade earlier. League deciders, FA Cup finals, the latter stages of European competition – you name it, Charlton had first-hand experience of it all. Well, nearly all. The World Cup final was new territory for the twenty-nine-year-old. A notoriously early riser, he found himself pacing the room he shared with Everton left-back Ray Wilson and that just wouldn't do. He needed to do something to distract him from the date with destiny he had lined up at 3 p.m. that afternoon.

He convinced Wilson to join him in getting out of the team's hotel HQ for a short while. A couple of days earlier, Charlton had bought a new shirt from a local shop but, on reflection, it wasn't really to his liking and so, hours before the biggest game in the history of English football, he decided to return it.

Off the pair went, down Parson Street and into Hendon town centre, forcing stunned onlookers into a succession of double-takes. Some stopped to wish them luck. Most, though, left them to go about their business, perhaps sensing that this was the players' way of normalising a most abnormal day.

After around an hour, they returned to the hotel where their teammate, Fulham full-back George Cohen, was reading – and, at Ramsey's insistence, replying to – some of the fan mail that had been steadily piling up.

It had been a broadly successful shopping trip. Charlton had managed to get his shirt changed and had also bought some cufflinks, a gift for his friend José Augusto, the tricky Portuguese winger, whom he would see at a banquet hosted by FIFA that night. More importantly, the trip had helped kill time.

It was just after 1 p.m. when Charlton and his teammates boarded the team bus and set off for Wembley. A police motorcycle escort accompanied them on their way as fans banged on the sides of the coach and roared their encouragement. As they passed the Hendon Fire Station, the freshly polished bells rang out in support.

This was Charlton's third World Cup. His first, in Sweden in 1958, had ended in heartache when the Soviet Union defeated England in a playoff to advance to the knockout stages. In Chile four years later, he scored in a 3–1 group stage win over

Argentina as England made it to the quarter-finals only to lose 3–1 at the hands of eventual winners, Brazil. This, though, was different. The quiet groundswell of optimism that had been building behind Ramsey's men in the months leading up to it had gathered momentum as the tournament had worn on. A goalless draw in the opening match with Uruguay had been followed by back-to-back 2–0 wins over Mexico and France as England breezed through the group stages. A bad-tempered quarter-final with Argentina was settled by a late Geoff Hurst goal, which set up a semi-final with inspired debutants Portugal. Charlton bagged a double only for a late Eusébio penalty to set up a tense finish. Portugal, who would finish the tournament as top scorers, threw everything they could at Gordon Banks' goal as they searched for an equaliser. But it wasn't to be. Full time: England 2, Portugal 1.

And so here they all were, sitting on a coach, getting ready for the biggest day of their lives. West Germany awaited. Immortality beckoned.

Charlton's mind drifted back to a conversation he'd had with a farmer from Herefordshire a few days earlier. 'Bobby,' he said, 'you and your teammates are playing for all of us. You'll win the game and collect the trophy but all over the country, in towns and villages, amateur players like me will be able to puff out their chests and say, "We are the champions of the world."'

On an unfamiliar day, Charlton took comfort in familiar habits. He and Wilson had long since developed their own pre-match ritual. Their kit was always in the same bag and always brought from the hotel by Wilson. He would hand Charlton his boots – one at a time – before giving him an ammonia inhaler to clear his nose. Finally, when the buzzer sounded inside the dressing room, summoning the players to line up in the tunnel, Charlton and Wilson would turn to one another, shake hands and wish each other luck. Today was no different.

PROLOGUE

As the two teams emerged onto the pristine pitch, the screams of 96,924 spectators melting into one cacophonous roar around them, Charlton's mind wandered again, this time back to his debut at Wembley as a fifteen-year-old playing for England schoolboys. The memory made him smile. So, too, did the sight of older brother Jack – playing behind Bobby in the centre of defence – going through one of own pre-match rituals. Jack had to, *had to*, score before the match kicked off. That was his thing. So long as he blootered a ball into the net, everything would be fine. As the other twenty-one players on the pitch loosened up in their own ways, Jack found a ball and sent a shot sailing over the goal. Panicked, he quickly grabbed another ball and tried again. In it went. *Phew.* One less thing.

As Siggi Held and Wolfgang Overath made their way to the centre-circle, ready to get the match started, more than thirty-two million people across the UK settled down behind their television sets, eyes trained on Charlton and co.

At precisely 3 p.m., as scheduled, Swiss referee Gottfried Dienst blew on his whistle. BBC television commentator Kenneth Wolstenholme took over.

'The rain has stopped; the excitement is intense. The ground in many places is soft and the 1966 World Cup Final is under way.'

* * *

AT CHORLTON-CUM-HARDY, Denis Law's plan was unravelling. *Fast.* Pre-occupied by wondering how the game was going, he found it hard to focus on golf. One poor shot followed another. And another. And another. And it was still raining. John Hogan, meanwhile, was enjoying the round of his life.

With several holes still to play, Hogan had established an insurmountable lead. Twenty-five pounds down the drain, just like that. But Law's day was about to get worse.

As the pair rounded the corner of the dogleg eighteenth hole, the clubhouse beyond the final green came into view. The cheers and celebrations from within spoke for themselves. Spotting Law, jubilant club members held up four fingers on one hand and two on the other; their grins as wide as the first fairway, their pint glasses as full as the bunkers.

You didn't need to be a codebreaker to crack their cipher.

England four, West Germany two.

Alf Ramsey's men had won the World Cup.

Law shook his head, sighed and muttered the only word he could muster.

'Bastards.'

ONE

SO MUCH BICKERING

JOHN PRENTICE landed at Prestwick, got off the plane and walked straight into trouble. It was 4 October 1966 and the Scotland national team manager was returning from New York where he had spent the last few days holding talks with the owners of Vancouver FC, a new franchise with ambitions to join the North American Soccer League (NASL).

A North American audience of more than one million had tuned in to the 1966 World Cup giving opportunistic entrepreneurs both the idea and the confidence to launch a first-ever professional league in the hitherto soccer-sceptic States.

One of those was to be in Vancouver and owned by Brigadier General Ted Eakins. With the inaugural NASL season set to begin in the spring of 1968, Eakins was hard at work building the foundations for his new football franchise. One of the first items on his agenda? Appoint the right manager.

After Coventry City head coach Jimmy Hill had rebuffed his advances, Eakins' focus drifted north to Scotland where he quickly identified Prentice – picked for the national team job only four months earlier – as his man.

The Shotts man's credentials were impressive, for sure. Between 1944 and 1960, he had enjoyed an impressive career as a wing-half for Heart of Midlothian, Rangers, Falkirk and Dumbarton. In addition to two league titles, he had also won the Scottish Cup with Rangers in 1953, a trick he repeated four years later as captain of Falkirk. With his playing career winding down, he was appointed manager of Arbroath in 1960 aged just thirty-three.

In November 1962, only two months after he resigned from the 'Red Lichties' – apparently in protest at Arbroath Town Council's refusal to allocate him a house – Prentice was appointed manager of First Division Clyde. The Glasgow outfit were relegated that season but, in his first full campaign in charge, Prentice guided them straight back into Scottish football's top flight and consolidated their position the year after that.

His relative success with a group of part-time players made him a man in high demand and, when Willie Waddell and Eddie Turnbull both turned down the chance to succeed Jock Stein as Scotland manager in 1966, the Scottish Football Association (SFA) turned their attention to Prentice.

He was appointed in March and, little more than a week later, took charge of the country for the first time in a British Home Championship title decider at home to England. A more intense baptism you would struggle to imagine.

Most pundits made Scotland favourites for the match. The received wisdom was that Alf Ramsey and his English side already had one eye on the upcoming World Cup they would host that summer. Combine that with their poor recent record against Scotland – three defeats and a draw in their previous four matches, no victories at Hampden since 1958 – and it was hard to argue a case against the Scottish optimism.

As it so happened, England ran out 4–3 winners, claiming the British Home Championship title for a third successive year and consigning Prentice to a debut defeat. Further losses followed at the hands of the Netherlands in May and Portugal in June, before a 1–1 draw with reigning world champions Brazil provided the beleaguered new boss a first 'result' of any significant note.

It was around this time that Vancouver made their move. Prentice had been Scotland manager for only three months and four matches but Eakins was confident he could tempt him to cross the Atlantic. For one thing, he was prepared to offer him full managerial control. At this time, the Scotland team was still being chosen for him by an SFA selection committee and, so far, talk of that changing had amounted to nothing more than just that: talk. There was also the promise of a return to club football and the cut and thrust of matches every week, not to mention the prospect of being part of a potentially huge new project in the shape of the NASL. The £5,000-a-year salary – more than Prentice was making in charge of Scotland – was no doubt a juicy carrot, too.

Events of that summer caused the landscape to shift dramatically, however. England's historic World Cup victory, masterminded by the soon-to-be 'Sir' Alf Ramsey, finally convinced the SFA powerbrokers that it was time for the Scottish national team to operate in a way that mirrored the new world champions. Whilst deeply envious of the Auld Enemy's success, the powerbrokers at Park Gardens in Glasgow swiftly concluded that if England could win the World Cup, so could they. *Let them have their moment. We'll get ours in Mexico in 1970.* Scotland had the players and now, thanks to England, they had the blueprint. All they had to do was follow it to the letter. Finally, in September 1966, they handed Prentice the autonomy he wanted. Going forward, he and not a selection committee would choose the Scotland team.

Vancouver, though, were not for giving up. While the SFA dithered and delayed, they persuaded Prentice to fly to the United States for further talks.

Ten days after agreeing to the SFA's new terms, he did just that, returning on 4 October to a media storm. The suggestion was that he was not fully committed to the job with Scotland and that he had travelled to the USA without the permission of the SFA.

Not so, countered Prentice who insisted that he made the trip with the blessing of association president Tom Reid.

'When he heard the story, he said he would not stand in my way,' an indignant Prentice told the reporters who had gathered to greet him at Prestwick Airport. 'The only crime I have committed is to try and better myself. All I want is security for myself and my family.'

The original approach from Vancouver, he added, had come amidst continued uncertainty over his position with Scotland and that reports he had been handed a deal to lead the team into the 1970 World Cup were wide of the mark.

Nonetheless, he was not prepared to discuss his future on the runway. He said: 'I've already made up my mind about the offer [from Vancouver] but I wanted to discuss it with my wife and inform the SFA before announcing it. There is no point in wasting time, although the Canadians have given no deadline for my answer.'

The newspapers had just gone to print with Prentice's remarks when the SFA's selection committee raced to convene a meeting. Less than forty-eight hours after Prentice's plane touched down, his future as Scotland boss was being thrashed out inside Hampden Park. Many in the room articulated their disillusionment at having been kept in the dark over their manager's trans-Atlantic dash, adding that it was humiliating to learn of it through the papers. Others who had supported the appointment of the country's first full-time and autonomous manager felt let down. It didn't take them long to reach the inevitable conclusion.

No sooner than he was in, Prentice was out.

In a 121-word statement, SFA secretary Willie Allan confirmed the news. 'We appreciate that a young man, especially one with a wife and young children, is entitled and can be expected to look to the future,' read the missive. 'Nevertheless, having in mind the nature of Mr Prentice's position as team manager, they do feel that when he freely reached agreement with them on 13 September as to his position with the Association, he should, in fairness to them, have disclosed that he was at that time interested in an appointment elsewhere.

'Those present when the committee met on Thursday were unanimous in the conclusion they reached.'

Prentice was en route to Roker Park to take in Sunderland's home match with West Bromwich Albion when his sacking was announced. In a *Sunday Mail* cover story that weekend, he gave his version of events. Speaking from his Edinburgh home, he said that he had been offered the chance to resign but had refused. 'There was intrigue going on while I was in Canada,' he said. 'I thought a smear campaign started against me a few days after I went away.

'I am now finished at the SFA. I won't go back next week. I didn't even have an office. It was not an easy job and the road was rough. I did not want the job initially but after several approaches I eventually took it because someone had to do it.

'This is an unfortunate conclusion to the whole affair. I've enjoyed the six months up to a point but there were difficulties and snags which I'm not prepared to talk about.'

Whilst SFA secretary Allan resisted the opportunity to respond to Prentice's remarks, insisting he did not 'wish to become a party to any mud-slinging', the association's president made no such concessions.

'John had little to complain about,' Reid insisted. 'He had the full support of the selection committee and me. He had the complete say in team selection. He had absolute power. That's more than Andy Beattie ever had in 1954 when I was chairman of the selectors.

'All these things Prentice has complained about are petty things. He talked, for instance, about being offered a room in the basement or a room upstairs. The room in the basement was only a temporary affair. The alternative room upstairs was mine, and I was quite willing to give it up.

'Surely the main thing was to build Scotland a team we could be proud of.

'Prentice was quick to come and ask me at 10 o'clock at night for permission to go to Canada. But he didn't have the courtesy to phone me when he came back and tell me what happened. Fair's fair.'

If anybody was surprised at the mess the Scottish national team found itself in, they shouldn't have been. Less than a year earlier, Jock Stein had vacated the post – which he had occupied on a part-time basis – after enduring stinging criticism following his failure to lead Scotland to the World Cup finals in England. A 3–0 defeat away to Italy in the qualification decider in December 1965 proved to be the last straw. In a parting shot, Stein remarked: 'If they were to give me the entire gate of the Scotland-England match, I would still refuse to be manager.'

There was an increasingly wide-held belief that the position had become a poisoned chalice. Prentice had been the fifth person to occupy the post in just eight years, following Andy Beattie, Matt Busby, Ian McColl and, most recently, Stein. Between them, they had taken charge of only fifty-three games.

In his report for the *Aberdeen Evening Express*, James Forbes called the Prentice saga 'just another sorry chapter in the history of Scottish international football'.

'How can good playing results be expected when there is so much bickering off the field?' he asked. 'To most people, it appears that Prentice, having got permission to investigate the prospect of another job, finished up being sacked for doing so. Under the circumstances, he may feel that he is better out of it.'

Compounding Scottish misery was the fact that the national team's turmoil was diametrically opposed to the glow of success their counterparts south of the border were basking in. It was not that the English had better players, as such. There was a widely held belief that players such as Denis Law, Billy Bremner and Jim Baxter were, at the very least, the equal of anything that Ramsey's men had to offer. It's just that their undisputed talents were being woefully compromised by rampant mismanagement. And for that, you could blame the SFA.

'Despite England's success in the World Cup under the sole control of manager Alf Ramsey, there are still plenty of Scottish officials of the opinion that a full-time manager isn't necessary,' added Forbes. 'No doubt their view of the Prentice affair will have convinced them that they are right.'

The situation prompted the *Daily Record* to conduct a multi-part investigation that it sensationally branded 'Soccerprobe'. With the national team in disarray yet again, its reporters canvassed the opinions of some of the shrewdest and most highly respected managers in the game.

Leeds United boss Don Revie called on the SFA to resist the temptations to resist regressing to old habits. 'The first step to making Scotland great again must be to appoint a full-time boss,' he said. 'A supremo, a man with the powers and strength of conviction and character as Alf Ramsey.

'Surely Alf proved during the summer that a one-man boss is the only way to succeed in football now. If Scotland could find someone like him, give him the same complete control, I'm sure that in a couple of years Scotland will be a really great side. There must be plenty people around who'd give their right arm to be in charge of a team who could call on players of the class of Jim Baxter, Denis Law, Billy Bremner, Bobby Lennox, Willie Bell, Eddie McCreadie, Willie Henderson and so on.

'When I run over these names, I'm convinced that potentially the talent which Scotland has available is second to none.'

Tommy Docherty, the Chelsea manager and former Scottish international, agreed. A no-nonsense, uncompromising disciplinarian, Docherty made the difficult task of maintaining order amongst the London club's galaxy of £100-a-week stars look easy. That was a quality he believed the next Scotland boss would need.

'I'm 100 per cent in favour of Scotland having a full-time manager,' he said. 'But he'd need to be a hard man. He'd have to make it perfectly clear from the start – both to the SFA and to the players – that he was boss.

'One man in complete and utter control is, in my opinion, the only cure for Scottish football's international ailments. We have the players, no doubt about that, but they need to be moulded. The wonderful talent we have would need to be channelled in the right direction.'

Docherty called for the new boss to be given a long-term contract – four, perhaps even five years – as well as sole responsibility for team selections, freedom to appoint his own staff and closer contact with the international set-ups at all age grades, from schools upwards.

'In my view, he ought to visit clubs, train with the players for a couple of days, arrange full co-operation with the club managers and really get to know everything that's going on that affects his job. He'd also need to travel abroad, get into the swing of things at every level, make every Scot who's playing top-class football anywhere feel that he is part of the plan to make Scotland's international team the best in the world.'

Grimly, Docherty added: 'Although it hurts to say this, Scottish football is 100 years behind the times. Change has to come and it's too bad if some people have their feelings hurt. It's an old saying but it's true: there is no place in football for sentimentality.'

Since standing down from the Scotland manager's post due to ill health, Matt Busby had taken over at Manchester United, where he had an embarrassment of riches at his disposal. He had led the Old Trafford club to four First Division titles, two FA Cups and four Charity Shields. Even better was to come. When it came to maximising the potential of players such as Bobby Charlton, Nobby Stiles, George Best and Scots like Denis Law and Paddy Crerand, he was a man almost without equal.

'If Scotland want to compete in the big time – and it's really big time these days – then the obvious thing to do is appoint a full-time manager,' said Busby. 'If the SFA don't realise the job means working twenty-four hours a day, they might as well give up any ideas of serious competition. In my opinion, anything less than full-time in modern football is just playing at it. Any managerial job means a lot of time and effort but a national manager must be prepared to devote more time than anyone.

'He needs to be continually on the move, keeping in touch not only with the established stars but also with up-and-coming youngsters. Scotland is still producing the raw material. In the hands of the right man as full-time manager, I see no reason why Scotland, come the 1970 World Cup, should not have an extremely good side.'

Liverpool manager Bill Shankly – like Docherty and Busby, a proud Scot – echoed the sentiments of his counterparts. 'A full-time manager is a must,' insisted the man who had led the Anfield side to First Division glory for the seventh time in the season just ended, despite having only fourteen players in his squad. 'His main task as I see it would be to go to any lengths to find every possible piece of international material. Not only the Denis Laws and the Billy Bremners, but all the promising youngsters. Then he'd need to find the blend. A lot of good youngsters with a few auld heids is the answer. But the only way to get a good international blend is to have a man working full time on the job. Half-measures are no use.'

The consensus was unmistakable. And yet fears persisted that the SFA, stung by the Prentice affair, would retreat to familiar ground. They had fallen at the first hurdle in their attempts to emulate the English and each minute that ticked by was a minute closer to Mexico . . . if they even made it that far. And as Revie had been quick to point out, it could take up to two years for the new man's ideas and tactics to pay dividends.

Of much more immediate significance was an upcoming clash with Wales at Ninian Park in Cardiff, the opening fixture of the 1966/67 British Home Championship, which would form the first half of the qualifying stages for the 1968 European Championship. Introduced in 1960, the pan-European contest was the brainchild of French Football Federation secretary-general Henri Delaunay and was designed to fill the competitive international void created by the World Cup's four-year cycle.

None of the home nations had qualified for the first two editions of the championship and so 1968 represented an opportunity for Scotland to both one-up their UK rivals – England, most notably – and restore some of the national pride that had been wounded by seeing Alf Ramsey's men win the World Cup in '66.

Getting off to a winning start against Wales was essential, so not having a manager in place was less than ideal. No sooner had Prentice been relieved of his duties than a host of big names were linked with the job. Tommy Walker, recently sacked by Heart of Midlothian, was one of the first. Dundee United boss Jerry Kerr, as well as Willie Cunningham, the Irish manager of

Dunfermline, and former Third Lanark gaffer George Young were also rumoured to be in the running.

Complicating matters was the fact that the Scottish job wasn't the only high-profile open vacancy in Scotland. Rangers, indeed, were rumoured to be looking for a new coach to assist manager Scot Symon and, with the financial clout of the Lawrence family who owned the Ibrox side, they would surely win any bidding war with the SFA for the top talent.

In the end, the SFA appointed Kilmarnock boss Malky Macdonald on an interim basis. He had proven himself to be a safe pair of hands months earlier when he had taken charge of the Scottish League side that beat England 3–1 at St James' Park in Newcastle. He didn't want the job full-time, though. Not then and not now. As well as being under contract with Kilmarnock, he had no ambitions to be the Scotland boss. But sure, he'd happily help in the meantime. And 'helping out' meant taking charge of a team picked for him for Wales by the selection committee.

The onlookers' worst fears looked like they were coming true.

Prentice, meantime, turned down the Vancouver job and, shortly thereafter, said no to an £8,000-per-year offer to take charge of the New York Football Club. Talks with St Mirren and Dundee also broke down before finally, two months after his sacking by Scotland, he took over at former club Falkirk. The 'Bairns' were scrapping it out at the wrong end of the table and believed former captain Prentice was the man to help preserve their place in the top flight.

The Brockville dugout was reoccupied as the one at Hampden continued to lie empty. A sorry situation for any country – not least one harbouring hopes of becoming world champions within the next four years.

TWO

THE WINTER GAME

THE FIRST FORMAL MATCH BETWEEN England and Scotland also has the unique distinction of being the first such contest between any two recognised nations.

It took place in 1872 at the home of the West of Scotland Cricket Club in Partick, a bustling community on the north bank of the River Clyde in Glasgow.

Five different fixtures contested by teams representing the two countries had been staged between March 1870 and February 1872, the first of those at The Oval, which resulted in a 1–1 draw. However, most of the players selected for the Scottish side were 'internationals' from the London area, which was met with a mixture of resentment and indignation in Scotland. There was, they argued, a far deeper pool of talent north of the border than these matches had showcased.

The man responsible for the scheduling of the games, Football Association secretary Charles Alcock, tended to agree. However, he was adamant that he had done his best to make the contests as competitive as possible, placing adverts in leading

Glasgow and Edinburgh newspapers for players to take part.

In an open letter published by *The Scotsman*, he reiterated his position.

'I must join issue with your correspondent in some instances,' he wrote. 'First, I assert that of whatever the Scotch eleven may have been composed, the right to play was open to every Scotchman, whether his lines were cast North or South of the Tweed and that if, in the face of the invitations publicly given through the columns of leading journals of Scotland, the representative eleven consisted chiefly of Anglo-Scotians . . . the fault lies on the heads of the players of the north, not on the management who sought the services of all alike impartially.'

He added: 'To call the team London Scotchmen contributes nothing. The match was, as announced, to all intents and purposes between England and Scotland.'

Nonetheless, he ended his missive by offering another challenge, this time to be staged in the north of England – but with one significant condition. Taking issue with the size of Scottish football teams at the time – many of which were rumoured to exceed the 11-a-side line-up preferred in England and which would become the internationally codified standard in 1897 – Alcock wrote: 'More than eleven, we do not care to play as it is with greater numbers. It is our opinion the game becomes less scientific and more a trial of charging and brute force.'

This time, Alcock's bait caught a bite. In the absence of a Scottish Football Association to sanction the match, Queen's Park, Scotland's oldest football club and by common consent its finest, took up the gauntlet instead. As a gesture of goodwill, the FA consented to the match being played in Glasgow 'in order to further the interests of the Association in Scotland'.

A date for the game was set – 30 November 1872, by coincidence (or perhaps not) St Andrew's Day – with the

West of Scotland Cricket Club selected to host ahead of the Glasgow Academical Rugby Club, who offered their ground at Burnbank free of charge. The Queen's Park Recreation Ground at Crosshill, where Queen's Park played and from which they took their name, was not considered and it wouldn't be until 1873 that the original Hampden Park would open.

The Scottish side for the match was chosen by goalkeeper and captain Robert Gardner. He picked a line-up comprised entirely of his Queen's Park teammates having reportedly been unable to obtain the services of two English-based Scots – Arthur Kinnaird of The Wanderers and Henry Renny-Tailyour of the Royal Engineers – for the clash. The side also featured siblings: twenty-eight-year-old James Smith and his younger brother Robert.

Alcock, meantime, chose the English XI from nine different clubs. It included Reginald Welch, part of the all-conquering Wanderers side that had won the first-ever staging of the FA Cup earlier in the year. Harrow Chequers' Monty Betts, Alec Morten of Crystal Palace and another Wanderers player, Thomas Hooman, had also been chosen but were forced to withdraw due to illness. Alcock might even have been tempted to pick himself but for an injury he was carrying.

Anticipation for the match reached a crescendo as the day dawned and, as the 2 p.m. kick-off approached, close to four thousand excited spectators had crammed into the ground on Hamilton Crescent, each of them paying a shilling for the privilege – approximately £6 in today's money.

Finally, after a twenty-minute delay to the scheduled start time, the two teams emerged under heavy skies. The Scots wore dark blue jerseys (originally the colour of Queen's Park) adorned with a Scottish lion for a badge and accompanied by white knickerbockers, blue-and-white striped stockings, and red cowls. Their guests, meanwhile, were as resplendent in their white jerseys – each of which featured the arms of England by way of a badge – with dark blue caps, and white trousers and knickerbockers.

The Scots won the toss and elected to make England shoot up the brae of the ground in the first half. It was the visiting captain, twenty-two-year-old Cuthbert Ottaway of Oxford University, who got proceedings under way, launching the ball deep into Scottish territory, and, in so doing, he quite literally kick-started international football as we know it today.

Alas, this match would not be remembered were it not for its historical significance. These days, commentators might be inclined to refer to it as 'one for the purists'. A classic, it was not. The conditions had much to do with that. Despite dry weather on the day of the game, torrential rain in the days leading up to it rendered the ground extremely soft and it didn't take more than a few minutes for it to start carving up.

Despite the best efforts of both sides, the game ended in a goalless draw, Robert Leckie's late shot that landed on top of tape strung between two posts in lieu of a proper crossbar the closest either team came to breaking the deadlock. As it turned out, there would not be another scoreless game in the following 85 matches between the two nations, the April 1970 clash at Hampden the next 0–0 draw they would contest.

The lack of goals, however, was of little consequence to those who were there to witness the occasion. The *Aberdeen Journal* reported that 'it was allowed to be the best game ever seen in Scotland'. Sport magazine *The Field* wrote that 'the result was received with rapturous applause by the spectators and the cheers proposed by each XI for their antagonists were continued by the onlookers until the last member of the two sides had disappeared'. The same report added: 'The match was in every sense a signal success, as the play was throughout as spirited and as pleasant as can possibly be imagined.'

That's not to say every major news outlet in the country covered the fixture with such gusto. The *Manchester Guardian*, for example, published a 124-word match report, which ran on the same page as a far more substantial feature on the Birmingham Cattle Show. *The Times*, meanwhile, dedicated most of a page in its next edition to the cattle, with the football overlooked completely.

Despite that, the match had proven both interesting and stimulating enough for a return fixture to be arranged for March 1873, this time at The Oval in south London. Again, a large crowd turned out – approximately three thousand in all – and, within minutes of kick-off, they were treated to the first goal scored between the two sides. A shot at goal by Charles Chenery of Crystal Palace forced Robert Gardner in the Scottish goal into a mistake which Wanderers' William Kenyon-Slaney capitalised upon to give the English the lead. His clubmate Alexander Bonsor doubled their advantage soon thereafter, only for Scotland to hit back through Henry Renny-Tailyour and William Gibb.

Second-half goals from Kenyon-Slaney and Chenery thwarted the Scots' endeavours and handed a first victory to the hosts. Once again, however, the real winner had been the game itself. A match report in the *Bell's Life and Sporting Chronicle* noted: 'If any proof were necessary to evince the growing popularity of the winter game of wielders of the willow, there was sufficient evidence on this occasion to convince the most sceptical that football, if only aided by fine weather, is a game that could take its place among the leading pastimes of the day.'

And so it proved. As the nineteenth century gave way to the twentieth, there had been twenty-eight official matches between the two nations, England winning nine, Scotland thirteen, and six ending in a draw.

The success of the fixture even emboldened the various

football associations of the constituent nations of the United Kingdom to create the world's first international football tournament, the British Home Championship, which debuted in 1884 and continued to take place for the next hundred years.

Crucially, the turnstiles kept on spinning, forcing organisers to take the now-annual fixture to venues that were bigger and better equipped to satisfy demand. Hampden Park (the first) made its debut in 1878. Sheffield's Bramall Lane did likewise in 1863. Ibrox Park and Celtic Park in Glasgow each got their shots. So, too, the Athletic Ground in Richmond, Ewood Park in Blackburn, and Goodison Park, the Liverpool home of Everton FC.

All the while, the attendances went up and up and up. By 1880, an estimated 15,000 watched on. That had doubled to 30,000 by 1890. In the final match of the century, more than 40,000 eager fans squeezed into Villa Park in Birmingham to see goals from Gilbert Smith of Old Carthusians and Bury's Jimmy Settle cancel out an effort from Rangers' Robert Hamilton to give the hosts a 2–1 win.

Suffice to say, *The Times* and *The Guardian* had also started to pay more attention by this point, the former gushing about the 'high traditions of excellence' and 'the finer arts of football' the match had demonstrated.

Changed days, indeed. And they were about to change some more.

THREE

BROWN AMATEURISM

IN THE FINAL YEARS OF THE 20TH CENTURY, football experienced a sudden, seismic surge both in its popularity and its global reach.

The first club outside of the British Isles, Kjøbenhavns Boldklubb, was formed in Denmark in 1876. Switzerland and the Netherlands followed suit three years later with St Gallen and Haarlemse FC, respectively. Belgium got its first club in 1880 (Royal Antwerp), France in 1881 (FC Girondins de Bordeaux), Argentina in 1887 (Gimnasia) and Germany, also in 1887 (SC Germania, better known today as Hamburger SV).

With that increase in formal domestic competition came clamour for more international competition. Initially, the Olympic Games satisfied that demand. Football made its debut on the programme at the second modern Olympics in Paris in 1900. However, this tournament, along with that of 1904 in St Louis and the 1906 Intercalated Games in Athens, were contested by various clubs and so-called 'scratch teams'. It was not until the London Games of 1908 that a 'proper' international tournament was staged by the Football Association. Only five nations were represented: Denmark, France, Great Britain, the Netherlands and Sweden. By the 1912 Games in Stockholm, that number had increased to eleven. When the Games resumed following the First World War in Antwerp in 1920, thirteen nations took part. The Olympics had established itself as the pinnacle of international football.

Trouble, though, was brewing. The 1920s saw football transition towards professionalism, something that was very much at odds with the 'amateur' spirit of the Olympics. The matter reached a head in the build-up to the 1924 Games in Paris. As debates raged over what did and didn't constitute 'amateurism', the British football associations issued FIFA – the game's global governing body and, beginning in 1924, the organisers of the Olympic football competition – with an ultimatum: either accept our definition of what it is to be an amateur and consider any player receiving remuneration of any kind to be a professional, or we're out. FIFA refused and, true to their word, the British associations withdrew from the Games in protest. Denmark did likewise.

Another interesting thing happened at that Games that would have a significant bearing on the direction of international football. Uruguay entered the Olympics, the first South American nation to do so. The previous December, the men from Montevideo won the 1923 Copa America, an international tournament open to all South American nations. They, along with Argentina, Paraguay and Brazil took part. Uruguay won all three of their matches, scoring six goals and conceding only one.

Yet they arrived in Paris as virtual unknowns. They were from the other side of the world at a time when that might as well have been light years away. Who, either in France or at FIFA, could confidently say whether or not they were 'amateurs'? Uruguayan author Eduardo Galeano maintained that they were. In his book, *Football in the Sun and Shadow*, he wrote: 'Pedro Arispe was a meatpacker. José Nasazzi cut marble. "Perucho" Petrone was a grocer. Pedro Cea sold ice. José Leandro Andrade was a carnival musician and bootblack. They were all twenty years old or a little older, though in the pictures they look like old men. They cured their wounds with salt water, vinegar plasters, and a few glasses of wine.'

As it turned out, the issue of where amateurism ended and professionalism began was causing as much of an issue in South America – Uruguay included – as it was in more or less every other country where the game had become popular.

Leagues and clubs insisted that they were, in fact, amateur endeavours but those who cared to look more closely knew better. This was a time of 'brown amateurism', a shady means by which clubs circumnavigated the more general ban on payments by finding other ways for money to change hands. 'Brown' envelopes and the like. Long story short, the Uruguayan team that arrived in France for the 1924 Olympics represented the very best that the country had to offer and was supported by a staff of expert personnel. A doctor and physical trainer ensured that the players were kept in peak physical condition. They stayed away from the Olympic Village in Paris, preferring to stay in a château in the neighbouring town of Argentuil instead. They warmed up for the Games with nine friendly matches against teams from Spain. They won all nine.

When the Games began, Uruguay were simply too good for their genuinely amateur opponents. They brushed aside Yugoslavia 7–0 in their opening match. A 3–0 win over the United States followed, before hosts France were convincingly dispatched, 5–1 the score. That set up a semi-final against the Netherlands, where a 2–1 win put the Uruguayans through to the gold medal match against the Swiss. Another three goals later, Uruguay were champions. In five matches, they'd scored twenty goals and conceded only two. Pedro Petrone finished as the tournament's top marksman with seven goals to his name. He was two days shy of his nineteenth birthday when he received his gold medal. He remains the youngest football gold medallist in the history of the Games.

As the players took a lap of honour – the first football team to celebrate victory in such a manner – the eulogising was well under way. Writing in *L'Equipe*, Gabriel Hanot noted: 'The Uruguayans are supple disciples of the spirit of fitness rather than geometry. They have pushed towards perfection the art of the feint and swerve and the dodge, but they know also how to play directly and quickly. They are not only ball jugglers. They created a beautiful football, elegant but at the same time varied, rapid, powerful, effective.'

As impressive as it had been, the Uruguayan Olympic victory was problematic for FIFA. On the one hand, questions persisted over the legitimacy of the side's amateurism. On the other, if they represented the best footballers the world had to offer – and it appeared they did – then they and everybody else deserved a bigger, fairer platform. *To hell with amateurism,* FIFA concluded. *Let's create a tournament where the world's best players can all take part.*

On 25 May 1928, members of FIFA, led by their French president Jules Rimet, met in Amsterdam and voted in favour of staging the first World Cup in 1930. After Uruguay offered to pay for all travel expenses, the Olympic champions were selected as hosts for the inaugural tournament.

A new era for international football had just been ushered in.

For the SFA, the decision was particularly interesting. There had been, for some time, simmering unrest about the extent to which Scotland had been represented on British Olympic teams.

For example, after a side made up entirely of English players contested the 1908 Games, the SFA passed a resolution to 'protest against one National body in the British Isles being termed the United Kingdom or playing as such without the consent of the other three National Associations'.

Noses were out of joint, basically.

At a subsequent meeting of the International Football Association Board, the FA explained that this had been a name given to them by the 'authorities'. Nonetheless, the 'Great Britain' football team that contested the next two Games – in 1912 and 1920 – continued to be made up exclusively of Englishmen. It wasn't until the 1932 Games that the first players from elsewhere in the United Kingdom – four Scots – made the squad.

By then, the first World Cup had been staged, as planned, in Uruguay and won by the hosts. However, if that tournament was meant to represent an opportunity for Scotland (and Wales and Northern Ireland for that matter) to emerge from the shadow of England and strike out on their own, it didn't.

The SFA, along with the representative bodies of the other Home Nations, all withdrew from FIFA over concerns about its definition of amateurism. As far as the Brits were concerned, the rise and rise of the Uruguayans, in particular, had created an uneven playing field and one they refused to support. Consequently, the inaugural World Cup – already hit by the decision of several European countries to stay away on account of the prohibitive two-week boat journey to South America – took place with only thirteen teams.

According to some historians, that principled stand potentially cost Scotland the opportunity to win the tournament. 'If Scotland were to have won a World Cup, then 1930 was not just their best chance, it was their only chance,' claimed Simon Turner. 'Not only did they have one of the most talented groups of players that the country is ever likely to produce, but they could also have competed in a tournament which many of the best teams in the world had declined to attend.'

Failure to resolve the dispute with FIFA prompted the Scots' boycott of the 1934 and 1938 editions of the tournament. It was only following the Second World War that tensions eased, with the Home Nations re-joining FIFA in 1946. Consequently, all were eligible to enter the 1950 FIFA World Cup in Brazil, with places in the tournament awarded to the top two finishers in the 1949/50 British Home Championship. Remarkably, the SFA took issue. Scotland, they insisted, would only be attending the finals if they won the competition. Second place, as far as they were concerned, was tantamount to being first loser. It was a breathtakingly intransigent, mulish approach. After beating Ireland 8–2 in Belfast and Wales 2–0 in Glasgow, the Scots were guaranteed one of the two places on offer. The worst they could finish was second. And so to the final match at home to England. A goal from Chelsea's Roy Bentley shortly after the hour at Hampden settled the contest. Having won all three of their games, England topped the table, with Scotland second.

True to their word, and despite the pleas of several of their players, which were echoed by England captain Billy Wright and several of his teammates, the SFA politely declined their World Cup place. It was, as the great sportswriter Brian Glanville later observed, an act of 'baffling insularity and pique'.

It wasn't until 1954 that Scotland participated in the World Cup. Despite finishing second to England in the 1953/54 British Home Championship – the tournament again acting as the qualifying competition – the SFA blazers relented and allowed a team to travel to Switzerland. It proved to be an unmitigated disaster. Despite FIFA allowing twenty-two-man squads at the tournament, the Scots sent just thirteen players, two of whom were goalkeepers. They were heavily outnumbered by SFA dignitaries, who travelled in large numbers with their wives. Following a 1–0 defeat to Austria in the Scots' opening match, team manager Andy Beattie resigned in protest at the haphazard organisation, leaving the team physio in charge.

Compounding matters was the ill-suited kit the Scottish players travelled with. Their hard boots put them at an immediate disadvantage to other sides who wore more modern, lightweight boots, whilst their heavy cotton shirts and shorts were entirely inappropriate for the conditions. One of the players, Tommy Docherty, later claimed that he had lost half a stone during the playing of the national anthems in their second match with defending champions Uruguay in Basel.

'The heat was incredible and we were drenched in sweat,' he revealed. 'At half-time, we had to get into a lukewarm bath to cool down. We just weren't prepared.'

By then, they were already two-nil down.

'We weren't given a run down on who were their dangerous players or anything like that,' added Docherty. 'Although I was told to man-mark their star player, Juan Alberto Schiaffino. No-one told me how good he was, I couldn't get near him. It was a shambles. That's the only way to describe it.'

In the end, the Uruguayans ran out 7–0 winners – to date, Scotland's heaviest defeat in a World Cup finals match – and no sooner had it begun than the side's first foray into the competition was over. Two games, two defeats, no goals scored, eight conceded. It was a grim wake-up call.

Compounding the Scots' misery was the fact that England advanced out of their group, reaching the quarter-finals where they, too, were put to the sword by Uruguay, albeit by a less emphatic score.

'That 7–0 defeat was hugely embarrassing for Scottish football,' explained Richard McBrearty, the curator of the Scottish football museum at Hampden. 'Before 1954, there had been the attitude that the Home Internationals was the biggest tournament. Now, the SFA and Scottish teams realised how far behind other nations we were and started to learn from them in terms of training, playing style and even what boots and kit to wear. All of a sudden, the window to the world was open.'

Four years later, they got a chance to make amends when they qualified for the 1958 World Cup in Sweden. The intention was for Manchester United manager Matt Busby to take charge of the team for the finals. However, the severe injuries he had sustained in the Munich air disaster that February forced him to withdraw, leaving trainer Dawson Walker at the helm.

The Scots got off to a reasonable start in the tournament, drawing 1–1 with a Yugoslavian side that had beaten England 5–0 in a warm-up match. Two of the Scottish players who sat out that game – Docherty and Archie Robertson – were sent to spy on their next opponents, Paraguay. They reported back that, despite losing 7–3 to France, the South Americans were 'rough and fit and good'. Scotland's best hope of beating them, they observed, would be to try and match their physicality.

For reasons best known only to him, Walker had other ideas.

He left out known scrapper Dave Mackay, Sammy Baird and Docherty, preferring instead to field a slim, small, lithe forward line. The outcome was exactly as predicted. Paraguay swatted aside their diminutive opponents, winning 3–2 to leave the Scots needing a miracle against France in their final game to advance in the competition. It didn't happen. Real Madrid's Raymond Kopa opened the scoring before Scottish defender John Hewie rattled the woodwork with a penalty. The mercurial Moroccan-born Just Fontaine added a second before Baird grabbed a late consolation, scant though it was.

Another World Cup, another early exit.

'We flew back, dispersed at the airport and that was it,' Hewie later revealed. 'I got a train back to London and saw my eldest daughter, Alison, for the first time.' She had been born whilst the team was in Sweden. 'My wife, Rachel, told me how embarrassed she'd been that I'd missed. We'd just got a new television and all the neighbours had been round to watch the France game. I do still wonder what might have happened had it gone in.'

In the qualifiers for the 1962 World Cup in Chile, a skilful Scots side boasting the likes of Jim Baxter, Paddy Crerand, Denis Law and Ian St John led 2–1 in a play-off before losing in extra time to a Czechoslovakia side that went on to reach the final that year.

Then, of course, there was another qualifying near-miss – this time at the hands of Italy – ahead of the 1966 finals in England where . . . well, you know the rest.

Having played such a pivotal role in the foundations of international competition, a series of missteps, misfortune and misdirection resulted in Scotland suddenly lagging dramatically behind countless other nations, not least their biggest rivals – England.

Egos were bruised, pride was battered, feelings were hurt.

Scores? Scores were to be settled.

FOUR

EURO VISION

THE UNION DES Associations Européennes de Football – UEFA, for short – was established in Switzerland in 1954. The brainchild of the Italian, French and Belgian football authorities, UEFA was intended to foster unity and solidarity in the post-war European football community. It was a way to share ideas and opportunities, not to mention better protect European interests at a time when FIFA – football's global governing body – was adding new members on a seemingly continuous basis.

In particular, European football executives observed how an alliance formed in 1916 by their South American equivalents had benefitted each of its constituent nations. Besides anything else, it had enabled them to examine key agenda items and discussion points well in advance of FIFA's biennial congress and adopt a common, mutually advantageous position on them. To avoid tumbling down football's global food chain, it was evident that Europe needed to follow the Confederación Sudamericana de Fútbol (CONMEBOL) blueprint.

The idea struck a chord with other national football authorities across the continent, with the result that thirty-one different associations were recognised as founding members. (The subsequent fragmentation of the Soviet Union, Yugoslavia and Czechoslovakia meant that, by the mid-1990s, UEFA had grown to comprise more than fifty members.)

Whilst its primary objective was to better defend the interest of European football as a whole, the formation of UEFA also prompted the creation of several new competitions, such as the European Champion Clubs' Cup (the forerunner to the present-day UEFA Champions League) in 1955 and the European Nations Cup, now better known as the UEFA European Championship, in 1960. Work on the latter, in fact, began within four months of UEFA's incorporation when a sub-committee was tasked with drawing up plans for a European national team competition. A confederation without its own competition, they reasoned, wasn't much of a confederation. FIFA had the World Cup. CONMEBOL had the South American Football Championship (later renamed the Copa America). UEFA needed something, too.

Henri Delaunay, the secretary-general of the French Football Federation and one of the principal architects of UEFA, first proposed a pan-European international competition in 1927. 'Our mosaic of European countries needs this outlet for sporting expression,' he said in 1954. 'We cannot continue living in an atmosphere of routine and obsolescence.'

The trouble Delaunay had was that there already existed successful, established and popular international football tournaments. The Central European International Cup, for example, had been running since 1927 and brought together the national teams of Austria, Hungary, Italy, Czechoslovakia, Switzerland and Yugoslavia. It was the brainchild of Austrian pioneer Hugo Meisl, who had also invented the Mitropa Cup, a knockout competition for club teams from central European countries, which also began in 1927. Then there was the British Home Championship, contested since 1883 by England, Scotland, Wales and Ireland.

A new international event posed an existential threat to those competitions and so, understandably, their respective governing bodies were opposed. So, too, were many of the most influential club sides across the continent, who were reluctant to release their players for any more international matches than was necessary.

After Delaunay's death in 1955, his son Pierre replaced him as the head of UEFA and, determined to honour his late father by realising his ambition, pressed ahead with plans for a new quadrennial competition. In 1957, a vote of UEFA members went narrowly in favour of the project. Still, the objections rained down. Ottorino Barassi, representing the Italian football association at the 1958 UEFA general assembly, shared his concern that such a tournament might 'excite national passions'. Only twelve years removed from the end of the Second World War, was it not irresponsible to create such a volatile tinderbox?

Delaunay was unmoved. 'Whether we like it or not,' he insisted, 'the momentum is uncontainable. The European international competition will take off in the end, and sooner or later it will have the virtually unanimous backing of the associations.'

On 6 June at the Foresta Hotel in Stockholm, under the direction of UEFA vice-president Gustáv Sebes, the qualifying draw for the inaugural European Nations Cup took place. A total of seventeen associations entered. Amongst those who abstained were England, Scotland, Wales and Ireland. West Germany, Italy and the Netherlands did likewise.

Of the seventeen countries who attempted to qualify, four made it to the finals in France. The hosts, Yugoslavia, Czechoslovakia and the Soviet Union. Thanks to an extra-time winner from Viktor Ponedelnik, it was the Soviets who ran out triumphant, defeating Yugoslavia in front of a crowd of 17,966 at the Parc des Princes in Paris.

Despite controversy in the build-up to and, indeed, during the event – Spain, for example, were disqualified after refusing to travel to the Soviet Union for a qualifying match on political grounds – the first European Nations Cup was a broad success. The twenty-nine matches it comprised were watched by more than one million spectators, averaging just over 37,000 per game. Where it had failed to connect with many of those running European football, it had succeeded with those who consumed it. That was impossible to ignore. As a result, twenty-nine out of a possible thirty-three national associations signed up for the next edition in 1964. As before, the competition was structured so that countries played teams over two-legged, home-and-away matches until the semis, where the final four teams would move on to the finals.

Amongst those to enter were England, Wales, the Republic of Ireland and Northern Ireland. Scotland continued to abstain. England and Wales both failed to make it through the preliminary qualifying round, with Northern Ireland bowing out in the last 16 and Spain accounting for the Republic in the quarters. Spain, indeed, went on to win the tournament, defeating the defending champions from the Soviet Union in front of almost 80,000 supporters in Madrid.

Ahead of the third edition in 1968, the competition changed its name from the 'European Nations' Cup' to the 'European Championship'. By this point, Delaunay had been proven correct; the tournament did have uncontainable momentum and the backing of almost all associations. The success of European nations at the 1962 World Cup – where Czechoslovakia lost in the final, Yugoslavia reached the semis and four others made it to the quarters – might have had something to do with that. So, too, the emergence and almost immediate popularity of the club-based European Cup. Whatever problems UEFA might have had, piquing the curiosity of football fans clearly was not one of them.

Consequently, a new qualifying structure for the 'Euros' was adopted ahead of the 1968 edition, the two-legged home-and-away knockout stage being replaced by a group phase. Thirty-one teams were divided into eight groups: seven of four teams and one of three. Each group winner would progress to the quarter-finals, to be played in two legs on a home-and-away basis, with the winners of those matches proceeding to the final tournament.

In a bid to satisfy all parties and protect various competing interests, UEFA agreed to use the British Home Championships of 1966/67 and 1967/68 as a qualifier, much like the 1950 tournament had been used for the 1950 World Cup. England, Scotland, Wales and Northern Ireland were all put in Group 8, with the results from those two editions of the competition being combined to determine the qualifying for the championship.

Suddenly, Scotland – the pride of the nation bruised by years of under-representation and underperformance on football's global stage, not to mention England's World Cup victory in 1966 – had a new prize to contend for. They had cause to feel optimistic about their prospects, too. After all, they had won the British Home Championship thirty-five times, most recently in 1963/64, when they, England and Northern Ireland shared the spoils. With the talent at their disposal, all they needed was for the SFA to create the right environment for them, starting with employing the right man to lead them.

Right up until he had boarded that flight to New York, it looked as though John Prentice could be that man, but there would be others, of that there was no doubt. Make the right appointment, get the best out of the world-class players the country unquestionably had and who knows, maybe Scotland would travel to Italy at the expense of their biggest rivals – Alf Ramsey's self-styled 'World Champions' – in 1968. Hey, perhaps they would even win it. Wouldn't that be something?

Yeah. That would show them.

Wouldn't it?

FIVE

WEAK, PUNY AND BESPECTACLED

AS DAWN BROKE IN CARDIFF on 22 October 1966, the acute pain of the previous day's tragedy, occurring just twenty miles north of the Welsh capital, was felt anew.

High above the village of Aberfan, near Merthyr Tydfil, seven colliery spoil tips had been built on top of a natural spring. Weeks of heavy rain – around six inches in all – had created an unsustainable build-up of water in Tip Number Seven. A little after nine o'clock that fateful Friday morning, the pressure told and the tip burst. Around 140,000 cubic yards of thick, black slurry slid 700 yards down the mountainside, moving at twenty miles an hour and in waves that were thirty feet high in places.

At the foot of the mountain, lessons had just begun at Pantglas Junior School. Before anybody had time to react, the building and a row of houses near it were smothered by the mudslide, trapping and suffocating almost all within them.

A total of 144 people were killed, 116 of them children, mostly aged between seven and ten. Minutes earlier, they had been at morning assembly where they had sung 'All Things Bright and Beautiful' in perfect, innocent unison.

People from neighbouring towns and villages threw shovels into the back of their cars and raced to the scene, desperate to help. By the time they arrived, it was already too late. After 11 a.m. – less than two hours after the building had been hit – no one else came out alive.

It was an utterly catastrophic, heart-breaking event that resonated far beyond the valleys of South Wales. The unspeakable sadness of it all was summed up just over a week later when Her Majesty Queen Elizabeth II visited to pay her respects. The visibly emotional monarch – whose sons Andrew and Edward were aged six and two at the time – was handed a small posy of flowers by a young girl. The accompanying card simply read: 'From the remaining children of Aberfan'.

To widespread incredulity, as exhausted rescuers continued to dig in vain for survivors, the opening match of the seventy-third British Home Championship went ahead as scheduled less than half an hour away. As one member of the SFA delegation was heard to remark, 'Life, I suppose, must go on.'

Not everybody agreed.

Of the anticipated crowd of 50,000, little over 33,000 passed through the turnstiles. Many of those who might otherwise have gone stayed away out of respect and solidarity with the population of Aberfan. Others were just too emotionally shattered by the devastation of it all. As TV commentator Kenneth Wolstenholme put it: 'Many people in Wales have no heart for football today.'

In his match report for *The Herald*, Raymond Jacobs noted that the tragedy had 'overshadowed' the game 'to an extent probably unique in international football'. He observed 'a national grief in which skies of thick grey joined heavily'.

Gair Henderson of the *Evening Times* described Cardiff as 'a city of silence and mourning'. He wrote: 'Normally by breakfast-time, the streets are packed with hundreds of singing Scots, but today they were quiet – part of the mourning that is being shown throughout Wales.'

Both sets of players wore black armbands as a mark of respect to the victims and a two-minute silence was observed prior to kick-off. Nobody wanted to be there, not least Denis Law. The Scotland forward was amongst those struck dumb by the decision not to postpone. 'Can you imagine, under those circumstances, having to play a game of football?' he would later remark. 'All the while the death toll rose. It was just horrendous. To be honest, the game meant nothing.'

The match yielded the thirty-sixth of Law's fifty-five Scotland caps. Born in Aberdeen in February 1940, he was the youngest of seven children born to George Law, a fisherman, and his wife, Robina. A penurious family, the Laws lived in a council tenement in Printfield Terrace in the Woodside area of the 'Granite City'. So poor were they, in fact, that young Denis went barefoot until he was twelve. When he did finally get shoes, they were seldom better than well-worn hand-me-downs.

'Whenever I look back at how life was lived when I was a child, it's all quite amazing,' he would later acknowledge. 'Our house had no carpet, no central heating and no TV. There was a pantry instead of a fridge, and I have difficulty recalling eating any food during the week other than soup and a bit of pudding.'

He regularly shared a bed with at least two of his siblings and baths were reserved for Sunday nights because that was the only time when there was hot water.

Born shortly after the outbreak of the Second World War, some of Law's earliest memories involve scrambling into shelters with his family when the air-raid sirens went off to alert of an imminent attack by the German forces. He recalls Aberdeen, with its nearby RAF base and North Atlantic shipping port, being 'a bit like a dartboard for the Luftwaffe'. Thankfully, the family survived the conflict with no casualties.

Law's other main childhood recollections centred around football. Despite his father having no real interest in the game, Denis and his three older brothers – John, Joseph and George – were forever kicking a ball about. George, in fact, was particularly talented and might even have had a professional career of his own had he not suffered a serious leg break when he was eighteen.

The brothers started following Aberdeen FC and, when they could afford it, they walked to nearby Pittodrie Stadium to watch their heroes in action. Other times, they used to watch the non-league teams playing in the local Highland League.

Law grew up idolising George Hamilton, a prolific inside-forward who scored over one hundred goals for Aberdeen across two spells. Then there was Paddy Buckley, a lightning quick forward whose seventeen goals helped Aberdeen win the Scottish football league for the first-ever time in 1954/55, not to mention his strike partner Henry Yorston.

'All we wanted to do was play football,' Law recalled. 'We would play on the way to school with an old bald tennis ball – or a tin can if we didn't have a ball – knocking it off the walls as we progressed, and then back home again in the afternoon. When the homework was done, it was back out to play again in the street, using lampposts and a grid as goals. If a guy had a football, he was the king. He'd be the one to pick sides and be the captain.'

A bright student, with a particular aptitude for English, science, geography and technical drawing, Law did well enough at primary school to qualify for a place at Aberdeen Grammar School. Just one problem. Football wasn't on the syllabus. Rugby? Sure. Cricket? Absolutely. But football? Afraid not. For Law, such a prospect was simply unthinkable. *No football?* Finally, after much lobbying, he persuaded his parents to let him go to Powis Junior Secondary School (now the St Machar Academy) instead.

For a time, Law harboured hopes of becoming a draughtsman or an architect when he left school. His father's tales from the boat put him off going to sea, while the idea of becoming a footballer seemed too far-fetched. 'In those days in Aberdeen, youngsters just didn't dream of becoming a footballer,' he said. 'That destiny was for another band of people altogether during my childhood.'

That started to change when he met Bill Durno. Powis Secondary's technical teacher, Durno also ran the school football team and quickly moved Law from full-back, where he generally played up to that point, to inside-left. It was an inspired move. Despite the cruel taunts of other players, who mocked his terrible squint and called him names like 'Cockeye', Law flourished in his new position. So much so that he was called up to travel to Ireland with the Scotland Schoolboys in 1953.

It was during the 1954/55 season, as his beloved Aberdeen – Buckley, Yorston and all – were making history, that Law got his big break. Huddersfield Town, who were going well in the English First Division, were managed by a fellow Aberdonian called Andy Beattie. As it so happened, his brother Archie lived a mile or so from the Law family and, from time to time, would go to watch matches involving local youngsters. At a time when Scottish talent scouts were as rich in supply as hen's teeth, Archie Beattie would keep tabs on up-and-coming players in the north-east of Scotland and send the most promising ones down to Yorkshire for his brother Andy to assess. Impressed by what he had seen in the local ranks, Archie tapped up Law in March 1955.

At first glance, he seemed an unlikely candidate for the rough and tumble of professional football. In addition to his squint, which forced him to wear glasses when he wasn't playing football, he was only 5'3" and, by his own estimation, weighed eight stone soaking wet. He was just a wee fifteen-year-old boy. To begin with, Andy Beattie agreed. He took one look at Law and, for a moment, wondered if this was Archie on the wind-up. 'Never did I see a less likely football prospect,' he would later say. 'He was weak, puny and bespectacled.'

Law was accompanied on the trip to Huddersfield by his older brothers. As a family, the Laws had never travelled further than Stonehaven – a coastal town fifteen miles south of Aberdeen – so travelling to England was a heady adventure, not to mention an almighty culture shock.

Despite Beattie's initial misgivings, Law spent a week with the 'Terriers' where he took part in a succession of five-a-side matches, presumably, he later reasoned, to assess whether he was as fragile as he looked. At the end of that week, and much to his surprise, the club made him an offer. 'Archie came to my house to see my mum and they sent me out while they discussed my future,' he recalled. 'He assured her that the club would put me in digs and keep an eye on me, and she was fully aware that I was into football, that it was what I enjoyed doing most.'

On 3 April 1955, Law signed with Huddersfield Town. It was a huge milestone both for him personally and, in time, Scottish football more broadly. Another significant thing that happened early in his Huddersfield career was the opportunity to get corrective surgery on his squint. Law had been on a waiting list for the procedure for almost two years by the time the call came in.

'I cannot emphasise enough what an incredible moment in my life that was,' he said. 'It completely changed things for me. Suddenly, I had the wherewithal to look people, literally, straight in the eye. Suddenly, I had confidence. I felt like a new man.'

Law's new-found self-belief was diametrically opposed to the mood around Huddersfield. Having finished mid-table in 1954/55, the side suffered the ignominy of relegation the following season. Its ageing squad was full of players in their thirties who were no match for the likes of Manchester United, whose 'Busby Babes' won the league that year with an average age of just twenty-two.

A disappointing start to life in the Second Division saw Andy Beattie vacate the manager's office, his place taken by his assistant and fellow Scot Bill Shankly. Far from being despondent or concerned about his own future, Law thrived under Shankly and made his first-team debut away to Notts County on Christmas Eve 1956, just a few weeks short of his seventeenth birthday. Huddersfield won 2–0 and Law kept his place for the visit of the same opponent just two days later. It was a dream home debut, Law scoring in a 3–0 win. It was to be the first of sixteen goals he scored for the old Leeds Road outfit.

Despite his good form, Law missed out on a place in the Scotland squad for the 1958 World Cup in Sweden but was handed his international debut later that year by interim Scotland boss Matt Busby. The Manchester United manager led the side for two games and, a huge admirer of Law (he reportedly had a £10,000 bid for the young forward rejected by Andy Beattie early in his Huddersfield Town career), picked him to face Wales in Scotland's opening match of the 1958/59 British Home Championship. Once again, Busby demonstrated his knack of spotting young talent, Law scoring the second in a 3–0 win. He featured in the next match the following month against Northern Ireland at Hampden. The sides drew 2–2 as Law's parents watched on from the stands, the first and last time they ever saw their youngest son play professional football. His first taste of playing England came at Hampden in 1960, his former Huddersfield boss Beattie picking him to lead the line alongside Ian St John, Alexander Young, Graham Leggatt and Andrew Weir in a 1–1 draw.

By then, he was playing his club football for Manchester City, the Maine Road men swooping to sign him in March 1960 for a British record transfer fee of £55,000. He spent little more than a season there before moving to Italian outfit Torino. The £110,000 deal was a record fee for a transfer involving a British player. His time in Turin was almost as brief. Despite his popularity amongst supporters, who voted him the number one foreign player in Serie A ahead of the likes of Fiorentina winger Kurt Hamrin and Inter Milan midfielder Luis Suarez, Law's time there ended acrimoniously when he was sent off during a match against Napoli. After the game, he was told that the Torino coach, Beniamino Santos, had in fact ordered the referee to send him off, so angry was he that Law had defied his orders by taking a throw-in. In July 1962 he signed for Manchester United for £115,000 – another British record transfer.

He found a club that was still in the process of grieving and rebuilding following the Munich air disaster of 1958 that claimed the lives of twenty-three people, eight of them Manchester United players. They spent most of Law's first season scrapping it out at the wrong end of the table and, ultimately, only avoided relegation by three points. They made up for their poor league form by winning the FA Cup – Law scoring the first goal in a 3–1 win over Leicester City – and qualifying for the Cup Winners' Cup the following season.

The Scot's free-scoring form early in the 1963/64 season earned him a call-up to play for a Rest of the World XI to face England at Wembley as part of the FA's celebration of the 100th anniversary of association football. With fellow Scot Jim Baxter named amongst the reserves, Law lined up alongside some of the game's greatest-ever players – Soviet goalkeeper Lev Yashin, Portuguese star Eusébio, and Real Madrid icon Alfredo di Stefano – and scored the side's only goal in a 2–1 defeat. Despite a twenty-eight-day suspension for a red card against Aston Villa,

Law finished that season with forty-six goals in all competitions, a Manchester United club record that still stands to this day.

He helped himself to twenty-eight league goals the following year, finishing as the top goal scorer in the First Division as the Old Trafford side won their sixth league championship and first since Munich. A dream year for Law was rounded off when he won the Ballon d'Or, an individual award presented annually to Europe's top player (and more recently expanded to include any player playing for a European club). Chosen by football journalists, Law was the clear winner, finishing ahead of Inter Milan ace Luis Suarez and Real Madrid's outside-right Amancio. He was the first – and, to date, only – Scot to receive the honour.

At international level, he had become almost the first name on the Scottish team-sheet and, with twenty-five goals, including a record-equalling three hat-tricks, was already well on the way to becoming the country's top goalscorer by the time the 1966/67 British Home Championships got under way in Wales.

It was Law, indeed, who spared the blushes of Malky Macdonald and his men with a controversial equaliser just two minutes from time at Ninian Park. Welsh goalkeeper Gary Sprake spilled a goal-bound effort from Joe McBride into the path of Law, who slid along the rain-soaked turf and bundled the ball into an empty net. Afterwards, a furious Sprake insisted that the Scots' talisman had handled the ball in the act of scoring. 'He punched it in,' he demanded. 'There's no doubt about it. I was about to grab the ball when he flicked it into the net.' Welsh captain Mike England and Terry Hennessey backed up Sprake's claims.

Law was having none of it, dismissing the Welsh protests as 'nonsense'. 'The ball hit my chest and I put it in with my foot,' he said. It was a moot point. The referee saw nothing wrong with it and the goal stood. In truth, a draw was the least the Scots deserved from the match. For seventy-seven minutes, they had laid siege to Sprake's goal, forcing the Leeds United shot-stopper into a succession of stunning saves, particularly from debutant McBride. The Celtic man was unlucky not to win a penalty with a quarter of an hour to play after England brought him down inside the box. Minutes later, Ron Davies capitalised on a mix-up in the Scottish defence following a corner floated into the box by inside right Cliff Jones. Davies spun on a sixpence and slammed the ball past Bobby Ferguson to give Wales the lead. It looked as though Dave Bowen's men would hold on for a famous victory until Law's last-gasp heroics rescued a point for Scotland.

While the Welsh players protested the legitimacy of Law's equaliser, SFA officials were making a complaint of their own. They were unimpressed by what they saw as an overly physical approach from their hosts. Indeed, Welsh full-back Graham Williams was cautioned by referee Ken Dagnall after one particularly bad foul on winger Jimmy Johnstone.

'How can you play football against a team who pull you down every time you have the ball?' asked SFA president Tom Reid. Jock Stein, the Celtic boss and former Scotland team manager, described it as 'without any doubt, the dirtiest international game I have seen.'

Not that it really mattered. Not when you considered what the bereaved families of Aberfan were dealing with just a short distance away. This was a day when football was what football is: a diversion, a distraction, a ninety-minute interruption from the inflexible realities of life and death.

**

ACROSS THE IRISH SEA, Alf Ramsey's England strode out onto Windsor Park in Belfast in their first hurrah as world champions. Eighty-four days had passed since Bobby Moore, proudly holding the Jules Rimet Trophy above his head, had been carried around Wembley on the shoulders of his teammates. Ramsey named the same starting XI as had defeated West Germany that day for the clash with Bertie Peacock's Northern Ireland.

The build-up to the match, at least from an English perspective, had been soured by a clash with the Inland Revenue. The taxman had got wind of a £1,000 bonus that had been collected by each of the twenty-two players in England's World Cup-winning squad and decided that he quite fancied a slice of it for himself. It was left to captain Moore to take up the challenge on behalf of his teammates, even taking the matter to the courts where Mr Justice Brightman found in favour of the world champions. 'The payment had the quality of a testimonial or accolade rather than the quality of remuneration for services rendered,' declared the judge, as England's footballers extended their winning run beyond the pitch.

Back on grass, they faced a Northern Irish side determined to cut their UK partners back down to size and end a thirty-nine-year wait for a home win over the English. They certainly had the players to do so. In Tottenham Hotspur's Pat Jennings, they possessed an outstanding young goalkeeper, whilst, at the other end of the park, Derek Dougan of Leicester City and Manchester United's Machiavellian maestro George Best were capable of hurting any opposition.

The Irish battled hard but were simply no match for their more polished, more efficient opponents. Roger Hunt opened the scoring shortly before half-time, finally breaking Jennings' resolve with a half-volley on the turn. Jennings didn't reappear for the second half, an ankle injury forcing him to make way for Willie McFaul, and England capitalised on the hour mark when Martin Peters headed home a cross from Bobby Charlton.

The hosts' frustrations told in the closing minutes when Linfield's twenty-three-year-old winger Billy Ferguson was ordered off by Scottish referee Bobby Davidson for a wild lunge on Alan Ball, the youngster leaving the field in tears.

It all amounted to a workmanlike if not particularly standout performance for England and Ramsey was, for the most part, satisfied. 'I was happy to see that first goal but we are still finding it difficult to get the ball in the back of the net,' he told reporters. 'This was one of the better games in the British Championship, though latterly it got rather out of hand. Ireland played quite well with several good individual performances and, after the second goal, we played too loosely.'

Be that as it may, England had seized the early advantage, not just in the latest round of matches against their three closest rivals but in the race to qualify for the 1968 European Football Championship.

The world champions were on a roll.

SIX

AN IMMOVABLE OBJECT, AN UNSTOPPABLE FORCE

ON THE DOMESTIC FRONT, Celtic had started the 1966/67 season like a locomotive. By the end of October, they had won all seven of their matches in Division One, establishing a three-point lead over Malky Macdonald's Kilmarnock. They had done so in free-scoring fashion, too, scoring twenty-six goals and conceding only six. A first successful title defence in half a century was looking promising.

Perhaps as a portent of that, they retained the Scottish League Cup courtesy of a 1–0 win over bitter rivals Rangers in front of almost 95,000 fans at Hampden Park. They also had a Glasgow Cup final against Partick Thistle to look forward to in early November, whilst in Europe, they had eased past Swiss champions FC Zürich in the first round of the European Cup, 5–0 the aggregate score.

And all this after thumping a Manchester United side – featuring George Best, Denis Law, former Celt Paddy Crerand and newly crowned world champions Nobby Stiles and Bobby Charlton – 4–1 in a pre-season friendly.

Central to Celtic's early-season success was the Glasgow club's scintillating strike force. Jimmy Johnstone, Stevie Chalmers, Joe McBride and Bobby Lennox were a potent front four with an almost telepathic understanding of each other's abilities and movement. Come Halloween 1966, they had scored a remarkable fifty-six goals between them in just twenty-one games.

Former Motherwell man McBride had claimed the lion's share of those, with twenty-seven goals to his name by the time the guisers hit the streets. Lennox, however, wasn't far behind with fifteen – and the SFA selectors were starting to take notice.

Born in the Ayrshire town of Saltcoats in 1943, Lennox grew up no different to most other young boys in the west of Scotland at that time: football daft. He played every opportunity he got, and, when he wasn't on the pitch, he was in the terraces overlooking them. With Kilmarnock being the nearest 'big town' to the family home, Lennox regularly travelled to Rugby Park as much to see the visiting teams as the home side.

His first visit to Celtic Park came in August 1957 when he and a couple of friends took in the League Cup match between the 'Hoops' and Airdrie. In April the following year, he was one of almost 128,000 people who crammed into Hampden to see Scotland host England in the British Home Championship. Manchester United's Bobby Charlton made his debut for the visitors that day, scoring the third goal in a 4–0 England victory.

A few years later, Lennox was back at Hampden, this time to see Denis Law – then at Torino – play for an Italian League Select in a 1–1 draw with a Scottish League Select. As he was for many Scots, young and old alike, Law was Lennox's hero. 'Denis was a glamorous player,' he would later reflect. 'Almost God-like in comparison to the rest of the players.

'Watching those greats, I never thought that the level at which they were playing was within reach for me. I had long been determined to make it as a football player and had no doubts that I had the potential to do so, but I never imagined that I could reach the greatest heights in the game.'

He took the first significant step towards doing so barely a week after his eighteenth birthday. Having impressed in the amateur set-up, first with a local Ayrshire parish club called Star of the Sea and then with Ardeer Recreation in Stevenston, Lennox had been attracting interest from a number of senior clubs. He had trials with both Blackpool and Chelsea, and, closer to home, had offers from Motherwell, Greenock Morton, Falkirk and Kilmarnock. St Mirren took him on trial, too. He turned them all down. Ardeer Rec were owned at that time by industrial giant ICI, which meant they had facilities that were at least the equal of (and, in some cases, were superior to) many of the clubs that wanted to sign Lennox. He was in no rush to move.

He was rewarded for his patience in September 1961. As he walked off the pitch with his dejected Ardeer teammates one Saturday afternoon, Shettleston having trounced them 4–1 in a West of Scotland Cup tie, Lennox was approached by Celtic's chief scout, Joe Connors.

'Bobby,' he asked him, 'how would you like to put your future in the hands of Glasgow Celtic?'

He didn't need to ask twice.

The following Tuesday, Lennox and his father travelled to Glasgow where they had a meeting with Celtic manager Jimmy McGrory. By the time it was over, Lennox – who had turned eighteen just days earlier – was a Celtic player. He made his first-team debut for Celtic in March 1962, deputising for Stevie Chalmers in a 2–1 win over Dundee. It might have been a dream debut, not to mention an appropriate pre-indication of things to come, had the referee not chalked off his first-half goal for a dubious handball.

Despite impressing, that was Lennox's only appearance that season. Indeed, he struggled to establish himself in the side under McGrory. When he finally did so late in 1964, he was dismayed by news at the end of January 1965 that the Celtic boss was stepping down to be replaced by Jock Stein.

'I didn't take it well,' he would admit. 'I fretted that the new man, whom I did not know at all, might not fancy me as a player and that my hard-won place in the team might be in jeopardy.'

He needn't have worried. Far from being unconvinced by Lennox, Stein was, in fact, a huge fan and believed that Celtic had been making poor use of his talents, particularly his blistering pace. Until then, Lennox had largely been deployed as an inside-right whose main responsibilities were to link the midfield with the attack. He was, essentially, a creator of goals as opposed to a scorer of them. Before he had even assumed office at Parkhead, Stein – serving an eight-week notice period at Hibernian – instructed Celtic coach Sean Fallon to convert Lennox into an out-and-out centre-forward. No more would he have to work back into his own half. Instead, he was to conserve his energy for working in the opposition's final third.

It was a stroke of genius that paid almost instant dividends. Lennox finished the 1964/65 season with twenty-one goals in all competitions and starred in the Scottish Cup final as Celtic ended an eight-year silverware drought. The following campaign started just as brightly. By December, Lennox had scored fifteen times as Celtic challenged Rangers at the top of the league, beat them in the Scottish League Cup final, and cruised into the quarters of the European Cup Winners' Cup.

That form earned Lennox a first Scotland call-up, albeit in slightly chaotic circumstances. With Stein in interim charge of the international side and looking to guide them to the World Cup finals in England the following summer, the team travelled to Naples for a winner-takes-all qualifier with two-time champions Italy. After five matches in a group that also contained Poland and Finland, the two sides were locked at the top of the table on seven points apiece, albeit the Italians had a far superior goal difference. As far as the Scots were concerned, the objective was simple: win and go through.

Their prospects were weakened in the build-up to the game when both Denis Law and Jim Baxter were forced to withdraw through injury. Liverpool's former Rangers left-half, Billy Stevenson, did likewise and more soon followed. As they gathered at their Largs base, Stein's squad comprised only fifteen players. Reinforcements were required.

Lennox, still only twenty-two years of age, had been at the cinema in Saltcoats that evening with his girlfriend Kathryn. They had gone back to her parents' house in the town for supper when, around 10 p.m., there was a knock at the door. It was Scotland trainer Walter McCrae. Having made the dash from the team's HQ, he explained the situation to Lennox and asked him if he would report for international duty the following morning.

The drama didn't end there. The bus that took the squad from the airport in Naples to their hotel in Sorrento travelled around so many twisting coastal roads that a number of the Scots players ended up with travel sickness. Lennox was one of them. When they finally arrived at the hotel, he was sent straight to his room to recover. Even when he finally made it out of his sickbed the next day – the day of the game – he was unable to take part in training. Along with Willie Johnston, he sat helpless in the stands as the Scots slipped to a 3–0 defeat, goals from Ezio Pascutti, Giacinto Facchetti and Bruno Mora ending their World Cup ambitions. 'It was still pretty exciting just to be there,' admitted Lennox.

That was the final match in charge of Scotland for Stein, who was replaced by John Prentice in March 1966. Despite continuing to impress for Celtic – finishing the season with twenty-five goals in all competitions as the Parkhead men won the league and League Cup double, finished runners-up in the Scottish Cup and reached the semis of the European Cup Winners' Cup –

Lennox was overlooked by the new national boss. The British Home Championship match with England and friendlies with the Netherlands, Portugal and Brazil came and went without his involvement.

He was again surprisingly overlooked by Prentice's interim successor, Malky Macdonald, for the 1966/67 British Home Championship opener away to Wales before finally getting a long-awaited first 'proper' call-up for match number two, the November 1966 clash with Northern Ireland.

Lennox took the place of Celtic teammate Jimmy Johnstone for the visit of Bertie Peacock's men, one of two changes to the Scottish starting XI from the side that drew with the Welsh.

The other drew much of the limelight away from Lennox's debut – the decision to drop Jim Baxter. The Sunderland wing-half's place had been in some doubt after the trip to Ninian Park. Many observers felt that the Scottish team simply couldn't afford the luxury of playing both he and Denis Law. Both were capricious talents but, according to some, too often stifled each other's ability. That much had been evident in the draw with Wales. Something had to give. Or rather, someone. Unfortunately for the thirty-one times capped Baxter, fate, which had so often smiled upon him, chose a bad day for a scowl.

In his place came Celtic midfielder Bobby Murdoch, winning his fifth cap in the heart of the midfield alongside Billy Bremner. Macdonald kept faith with his club keeper Bobby Ferguson, with Celtic duo Tommy Gemmell and John Clark operating either side of Rangers' central defensive pairing Ron McKinnon and John Greig, the latter continuing as captain. Another Rangers man, Willie Henderson, was picked up front alongside Law and Celtic duo Lennox and McBride.

Lennox later admitted it was a relief to have familiar faces alongside him as he made his first Scotland start. 'Having so many fellow Celts in the side made the transition from club to country a particularly easy one,' he said. 'I felt right at home immediately. I was less overawed than I might have been.'

Whilst undoubtedly strong, Macdonald's line-up was, however, inexperienced. Combined, they boasted only 108 international caps between them, of which Law (thirty-six), Greig (nineteen) and Henderson (twenty-two) accounted for more than two-thirds. McBride was making only his second start, Gemmell and Clark their third, Murdoch his fifth.

By comparison, their opponents had 192 caps between them as Peacock made four changes from the side beaten 2–0 by England weeks earlier. Tottenham Hotspur's Pat Jennings kept his place in goal; John Parke (Sunderland), Martin Harvey (Sunderland) and captain Alex Elder (Burnley) were joined in a back four by Arsenal's Terry Neill; Manchester City man Johnny Crossan formed a midfield three with Huddersfield Town's Johnny Nicholson and David Clements of Coventry; Dundee's Sammy Wilson was joined up front by Leicester City's man mountain Derek Dougan and George Best, Manchester United's mercurial maestro.

Eight of the Irish starting XI had played in the last meeting between the sides at Ninian Park in October 1965, where goals from Dougan, Crossan and Willie Irvine helped the home side to a 3–2 win. In the twelve matches between the sides since Northern Ireland had formally separated (in a footballing sense) from the Republic of Ireland in 1951, Scotland had won six and the Irish three, with the remaining three drawn. However, two of those Irish wins had come in the last three matches. Little wonder most neutrals anticipated another close affair at Hampden.

In the build-up to the match, both sides were rocked by injury. Following Manchester United's 2–0 win over Sheffield Wednesday on the Saturday before the match, Denis Law and George Best were ruled out of the midweek clash in Glasgow. Law had sustained a shin injury, whilst Best had knocks on both ankles and a suspected broken toe.

'If the match were on Saturday, I would have had a chance,' said Best. 'But with only forty-eight hours to go, my chances are hopeless.' Team manager Peacock was equally despondent. 'I'm terribly disappointed that he's not playing,' he lamented. 'He is a big loss to our side.' Best's place was taken by Burnley forward Irvine, who had an adventurous journey north from Lancashire. Having received news of his last-minute call-up at 3.30 p.m. on the Monday afternoon, Irvine got the 5 p.m. train to Glasgow. However, his connection from Glasgow to the Irish side's base in Largs broke down, forcing him to complete the journey by taxi. It was the early hours of the morning by the time he made it to the team hotel.

There was no such drama for Law's stand-in, Stevie Chalmers. Brought in for his fifth Scotland start, Chalmers might not have had the same experience, market value or 'X factor' as the Manchester United man he had replaced, but in four previous appearances for Scotland he had scored three goals, including the opener in a 1–1 draw with world champions Brazil five months earlier. Plus, as a clubmate of fellow front-men McBride and Lennox, he slotted straight into the line-up.

On a cool, crisp evening on Glasgow's south side, Scotland started the brighter, Jennings doing well to keep out a strike from McBride. It was against the run of play that the visitors took the lead in the ninth minute. Nicholson received the ball twenty-five yards from goal and let fly with a speculative effort that flew past the despairing Ferguson.

Five minutes later, the Scots were back on level terms. After good work on the left, Lennox cut the ball back for his on-rushing Celtic teammate Bobby Murdoch to crash the ball home from twenty yards.

Northern Ireland almost restored their lead soon afterwards when Sammy Wilson flashed a header just past the post before Scotland edged in front with ten minutes of the first half remaining – and lo and behold, it was debutant Lennox who scored it.

A corner from the right was nodded down by McBride to Lennox who flicked the ball back over his own head and into the roof of the net from four yards out. 'I was delighted with it and jumped into Billy Bremner's arms,' he recalled. 'It was especially pleasing as Pat Jennings had made a terrific save from me earlier in the match. I had been clean through on goal and he had raced out to snatch the ball from my feet.'

Into the second half, the Irish tried desperately to get back on terms but the best chances fell to Scotland. The home side screamed for a penalty after Neill appeared to handle the ball inside the box, only for those claims to be waved away by English referee Jack Taylor. McBride and Henderson went close before Lennox should have helped himself to a second after being sent through one-on-one against Jennings. Instead of firing past him, the Celtic man instead tried to go around him and the chance was lost.

In the dying minutes of the match, Lennox thought he had won his side a penalty when he was brought down by Parke. Once again, Taylor turned away.

In the end, the Scots ran out deserved winners but were frustrated not to have won by a bigger margin. Nonetheless, it ended a sequence of five matches without a win, maintained their hopes of winning the British Home Championship, and (far more significantly) kept them in the running for a European Nations Cup place. Not bad for a team missing its two best players and without a permanent manager.

Up next? England, at Hampden Park, in April.

* * *

AS SCOTLAND WERE LABOURING to victory over Northern Ireland, Alf Ramsey's England – yet again represented by the same eleven players who had contested the World Cup final – were laying waste to a woeful Wales at Wembley.

Following a frustrating stalemate in a friendly with Czechoslovakia two weeks earlier, the sixteenth match since the summer of 1965 in which England had not conceded a goal, the majority of the 70,000-strong crowd turned up in anticipation of a straightforward victory. They were duly rewarded with a 5–1 rout, which extended the hosts' unbeaten record against their visitors to eleven matches.

Geoff Hurst continued his remarkable scoring record for his country, grabbing his sixth and seventh international goals in the first half. Wyn Davies pulled a goal back for David Bowen's side only for Bobby Charlton to restore England's two-goal cushion shortly before half-time with his forty-first international strike. An own goal by Terry Hennessey shortly after the hour made it 4–1 before Jack Charlton capped a fine performance with a late fifth.

The victory consolidated England's place at the top of the Home Championship and European Nations Cup qualifying tables. It also increased their unbeaten record at Wembley to eleven matches and was their nineteenth consecutive match without a loss. Not since Austria beat them 3–2 in a friendly in October 1965 had they tasted defeat. In that period, they had scored forty-two goals, conceded only ten, won sixteen times, kept twelve clean sheets and won the World Cup.

It was beyond any reasonable doubt that they were the best national team on the planet and, in Alf Ramsey, they had one of the most shrewd and meticulous managers, a boss beloved by players, fans and the media alike.

Three lions. One juggernaut.

Come ahead, Scotland. Come ahead.

SEVEN

THE KNIGHT ACROSS THE TABLE

A GRAND TOTAL OF 691 NAMES appeared on the 1967 New Year's Honours List but one stood out above all others. Alf Ramsey, the architect of England's World Cup victory five months earlier, was to become a knight of the realm. Arise, Sir Alf!

That the forty-six-year-old was given such royal acclaim was no great surprise. His methodical approach to management had brought football home. A proud sporting nation, starved of international success in the sport they cherished the most, gorged on the glory Ramsey had served them.

There was an honour, too, for his captain, Bobby Moore. Just weeks after winning the BBC Sportsview Personality of the Year award – the first footballer to do so in the twelve-year history of the prize – the West Ham man was made an O.B.E. Whilst many teeth were gnashed at the rest of England's heroes being overlooked, there was, still, appreciation and gratitude that Ramsey, in particular, had been recognised for his all-conquering efforts.

He became just the sixth 'Sir' in the 103-year history of English football, joining JC Clegg, Frederick Wall and Stanley Rous, as well as Stanley Matthews and Joseph Richards. Illustrious company, by any measure. Not that Ramsey was paying much attention.

'This honour,' he said, 'reflects on the whole of the team and is a wonderful tribute to all of British soccer.' It was trademark modesty from a man born into humility.

Born in Dagenham on 22 January 1920, Alfred Ernest Ramsey was the third of Herbert and Florence Ramsey's children. Herbert was a hay merchant who worked a smallholding, kept pigs and rode a horse-drawn dustcart. An archetypal 'rag-and-bone' man. The family's home had neither hot water nor electricity. The only toilet was an outdoor one. Even after the surrounding area was transformed, first by investment from London County Council and then the opening of the Ford Dagenham automobile factory in 1931, the Ramseys continued to live an anachronistic lifestyle. Indeed, it wasn't until the 1950s that their home was fitted with electricity, Florence reportedly being frightened of it. According to one of Alf's childhood friends, the family home was 'little more than a wooden hut'.

From the age of five, Ramsey attended Becontree Heath School. He and his brothers had to walk two hours from their home to get there and, to break the monotony of the journey, would kick a tennis ball to one another more or less the whole way there and back again. By the age of seven, he had been picked to play at inside-left for the school football team, often playing against boys twice his age. Far from being intimidated, young Alf revelled in the opportunity and, at nine years old, was converted to centre-half and named team captain. Despite his relative lack of pace, Ramsey was a terrific passer of the ball who studied the game forensically to improve his ability to read the play.

It was whilst he was at school that his older brother Albert took him to see his first-ever football match, a league clash between their beloved West Ham United and London rivals Arsenal. The next senior match he attended, he played in.

When he left school in 1934 at the age of fourteen, Ramsey became an apprentice at the local Co-op branch, delivering groceries on a bicycle. His Saturday afternoon shifts forced him to put football on the backburner for two years until he discovered Five Elms, a newly formed amateur team who played on Thursdays. It was around a year later that Ramsey was spotted by a scout from Portsmouth FC called Ned Liddell. He offered Alf, by now in his late teens, an amateur contract with the First Division outfit. Rather than sign immediately, Ramsey asked to take the forms home to examine that evening. He signed them later than night and returned them to Portsmouth by post. That was the last correspondence he had with the south coast side. He spent the next two years continuing to work at the Co-op and turning out for Five Elms.

Following the outbreak of the Second World War in 1939, Ramsey was drafted into the British Army in June 1940 and assigned to the Duke of Cornwall's Light Infantry. A shy, socially awkward young man, he was transformed by his military experience, later describing it as 'one of the greatest things that ever happened to me'. In his 1952 book *Talking Football*, he said: 'I learnt, in a few weeks, more about life in general than I had picked up in years at home.'

He spent the entire conflict in the UK on home defence duties. One of his earliest postings was to the Cornish town of St Austell, where, in addition to manning the beach defences, he captained the battalion's football team. In 1943, they were redeployed to Barton Stacey in Hampshire, where they came under the command of a Colonel Fletcher, himself an established footballer. Ramsey featured in the battalion side that was beaten

10–3 by Southampton in a pre-season friendly in August 1943. The following week, they took on the Saints' reserves, this time winning 4–1.

Some weeks later, Colonel Fletcher summoned Ramsey to his office. It transpired that Southampton had been back in touch. They needed a centre-half for their trip to Luton Town the next day and, having been impressed by him in his two matches against them, wanted to know if Ramsey was available.

Initially, he was reluctant. Senior football was a huge step up and, even though his battalion team featured a number of established players, such as Brentford's Len Townsend and Arsenal forward Cyril Hodges, he still didn't think he had enough experience to do Southampton justice. At Fletcher's insistence, he decided to give it a try. The following day, he signed amateur terms with the Saints – ironically, Portsmouth's biggest rivals – en route to Luton. It proved to be an eventful debut for the twenty-three-year-old. With Southampton leading 2–1, he gave away a penalty late on, allowing the hosts to equalise. Nonetheless, there was still time for his new side to grab a winner and Ramsey played three more times before his battalion was posted to County Durham at the opposite end of the country. When the unit came back to the south coast at the start of the 1944/45 season, Ramsey returned to Southampton for a trial. This time, his efforts earned him a contract on wages of £2 per match. With that, Company Quartermaster Sergeant Alf Ramsey was a professional footballer.

Injury prevented him from playing until December of 1944 and he went on to make eleven League South appearances that season. The following campaign, 1945/46, was the first football season to take place following the end of the war in Europe, and Ramsey started it in the new and unfamiliar position of centre-forward. Even so, he impressed, scoring twice in each of Southampton's first two games followed by a hat-trick in a

6–2 drubbing of Newport County. Military commitments once again intervened when, in December 1945, he was deployed to Palestine. He returned to England in June 1946 to two separate job offers: one, a continuation of his football career with Southampton; the other, a return to his pre-war gig at the Dagenham Co-op. After some fierce negotiating with Saints' new boss Bill Dodgin, who upped his wages, Ramsey joined Southampton for a third time and was formally discharged from the army soon thereafter.

The 1946/47 season saw the Football League resume at the expense of the inter-war leagues that had taken root during the conflict. Southampton found themselves in the Second Division, just as they had been in September 1939 when the British declaration of war on Germany led to the abandonment of the season and eventual suspension of the league. Ramsey began the season in the reserve team where he continued to persevere as a centre-forward. That changed when Dodgin and club trainer Sydney Cann made a decision that would alter the direction of his career in an extraordinary way. They converted him into a right-back. Cann had played in the position for Torquay United, Manchester City and Charlton Athletic, and he saw a great deal of himself in Ramsey. He took young Alf under his wing and helped to nurture him. 'I have never known anyone with the same quickness of learning as Alf Ramsey,' Cann once remarked. 'He was the type of player who was a manager's dream because you could talk about a decision and he would accept it and there it was, in his game.'

In October 1946, Ramsey made his full league debut in a Second Division clash with Plymouth Argyle, replacing regular starter Bill Ellerington who was forced to miss the game through injury. Southampton ran out 5–1 winners. When Ellerington recovered to full fitness, he reclaimed his place in the side only to break down again in January 1947 shortly before an away trip to Newcastle United. Once again, Ramsey deputised, and once again, he impressed. He retained his place in the side for the remainder of the season and was praised by Dodgin in a February 1947 interview. 'Alf Ramsey,' said the boss, 'is a player who thinks football, talks football and lives football.'

His teammates loved him, too. Eric Day, who spent almost his entire career playing on the wing for the Saints, said: 'He had a very, very good football brain. If he hadn't, he would not have played where he did because he was not the nimblest of players. He wasn't particularly brilliant in the air, because he did not have the stature to jump up. But he was a decent tackler and a great passer. He could read the game so well. That was his big asset.' Forward Ted Bates – subsequently dubbed 'Mr Southampton' – added that Ramsey possessed a 'razor-sharp brain' and said he 'would never get into a situation that exposed him'.

The following season, Ramsey was the only player to feature in all forty-two of Southampton's league matches. During the 1947/48 campaign, he captained the side on several occasions and, despite the Saints missing out on promotion to the top flight, finishing third behind Birmingham City and Newcastle United, he was part of a sixteen-man England squad that toured Switzerland and Italy. He didn't feature in any of the games but the trip was an important personal milestone for him nonetheless – the flight to Geneva was his first time on an airplane.

He didn't have to wait long for his second such expedition. No sooner had he returned from Europe with England than he was en route to Sao Paolo to join his Southampton teammates on a club tour of Brazil. The Saints had lost every game of the visit by the time Ramsey arrived and spirits in the camp were low. At Alf's suggestion, they decided to try a different approach for their next game with Corinthians. Instead of trying to play the Brazilians at their own sharp passing game, Ramsey recommended using long diagonal passes from deep to exploit gaps left by their opponents' defenders when they charged forward to join the attack. It worked. Southampton beat Corinthians 2–1.

Back in Blighty, Ramsey's impressive form continued and earned him a debut for England in a friendly with Switzerland in December 1948. The following month, he made what proved to be his final competitive appearance for Southampton in a 2–1 defeat to Sheffield Wednesday. In a friendly a week later, he slipped and injured his knee, allowing Ellerington to come back into the squad. Ramsey missed ten matches, during which the Saints won eight times and drew the other two. That prompted Dodgin to observe that Ramsey was 'going to find it very hard' to win back his place. Insulted, Ramsey demanded a transfer. He later admitted that he was so offended by Dodgin's remark that, 'for a fleeting moment', he considered quitting football altogether.

Reluctantly, the Southampton board relented and Ramsey was put up for sale. Liverpool, Luton Town, Burnley and Sheffield Wednesday all expressed an interest but, ultimately, it was fellow Second Division outfit Tottenham Hotspur who sealed the deal. Their manager Arthur Rowe swooped in May 1949 to sign him in a part-exchange deal, widely reported to have been worth a club record £21,000.

The move paid instant dividends for club and player alike. Tottenham began the 1949/50 season strongly, going undefeated in their first twenty-two games. Ramsey was a big part of the reason for that. He formed an immediate understanding with several players, amongst them wing-half Bill Nicholson, goalkeeper Ted Ditchburn and inside-right Sonny Walters. He also liked the fact that Rowe encouraged him to combine his defensive duties with regular forays into opposition territory.

The Londoners won the title with seven games to spare, winning promotion to the First Division for the first time since the 1934/35 campaign. It was the first major honour of Ramsey's career and, at the club's annual meeting ahead of their return to the top flight, Rowe told those in attendance that 'as much as anything else, I would rate our good time last year to the acquisition of Alf Ramsey'.

By Christmas of 1950, Spurs found themselves leading the First Division, with Ramsey in the form of his life. According to biographer Leo McKinstry, he 'was the master of strategy, the lynchpin of a side that built its attacks from the back, the scheming practitioner who put Rowe's plans into action'. His exceptional footballing brain earned him the nickname 'The General'.

By this time, Ramsey was well established as England's first-choice right-back and, in November 1950, had captained the side for the first time in a 4–2 British Home Championship win over Wales. He retained the armband for the 2–2 friendly draw with Yugoslavia the following week.

On 28 April 1951, Tottenham defeated Sheffield Wednesday 1–0 to win the English Football League for the first time in their sixty-nine-year history, a feat made all the more impressive considering they had done so in their first season following promotion from the Second Division. Ramsey was thrilled. 'I think fortune shone upon me very handsomely during the 1950/51 season,' he later wrote. 'After all, I was a member of one of the finest club teams in years.'

Tottenham made a strong defence of their title the following season, ultimately finishing second to Matt Busby's Manchester United. It was in the campaigns that followed that the wheels of the Tottenham juggernaut fell off. A tenth-place finish in 1952/53 was followed by sixteenth the next season. The fans that had saluted them as heroes just a couple of years earlier started to turn on the ageing members of the team, such as Ron Burgess, Nicholson and, yes, Ramsey. The latter's preference for keeping possession rather than clearing his lines infuriated sections of the Spurs support, never more so than in the FA Cup semi-final with Blackpool at Villa Park in March 1953. With the game evenly poised at 1–1, there was just a minute left on the clock when Ramsey steadied himself to play the ball back to goalkeeper Ditchburn when clearing it appeared the better option. The ball bobbled off his knee and bounced away from him, allowing Jackie Mudie to run through and score the winning goal.

Fans, media and even some of the Tottenham board queued up to savage him for the mistake. It was a blunder that haunted Ramsey for the rest of his career. He maintained that passing the ball back to the goalkeeper was the best option. He just got his execution wrong. Despite being linked with a return to Southampton – by now playing in the Third Division South – he stayed on at Tottenham and, in November 1953, made the last of his thirty-two appearances for England against the 1952 Olympic champions Hungary at Wembley.

The so-called 'Magical Magyars' were a formidable opponent and in the midst of what proved to be a thirty-one-game unbeaten streak that took them all the way to the 1954 World Cup final in Switzerland. England, meantime, had a proud record of having lost only once on home soil against foreign opposition, a 1949 defeat at the hands of the Republic of Ireland. The British media dubbed it the 'Match of the Century': the originators of the game against the world's strongest team.

As it turned out, it was a mismatch. With Ferenc Puskás, Nándor Hidegkuti and József Bozsik in full flow, the Hungarians thrashed their hosts 6–3. Ramsey scored a consolation from the penalty spot. It was his third and final goal for his country.

The following season, he was made Spurs' club captain following Burgess' move to Swansea City. By now in his mid-thirties, Ramsey was planning for a life beyond the pitch and had been promised a coaching role with Tottenham by Rowe. However, when ill-health forced Rowe to stand down in February 1955, Ramsey's options suddenly narrowed. 'I was thirty-five years old and obviously concerned about my future,' he later wrote. 'I really didn't know what was going to happen to me. I knew my days as a player were numbered and there was only one way things could go for me in this respect – downhill.' At the end of the 1954/55 campaign, having been overlooked for a coaching role by Rowe's replacement Jimmy Anderson and left out of a post-season tour to Hungary, Alf Ramsey announced his retirement from football.

Within weeks, he was back in the game. He was coaching in Southern Rhodesia in the 1955 off-season when Ipswich Town – then playing in the Third Division South – made him an offer. They were looking for a replacement for their long-standing boss, Scott Duncan, and wanted Ramsey to take over on a player-manager basis. 'I told them I would only concentrate on one job,' Ramsey later said. 'It would be impossible to play with the players I would be coaching.' The board agreed to his condition and he was appointed Ipswich boss on 9 August 1955, much to the delight of his former England teammate and captain Billy Wright. 'In appointing Alf to become their manager,' he said, 'Ipswich Town paid a tremendous tribute to intelligent football and footballers who think.'

A small, somewhat-unfashionable club, Ipswich was the ideal place for Ramsey to hone his coaching craft. Duncan had agreed to stay on as secretary, carrying much of the administrative burden that would otherwise have fallen to his successor. Most of the coaching staff remained in place, too, giving the club – and Ramsey – an essential layer of continuity. Still, there were challenges. The team had just been relegated from the Second Division and morale was low. The squad was ageing, too, and, despite having strong links to the local Cobbold brewing family, there was little money to invest in a rebuild. Ramsey would have to make the best of what he had.

'I had no plan for Ipswich when I went there,' he later said. 'The first thing I had to do was to forget my set ideas on how football ought to be played. My experience had been in the First Division. I soon found that what I faced at Ipswich was very different.'

His first game in charge was a dire display, prompting the local newspaper to brand it 'as poor a performance as one can recollect at Portman Road'. Things, though, soon improved and, in his first season in charge, Ramsey steered Ipswich to a credible third-place finish. The following season, they won the league, scoring over 100 goals in the process and earning promotion to the Second Division. They consolidated their position over the next three years with a trio of mid-table finishes before winning the league in 1960/61 and winning promotion to English football's top flight for the first time in their history.

Most pundits pinned them as relegation fodder the following season. How could they ever hope to compete with superior sides such as Burnley, Sheffield Wednesday and Ramsey's old club Tottenham, winners of the championship the year before? The answer lay in a formidable front three of Jimmy Leadbetter, Ray Crawford and Ted Phillips. Their goals fired Ipswich to the league title at the very first attempt. From the Third Division to champions of England in the space of just six years, it was, as the *Sunday People* newspaper declared, a 'SOCCER MIRACLE'.

'We're ordinary players, who play ordinary football and who concentrate on the simple things,' claimed Ramsey. Few agreed. This was the first time a club had won the championship at the first time of asking (with the exception of Preston North End who had won the inaugural title in 1888/89). It was an extraordinary achievement, a fairy-tale so far-fetched as to have been beyond the imagination of Hans Christian Andersen himself. As the players took it in turn to lift the trophy, Alf Ramsey's stock was rising.

In October of that year, with Ipswich having made a slow start to their title defence, the Football Association made their move. England's World Cup quarter-final defeat to Brazil that summer had prompted a fierce backlash against long-standing national boss Walter Winterbottom. The former Manchester United half-back had presided over four World Cups by this point and had failed to advance beyond the last eight. He had lost the dressing room with his academic approach and ninety-minute team talks and endured a tense relationship with the press. With little sign of progress on the pitch and a string of 'Winterbottom Must Go!' headlines in the newspapers, the FA dispensed with his services after seventeen years and 139 games in charge.

Top of their list to replace Winterbottom was his assistant Jimmy Adamson. When he turned them down, preferring instead to concentrate on extending his playing career, they turned to Ramsey. However, he too was reluctant. For one thing, he felt a loyalty to Ipswich that made him resistant to abandoning them midway through a season and, on a personal level, he was relishing the prospect of taking on the mighty AC Milan in the European Cup that November. He also wanted total control over squad and team selections. Throughout his tenure, Winterbottom had been 'manager' but selections and various other decisions were the responsibility of various committees. As far as Ramsey was concerned, that had to change.

The FA acquiesced. Yes, Ramsey would be allowed to combine his new national team responsibilities with seeing out the season at Ipswich, and yes, he would have the authority he demanded. In October 1962, he was confirmed as England's new manager. He formally took charge in May the following year.

In one of his first acts as national team boss, he named West Ham United captain Bobby Moore as England's new captain.

Like Ramsey, Moore came from a working-class background but at just twenty-two years old, there were some doubts over whether he could galvanise and lead a team comprising some of the best players – and biggest personalities – in the world. Bobby Charlton, Jimmy Greaves, Ray Wilson and the like. Nonetheless, he wore the armband for the first time away to Czechoslovakia on 29 May 1963. England won 4–2 and Moore entered the history books as England's youngest-ever skipper. It was to be the first of a record-equalling ninety matches he would lead his country into.

Failure to qualify for the European Nations Cup early in the opening match of Ramsey's reign was a blow but by no means a disaster. Rightly or wrongly, his focus was already on the next World Cup in 1966. As hosts, England automatically qualified for the tournament and the boss was determined to make the most of it. Indeed, he had caused a media frenzy at his unveiling when he confidently predicted that his side would win the Jules Rimet Trophy. By the time they lined up for their opening match of the tournament, against two-time winners Uruguay at Wembley on 11 June 1966, Ramsey had been in charge for thirty-eight games, winning twenty-four, drawing eight and losing only six. More significantly, they were unbeaten in their last ten matches and had lost only once in their last twenty-four. Favourites? Not quite. Most bookies were tipping Brazil at 9/4 but England were a close second at 9/2.

After playing out a stalemate with the South Americans in their opening game – the first time England had failed to score in a match at Wembley since 1945 – goals from Bobby Charlton and Roger Hunt gave Ramsey's men a 2–0 win over Mexico in their second match. They beat France by the same scoreline, Hunt grabbing a double, to advance to the knockout stages as winners of Group A.

That set up a clash with three opponents: Argentina on the

pitch, and both FIFA and the Football Association off it. FIFA were reportedly so incensed by a tackle made on Frenchman Jacques Simon by Nobby Stiles that they were lobbying the FA to have the Manchester United man dropped from the team. On the eve of the quarter-final clash with Juan Carlos Lorenzo's Argentina, Ramsey pulled Stiles aside on the training ground.

'I want to know whether you intended to kick the Frenchman,' he asked.

'I swear I didn't mean it,' replied Stiles. 'My timing was bloody awful. It must have looked bad but it was just bad timing. I didn't purposely kick the lad.'

'I believe you,' said Ramsey. 'I take your word as an Englishman.'

Satisfied, the England boss issued the FA's Senior International Committee with an ultimatum: *Either Stiles plays or I quit – right here, right now.*

'He was prepared to resign in the middle of a World Cup over me,' Stiles later remarked. 'I never found that out until after he died. What a man. From things that were said afterwards, I'm convinced that I would have lost my place under most other managers. But not Alf. He always stuck by what he believed in.'

The FA backed down and Stiles played. Prior to the kick-off, the combative, diminutive midfielder was pulled aside by Ramsey's two assistants, Harold Shepherdson and Les Cocker. 'Both of them said, very seriously, that Alf had put his reputation on the line for me and that I should do my utmost not to let him down,' he recalled. 'I was always inclined to be a bit excitable on the field, getting upset over bad decisions, that sort of thing, so I understood exactly what Harold and Les were on about. If I did just one stupid thing it would embarrass Alf and weaken his position.'

Whilst Stiles was able to maintain his discipline, the Argentines were not. In a bad-tempered match, the captain of

'La Albiceleste', Antonio Rattín, was sent off shortly after the half-hour by German referee Rudolf Kreitlein for what he later described as 'violence of the tongue'. Incensed by the perceived injustice – and, as far as he was concerned, bias towards England – Rattín initially refused to leave the pitch. When he finally did so, he sat on a red carpet that had been reserved exclusively for the Queen's use, much to the fury of the English players and fans. Two police officers eventually had to escort a still remonstrating Rattín down the tunnel and out of sight. His furious teammates spent much of the remainder of the match hounding, chasing and kicking out at anyone in an English shirt. By his own estimation, Stiles was spat at six or seven times by the opposition. Finally, Geoff Hurst, a replacement for the injured Jimmy Greaves, broke their resistance when he headed in a late winner. At full time, disgusted by what he had witnessed, Ramsey instructed his players to abstain from the customary swapping of shirts with the Argentines. 'It seemed a pity so much talent is wasted,' he subsequently said. 'Our best football will come against the right type of opposition – a team who come to play football, and not act as animals.'

The tournament's surprise package, Portugal, were then dispatched 2–1 in the semis to set up a final with West Germany. Under pressure to restore a fit-again Greaves to the starting line-up, Ramsey resisted. His instincts had served him well thus far and, as the biggest ninety minutes of his career approached, they were telling him not to change a winning team. Hurst kept his place and repaid the faith of his manager with the first-ever hat-trick in a World Cup Final. On a day of tension and expectation, drama and delirium, England won 4–2 after extra time to become world champions for the first time.

As captain Bobby Moore was carried around the Wembley pitch on the shoulders of his teammates and Nobby Stiles danced a jig of joy, Ramsey refrained from joining in the celebrations, preferring instead to watch from afar. 'This is for you players,' he told Bobby Charlton as the Manchester United man tried to persuade his manager to join in. 'You won it.'

Jack Charlton recalled: 'Alf had a huge smile on his face, a genuine big smile on his face. He grinned a lot, but sometimes when he grinned you didn't feel like it was a real grin, like when he was telling you that you couldn't do something. But this time, Alf had a real grin on his face. He looked very, very happy.'

Ramsey's innate ability to inspire was never more evident than at the end of the ninety minutes. Having conceded a late equaliser to force the game into extra time, the English players were as deflated as they were exhausted. Several of them fell to their knees on the pitch. At Ramsey's insistence, they all quickly got back to their feet and listened intently.

'He made a short but extremely effective speech,' Bobby Charlton later recalled. 'He said that we had won the game once but it had been taken away from us. Now, we had to go out and win it again. We had to make sense of the work and all of the sacrifices. We had to do something that would make us proud for the rest of our lives.

'He touched all the players. He reminded us of all that had been achieved in three years, how far we had come and, most of all, how it would be absolutely intolerable if the prize was allowed to slip away. I could feel life and determination return.'

'It was Alf Ramsey, our football "Svengali", who erased all our worries and always put us in the right frame of mind,' added Stiles. 'We were his puppets. He moulded us. And never once did he doubt that England would win the World Cup.'

Following news of his knighthood on New Year's Day 1967, the press – with whom he had maintained an often-fractious relationship – were quick to pay tribute.

The *Daily Mirror*'s Ron Wills wrote: 'Alf Ramsey began by believing in himself. In his ability to master the ways of the world. In his right to play football as he thought it should be played. Ipswich were given belief and the League championship of England was theirs. England were given belief and they mastered the might of world football. Through it all, Ramsey has often stood alone, almost aloof, seeking few favours but never forgetting friends.'

Wills' *Mirror* colleague Sam Leitch added: 'Sometimes, Alf Ramsey talks about the game in a way which the terraces might find hard to appreciate. The ball itself can become "this precious gem", while a goalless draw at Wembley saw England play, in Alf's opinion, "sheer poetry". But Ramsey gets through to the footballer in a way which those of us who are not his players will never understand.'

Indeed, for all that was known about Ramsey, he was hugely enigmatic, a trait that World Cup glory only succeeded in intensifying. He was notoriously sensitive about his working-class upbringing and went to extraordinary lengths to deny them, adopting an accent that the great football writer Brian Glanville once described as 'sergeant-major posh'. Some speculated that he had even paid for elocution lessons, so determined was he to put distance between 'Sir Alf' and 'Alf from Dagenham'.

'He tended to speak in a very poncey plum-in-the-mouth way,' noted former England international Rodney Marsh. 'It was all "Oh, hello Rodney and how are you?" To me it was all complete bollocks.'

Another football writer, Ken Jones, noted that, on one occasion, when Ramsey heard Bobby Moore and Jimmy Greaves mocking his accent on the team bus, he declared that he would 'win the World Cup without those two bastards'.

Throughout his tenure as England manager, he worked out of a small, basic office in the Football Association's headquarters in London, commuting back and forth every day from his family home in Ipswich.

Bizarrely, he also claimed to be two years younger than he really was throughout his career and for many years thereafter. For example, when he first joined Southampton, he told the club that he was born in 1922, not 1920. His logic was twofold: one, he figured it would improve his career prospects if people thought he was a little younger; two, he lost two years to fighting in the war so he invented this 'white lie' by way of self-compensation. It was only after he was knighted that he revealed his true age, his conscience preventing him from lying to Debrett's, the publisher of *Debrett's Peerage & Baronetage*.

No, nobody could ever have mistaken Sir Alf Ramsey for being a straightforward man. He was austere yet compassionate, principled yet dogmatic, innovative but practical. One thing everybody could agree on, however, was that he was a winner. A dogged, determined, uncompromising winner.

Lifting the World Cup? What many saw as the completion of a dream, Ramsey viewed as only the beginning. Anybody, he reasoned, could scale Everest. Staying there was another matter altogether.

Sir Alf was in no mood to budge. Not for anybody. And certainly not for Scotland.

EIGHT

HAVING A HAFFEY

CONTRARY TO A LONG-STANDING AND WIDELY HELD MISCONCEPTION, it was Sam Leitch and not David Coleman who erroneously observed that there would 'be dancing in the streets of Raith' after a large victory for the Kirkcaldy-based Raith Rovers in the 1960s. The gaffe has become immortalised in Scottish football – there is no such place as Raith – and yet it wasn't the biggest blunder of Leitch's broadcasting career.

Born in Great Yarmouth to a Scottish family, Leitch found fame as the long-time host of the football preview on the BBC's flagship Saturday sports show *Grandstand*. He also had a popular weekly column in the *Sunday Mirror* and used the 9 April 1961 edition to make a bold prediction about the following weekend's England-Scotland fixture at Wembley.

The match brought the curtain down on the 1960/61 British Home Championship and England were heavily fancied to prevail. Walter Winterbottom's men were on a four-game winning streak, during which they had scored a remarkable twenty-three goals.

Scotland, by contrast, had won only one of their last eight matches and were late arriving in London, travelling south on a Thursday night train from Glasgow after most of their players had played for their clubs on the Wednesday night. Several of them were nursing injuries as they boarded the locomotive. First-choice goalkeeper Lawrie Leslie, for example, had received eleven stitches to an eye wound following a clash of heads with Ayr United's Sam McMillan the previous weekend. Neither captain Eric Caldow nor Motherwell's Johnny McCann were at full fitness either but both were named in a young and hugely inexperienced line-up, nonetheless. With an average age of twenty-four, Ian McColl's side included four debutants: Bobby Shearer, Billy McNeill, John McLeod and Pat Quinn. They were a diminutive bunch, too, one reporter even going so far as to dub the team the 'Tiny Tots' and, with only a few exceptions, 'no bigger than bantam-weights'.

To most observers, England were clear favourites. McColl himself sounded less than confident in the Scots' prospects. 'I make no promises or prophecies,' he said, 'but go to the game with an open mind. I shall try to get the lads to do their best.'

Leitch, however, was far more optimistic. 'I predict that Scotland's wee blue soccer devils will shock England at Wembley,' he wrote in his newspaper column. 'Two of the tiny Scottish attack even told me that if England selected Peter Swan (centre half) and Mick McNeil (left back), the game was in the bag.'

England did indeed field Swan and McNeil. But they also had an inspirational captain in Fulham's John Haynes, not to mention the talismanic Bobby Charlton and free-scoring Jimmy Greaves, whose devastating form for club and country earned him a megabucks move from Chelsea to AC Milan on the eve of the match.

In front of a near-capacity crowd of 97,000, England took the lead after only nine minutes, Bobby Robson firing low into the corner from range. They doubled their advantage soon after through Greaves and were 3–0 up on the half-hour when Greaves pounced on a mistake by Scottish goalkeeper Frank Haffey, the Celtic man having been promoted to the starting line-up forty-eight hours before kick-off after Leslie failed to recover in time.

McColl's men rallied early in the second half and goals from Dave Mackay and Davy Wilson appeared to have turned the game on its head. However, another blunder by Haffey – this time, allowing a tame effort from Bryan Douglas to spill under his body and trickle over the line – made it 4–2 to England. After that, the floodgates opened. Bobby Smith helped himself to a hat-trick, Greaves completed his own and man-of-the-match Haynes grabbed another. Quinn's debut goal was barely a consolation for the Scots as England inflicted a heaviest-ever defeat on their fiercest rivals.

Years later, Denis Law described the 9–3 hammering as his 'blackest day' and admitted that he and his teammates had given their hosts 'the freedom of Wembley'.

'What a strange game that was,' he recalled. 'It should never have happened. England started well enough but we never felt out of it and we came back to make it 3–1 through Dave Mackay, and then Davie Wilson scored. At 3–2, England were rocking and we were back in the driving seat; we were still trailing, but we had our tails up. Honestly, they looked down and out. Then we conceded a stupid fourth from a free kick, and suddenly they were back in command.

'Can you imagine being in a Scotland team that is beaten 9–3 by the English? It might be just about acceptable in a schoolboy match, maybe even in a club match, but certainly not in an international match, and most definitely not at Wembley. For the rest of our careers, that result made the Scottish players all the more determined on the pitch, because we continually had to try to live it down. In fact, I think we're still trying.'

As the English team celebrated a thirty-third British Home Championship title with a lap of honour around the pitch – the inspirational Johnny Haynes carried shoulder-high by his teammates – the finger of blame for the defeat was already pointing to Scots goalkeeper Haffey.

'We were, to say the least, dodgy at the back with Frank having a nightmare game,' added Law. 'To this day, if a goalkeeper has a bad game, it is known as "having a Haffey". Once that fourth goal went in, they ran away with it.'

Goalscorer Wilson agreed. 'The fourth goal was the killer. The ball squirmed out of Frank's grasp and over the line. England were flying and we collapsed.'

The great Scottish sportswriter Hugh McIlvanney described the match as 'a personal tragedy' for Haffey, who incurred the wrath of Law when he tried to lighten the mood in the dressing room afterwards by performing Harry Lauder songs for his teammates.

'I always enjoyed a wee sing-song,' he admitted. 'So, it is a fact that I did a bit of warbling as we got a soak after the game. Remember, I was just twenty-two years old at the time. I had my whole career ahead of me. I could sing or I could melt into the deepest, darkest depression. I chose to sing. I was sitting there in the bath and all around me was doom and gloom, so I just started singing.

'Denis Law came over and said: "Damn it, big man, for a goalkeeper, you're a great singer."

'Don't get me wrong. I wasn't indifferent to what had happened to Scotland and a 9–3 defeat at Wembley was a very sad situation. I could have sung all night, but I was still shocked and stunned. I might have been trying to laugh it off – or even sing it off – but inside I was completely burned up.'

Haffey's haphazard attempts to put a brave face on the defeat only made him more of a scapegoat. As the team bus left the stadium after the match, scores of furious Scots fans lined

Wembley Way to jeer and heckle. Most of the players ducked below the window line to hide their shame. Haffey, by contrast, sat and grinned at the baying mob.

When the players arrived at King's Cross station later that evening, they found a cabal of Fleet Street photographers lying in wait. Whilst most had the good sense to walk straight past them, Haffey obliged the snappers' requests, foolishly posing beneath Big Ben as the iconic London clock's hands pointed to nine and three.

By the time the overnight sleeper pulled into Glasgow's Central Station, the Sunday newspaper billboards were standing guard outside every newsagent. 'SLAP HAFFEY' read one. 'HAPLESS HAFFEY' said another. Just as quickly, jokes started to fly. Amongst Rangers supporters, for example, the only correct answer to being asked for the time was to reply 'almost ten past Haffey'.

It was an afternoon and a result that would have a profound impact on the strapping big keeper. From the ecstasy of saving a Bobby Charlton penalty on his international debut a year earlier, his second appearance for his country turned out to be his last. He subsequently moved to Australia where he became a popular – and successful – cabaret singer. However, the demons of that Wembley defeat followed him Down Under. Countless times in the years that followed, his phone would ring with journalists looking to interview him about that fateful day. On every occasion, he politely declined.

Speaking to *The Times* in 2011, his son Ronnie remarked: 'Dad has long since reconciled himself to carrying the blame to his grave. He sat me down some years ago and told me all about it. He has rationalised events in his own mind, put the game to bed and will not discuss it again.'

Of course, not everybody believed the defeat was Haffey's burden to carry alone. Teammate Ian St John said: 'It wasn't all Frank's fault; a lot of strange things happened, Defensively, we were awful. I partially blame our manager, Ian McColl. It was only his second game in charge, and, for me, he hadn't a clue. At half-time, with us 3–0 down, Ian could not sort us out. He was out of his depth.'

Hat-trick hero Greaves agreed. 'It's true he had a poor game, but Frank wasn't the only Scot who didn't perform well that day. In truth, I don't think any international team of the time could have lived with England that day. My abiding memory is of Dave Mackay charging murderously at any Englishman in possession in the closing stages.'

'The goalie might have stopped a couple but we'd have run amok whoever was in goal,' added Haynes. 'These things happen. It all comes together and a team suddenly starts purring. We hit five in about ten minutes and, with Jimmy in that groove, we'd have beaten any team anywhere. It was very competitive until we hit that purple patch. Then, even the best keeper in the world wouldn't have denied us, not even if Gordon Banks and Peter Schmeichel had been in there together.'

Jimmy Armfield was well used to the rivalry between the two sides before stepping onto the pitch that day. The Blackpool team the enterprising right-back played for at the time had a large Scottish contingent and training would frequently take the form of England-Scotland five-a-side matches. 'They became so physical that the manager put an end to it,' he laughed.

Armfield made the thirteenth appearance of his England career in that 9–3 win and he, too, defended Haffey. 'He might have made a couple of mistakes but not half as many as the defenders around him. It is always too easy to blame your keeper. That performance must have been one of England's all-time best, certainly going forward. The runners and strikers were inspired by the endless stream of wonderful passes from Haynes and Robson. After running riot that day at Wembley, we beat Mexico 8–0 but then injuries weighed in and the selectors began tinkering. Had they not, I seriously think we'd have won the World Cup in Chile the following year.'

Even Lawrie Leslie, the man who was supposed to keep goal for Scotland that day, refused to single out Haffey for the defeat. 'It was a terrible game for us,' said the Airdrie man. 'Nobody played well.'

His wife Jeanette was less forgiving. 'I'll tell you this,' she said, 'even with both his eyes stitched shut, there is no way my Lawrie would have conceded nine goals.'

Decades later, Billy McNeill reflected on the international debut from hell. 'It was one of the lowest points of my career,' he said. 'My first painful lesson on just how cruel sport can be. Nothing will ever completely expunge the memory. What was essentially a proud moment, playing in my first international, turned out to be an absolute disaster. It was just one of those days when everything England attempted came off for them, while every mistake we made was magnified and punished in the most brutal fashion possible.'

For Law, the pain of that humiliating loss has never gone away. 'Looking at that horrendous scoreline now,' he recalled, 'it looks as though we were absolutely demolished but it just wasn't like that, as daft as that may sound.

'That day, Jimmy Greaves was, as ever, lethal. You might not know he was there for eighty-eight minutes, and he still might finish up on the scoresheet with a couple of goals to his name. Greaves was a different player compared to me and other forwards. He was the best pure striker, the best goalscorer, I have ever seen. When he had the ball in front of goal, there was always absolute panic among the opposing defence. They knew it was probably either going to end up in the net or miss by inches; there weren't that many chances he fluffed.

'I was a different type of player. I was an old-fashioned inside-forward, doing work all over the pitch, which included scoring goals. Greaves, though, was an out-and-out poacher. He just waited up front, prowling around the penalty area. I have always tried to judge a player's qualities by asking myself if I would like him in the opposition when I'm playing. I didn't want Greaves playing for the opposition team at any time. That's how good he was.'

As a teenager, Law watched England thrash Scotland 7–2 at Wembley in 1955, the agony of that particular defeat intensified by Fred Martin – who played for his beloved Aberdeen – being in goal for Scotland that day. He assumed that would be as bad as it would ever get. He was wrong.

'It was only my tenth match for Scotland, and I had only been on the losing side twice, both times by the odd goal, so it was a shattering defeat for me personally. I couldn't even return to Scotland with my tail between my legs like some of the others; not only did I have to go back to Maine Road, I also had to play against English players every week.'

Compounding Law's misery was the fact that television cameras caught him lashing out at Bobby Robson – in full view of Her Majesty the Queen, no less.

'He kicked me and I kicked him back. Fortunately, we shook hands and apologised to each other. I think it's written into your contract that, when you play at Wembley, you're not allowed to do things like that in front of the Queen, and one of the English papers made a big play on it.'

As it turned out, a breach of royal protocol – implicit or otherwise – was the least of Law's concerns; he and his teammates had to play three qualifying matches for the 1962 World Cup just weeks after their Wembley humbling. First up were back-to-back fixtures against the Republic of Ireland, followed by a trip to Bratislava to play Czechoslovakia. Question was, how would McColl and the team of selectors respond to the England loss? More specifically, who would carry the can?

Haffey was dropped. No great surprise. So, too, was Motherwell centre-half Bert McCann. According to his defensive partner Billy McNeill, McCann set fire to his visa for the forthcoming trip to Czechoslovakia in a London pub after the Wembley thrashing. He clearly suspected that Haynes, Greaves and co. had just ended his international career and, as it happened, he was right. Much more surprising, however, was the decision to omit both Mackay and Law.

'I was annoyed at being singled out amongst the forwards,' admitted Law, 'especially as we had scored enough goals to win a normal game. I always felt as an Anglo that I had to do something special to keep my place in the national side. Not a lot was said publicly by those who played south of the border but we all felt we had to do something special to get noticed. If somebody was going to carry the can, I thought it would be an Anglo. If you're in a team beaten 9–3 by your biggest rivals, somebody has to go – but it's a bit tough blaming the forwards.'

To make matters worse, as England were laying waste to Scotland, Law's Manchester City teammates were just across London playing West Ham United. The Maine Road outfit were struggling at the bottom end of the table and desperately wanted Law's services for their trip to the capital. To the annoyance of his manager Les McDowall, he insisted on playing for his country instead. 'I had never played against England at Wembley before and you never know when your last chance is going to come,' he reasoned. 'As it turned out, I wish I'd played for City.'

Over twenty years later, Law visited Sydney, Australia, with fellow Manchester United great George Best. The pair had formed a formidable after-dinner chat show which they decided to take on the road.

The late, great Best recalled: 'We were performing in Sydney and Frank Haffey turned up and, afterwards, he was engaged in a conversation with Denis in the car park of the hotel where we were staying. He asked: "Tell me straight, Denis, is it safe for me to come home now?"

'Solemnly, Denis thought about it for a moment, stroked his chin, shook his head and answered: "Not yet, Frank. Not yet."'

As far as Law was concerned, losing was always bad. Losing to England was worse. But losing to England by a record-breaking margin? Well, that was simply unacceptable. Fuelled by that humiliation, he made a promise to himself that, one day, he would get his revenge on the Auld Enemy and on their own turf, too.

9–3 was a score that simply had to be settled.

NINE

SEND FOR A SAINT

THE DECISION TO APPOINT BOBBY BROWN as Scotland's new manager caught most people by surprise, not least the Scottish football media. For all their contacts and tenacity, the top journalists of the day were blindsided by the decision. Writing in the *Evening Times*, Gair Henderson even admitted as much.

'The appointment,' he observed, 'is more than a surprise. It is something of a soccer bombshell. Outside of the inner circles of the SFA, Mr Brown's name had never been mentioned as a candidate for a job that pays £4,000 but carries with it worries to match the salary.'

Henderson, one of the best-connected sportswriters in the country, added that Brown had 'practically no experience of Continental football, either at a club or international level' and would require 'drive, personality and a ruthless determination to deal firmly with players who are international stars, and who have their own ideas of just how important that makes them.'

It was a typically fair summary. Few knew the Scottish football machine better. If Henderson thought that taking Brown from

St Johnstone and thrusting him into the national spotlight was a risk, then that's exactly what it was.

Brown was born in 1923 in the Stirlingshire village of Dunipace. Situated just a few miles north-west of Falkirk, local legend has it that the famous Scottish patriot William Wallace – yes, *Braveheart* – lived there in the 13th century with his uncle, who was a clergyman at the parish church. When Brown was six, his family moved to the tiny nearby hamlet of Torwood where he and his younger sister Agnes attended primary school.

Brown's father, James, was an engineer at the Bonnybridge power station and, like many of his colleagues, was a devotee of Falkirk FC. Every other Saturday during the football season, he would stand in the Brockville Park terraces cheering on the Bairns. Before long, he started taking his own bairn with him and it wasn't long before Bobby was bitten by the football bug. Any chance he got, he went down to an old, nearby farmstead where he would kick his tatty, odd-shaped football off a wall and catch it as it rebounded.

It wasn't long before those self-taught skills came in handy. When Brown was around eleven years old, he became a regular attendee at informal challenge matches arranged between men from Torwood and other nearby villages, such as North Bromage and Plean. The games were classic jumpers-for-goalposts affairs and, because none of the men wanted to be goalkeeper, Brown – or 'Wee Bobby', as they knew him – did so instead.

His first experience of 'proper', organised football came when he went to went to secondary school. The Larbert Village School team played matches every Saturday morning against other schools in the district and Brown kept goal for them until he moved to Larbert Central School.

When he wasn't playing football, he was watching it. In addition to keeping up appearances at Brockville, Brown also became a regular at Forthbank – home of King's Park, a Second

Division club that folded after the Second World War and which later reformed as Stirling Albion – as well as matches involving local junior sides, like Falkirk Violet and Raploch Hearts. Whilst most people's eyes were trained on the main goal threats, Brown's were fixed on the goalkeepers. He studied their movement, their positioning, their reflexes. Whatever they did, he took mental notes and filed them away for future use.

After passing his 'Qualifying' exams, Brown moved on to Falkirk High School where his PE teacher was Hugh Brown. By curious coincidence, Hugh was the father of Craig Brown, who would go on to become the Scotland national team manager between 1993 and 2001. A former footballer himself, Hugh took charge of the school team and ran it like a professional endeavour. He insisted on the boys showing up for games with boots buffed to a high shine. Squads for weekend matches were announced in the school gymnasium on Fridays. Strips were hung on individual pegs in time for the players arriving for the games. It was a slick, efficient machine that, very quickly, became a winning one. With local opposition being little match for the Falkirk High boys, Hugh Brown successfully applied for them to join the Glasgow and District League. Rather than continuing to be a big fish in a small pond, he wanted his players to swim with the biggest whales in the country.

Brown's impressive performances in goal earned him a call-up for the Falkirk District Schools team and then the 'Rest of Scotland' Schools. His local club, Falkirk, caught wind of his development, prompting their manager, former Rangers left-half Tully Craig, to invite him to start training with them during his final year at school. As much as he liked the idea of being a footballer, Brown wasn't totally convinced that there was a career in it and toyed with the prospect of becoming a PE teacher or policeman instead.

It was around lunchtime on 13 April 1940 that everything changed. Brown, now seventeen, was playing in a Glasgow

Schools League match that Saturday morning. At full-time, two men approached him with the most unlikely of requests.

Queen's Park, the oldest football team in the country, needed him to play in goal against Celtic, the nineteen-time champions of Scotland, at Celtic Park . . . that afternoon. It quickly emerged that Mustafa Mansour, Queen's Park's regular goalie and a student at Jordanhill College, had abandoned Scotland to support the war effort in his native Egypt. To make matters worse, the side's other keeper, Gordon Hamilton, was a lieutenant in the Territorial Army and had been called up for active duty.

Before he knew it, Brown was whisked away by car to Hampden Park where he signed his registration forms and joined his new teammates on the coach that travelled to Celtic Park. The match ended in a 4–4 draw and, despite shipping four goals, Brown impressed team bosses enough to merit a start in the remaining seven games of the season. He subsequently enrolled to train as a PE teacher at Jordanhill, where he planned to combine his studies with playing for Queen's, before an escalation in the conflict between the Allied Forces and Nazi Germany put normal life on hold.

Brown initially joined the Fleet Air Arm of the Royal Navy, where he trained to be a navigator on a Fairey Swordfish biplane torpedo bomber. The Swordfish, nicknamed 'Stringbag', saw frontline service throughout the Second World War and Brown might have, too, but for his talents as a goalkeeper. You see, whilst most of his training class saw active duty, Petty Officer Brown was transferred to the Royal Navy's physical training department at the instruction of Earl Alexander of Hillsborough, First Lord of the Admiralty and head of the Fleet Air Arm. The Earl had learned of Brown's ambitions, both in football and in teaching, and decided to give him the opportunity to continue his studies at Portsmouth College and, at the same time, turn out for teams such as Chelsea, Chester, Portsmouth and Plymouth Argyle in the Wartime League.

It was a decision that, potentially, saved Brown's life. He was one of seven Jordanhill College students who enrolled in the Fleet Air Arm. Five did not survive the war. As he would later admit, football kept him out of the firing line.

During his time on the south coast of England, Brown played in five wartime internationals for the Scottish national side, the first of those coming against England at Villa Park in February 1945. When the conflict ended, he returned to Scotland and resumed his career with Queen's Park where he shared the goalkeeper's jersey with up-and-coming Ronnie Simpson. In October 1945, with Brown in goal, Queen's won the Glasgow Cup for the first time in almost half a century courtesy of a 2–0 win over Clyde.

A 2–2 draw with Belgium at Hampden in January 1946 saw Brown earn the first of his five full Scotland caps and, for good measure, enter the history books as the last amateur player to earn a full cap for Scotland and the last to do so while a Queen's Park player.

At the end of that season, he moved across Glasgow to join Rangers. By now a qualified teacher, he signed part-time terms with the Ibrox side and, for the next ten years, combined goalkeeping with PE teaching. He played 296 first-team games, including a remarkable sequence of 179 in a row, and clocked up 109 clean sheets. His time with the club coincided with the historic treble-winning campaign of 1948/49, the first time in Rangers' history that they had won the modern trifecta of Scottish League, Scottish Cup and Scottish League Cup honours in the same season.

All told, Brown won five league titles, four Scottish Cups and two League Cup winner's medals with Rangers before his 'day job' finally took its toll. Legendary Ibrox manager Bill Struth wanted him to quit teaching and go into football fulltime. Brown refused and, in 1952, he lost his place to George Niven.

He made only a handful more appearances for the first team before joining Falkirk in 1956.

Brown spent two years with his boyhood club, at the end of which he hung up his boots and moved into management with St Johnstone. Ironically, he gave up teaching to take the job fulltime, inheriting a club that had finished eleventh in the old Second Division the season before. In Brown's first campaign, he steered the Perth side to sixth. The following year, he got them promoted into Division One as champions. Despite the goalscoring exploits of future Manchester United manager Alex Ferguson – the twenty-one-year-old finding the net five times – Saints were relegated in 1962 but Brown stayed on at Muirton Park and took them straight back up in 1963, where he respectably and successfully established them as a mid-table side.

Those nine years in charge of St Johnstone were some of the happiest days of Brown's career. In a professional sense, he had a supportive board who seldom interfered and, instead, trusted him to do the job for which he was hired. Off the pitch, he and his family had settled in the village of Stanley, around six miles north of Perth and situated on the banks of the River Tay. As a country boy at heart, Brown enjoyed the peace and quiet. When he wasn't taking his dogs for long walks in the surroundings hills, he was salmon fishing on the Tay. His wife, Ruth, became active in the local community, too, running the local Brownies troop.

After a while, though, Brown started to yearn for something more. In Jack Davidson's fantastic biography, he admitted: 'St Johnstone was a great learning curve and I always have the fondest memories of my time there. But I did begin to feel, as time went on, that the job – although highly enjoyable – was becoming less of a challenge. There was something missing. I was almost in too much of a "comfort zone" and needed a more demanding challenge.'

One evening, in February 1967, opportunity knocked. While out walking his dogs, SFA secretary Willie Allan phoned Brown at home and left a message with Ruth to call him back. When he did, he was stunned to be invited to interview for the Scottish manager's job. He duly did so and, later that evening, received a call – again at home, again from Allan – telling him the gig was his if he wanted it.

After much deliberating, he accepted. Despite the ordeal endured by his predecessor John Prentice and all the stories he'd heard about the SFA's overbearing office-bearers, it was, he decided, too good an opportunity to let slide. A once-in-a-lifetime opportunity, potentially. He just had one condition: he wanted complete control over team selection. His logic was sound. He had a clear vision and strategy that he believed could transform the side's fortunes – but he couldn't do it with somebody else's line-up.

To their credit, the SFA relented and, on 6 February 1967, the news was made official. Following St Johnstone's Scottish Cup tie at Aberdeen on 18 February, Bobby Brown would leave the club to become Scotland's first full-time manager. He signed a four-year contract worth £4,000 and was given an office on the second floor of the SFA's Park Gardens headquarters in Glasgow city centre.

'I feel particularly happy to be given this opportunity at the top level in football,' he said upon his unveiling. 'This is a tremendous step forward for me.'

He left with the reluctant blessing of St Johnstone's long-standing chairman Alex Lamond. 'Bobby Brown is a young man of excellent character,' he said. 'While we are sorry to see him go, we're delighted for him. He was a credit to St Johnstone and will be to Scotland.'

Hugh Nelson, the chairman of the international selection committee, pledged to give Brown 'every chance and all the backing from the SFA', while Jock Stein – who had vacated the Scotland manager's position little over a year earlier – offered his own best wishes. 'Bobby Brown is a good man who has done very well with limited resources at St Johnstone,' he remarked.

Brown officially started on 20 February with not a second to lose. In just under eight weeks' time, he would be taking his team to Wembley to face the best team on the planet, the reigning world champions.

The Auld Enemy.

The boy from the same Stirlingshire town as William Wallace suddenly had to lead his own troops into battle with the English.

The clock was ticking.

TEN

QUIVERING FAULT LINES

IT'S NOT ENTIRELY TRUE TO SAY that Bobby Brown's first game in charge of Scotland was the clash with England at Wembley in April 1967. Pedants, in fact, will argue that it wasn't even the first time he took charge against the Auld Enemy. It would be more accurate to say that the Wembley match was the first time Brown led the men's 'A' side. Prior to that, he had presided over the Scottish sides for two other internationals against England – an Under-23 match at St James' Park in Newcastle on 1 March, and a League XI fixture at Hampden a fortnight later.

Under-23 matches became a feature of international football following the creation of UEFA in 1954. Indeed, 1967 saw the introduction of a new European Under-23 international competition. It was staged, to varying degrees of formality, until 1978 when the authorities decided that the gap between Under-18 and Under-23 football was too large, whereupon they reduced the age limit to twenty-one.

Scotland made an inauspicious debut at Under-23 level. In February 1955, a side comprising several future full caps – amongst them Eric Caldow, Dave Mackay and Graham Leggatt – was humiliated 6–0 by England under the Shawfield Park floodlights in the southside of Glasgow. It was a humbling that earned the young Scots a savaging on the sports pages the next day. Gair Henderson of the *Evening Times* described their approach to the game as 'too casual' but insisted that a more worrisome issue extended far beyond that singular performance. 'We will have to start searching now for the talent of the future and, when we find it, nurse it along and bring it out in the English fashion,' he wrote. 'Otherwise, Scotland's colts will meet the same rapid-fire fate every time.' Writing in the *Dundee Courier*, Jack Harkness called the result 'a sad night for Scotland.'

James Forbes, of the *Aberdeen Evening Express*, was arguably the most withering. Blasting the Scots' 'lackadaisical attitude', he wrote: 'It was the first-ever game of its kind between the two countries and unless Scotland's officials are prepared to be more business-like, it ought to be the last. The 6–0 score in England's favour was no fluke, and had they not been merciful to the extent of trying to give all the forwards a goal near the end, it might have been double figures.'

It was a year to the day until the side got a chance to make amends, travelling to Hillsborough for a rematch with England. They did marginally better, losing 3–1. It wasn't until October 1957 that the Under-23s recorded their first win. Goals from Mackay, George Herd, Dan Currie and Alex Young sealed a 4–1 victory over the Netherlands.

By the time Bobby Brown took the reins of the national team, the Under-23s had played twenty games, winning six, losing eight and drawing six. However, England continued to confound. In eight matches against their nearest rivals, Scotland had managed only one victory, a 1–0 win in March 1961 at Middlesbrough's Ayresome Park. Scotland's goalscorer that night? One Denis Law. That, indeed, was England's most recent

Under-23 defeat and one of only two they had suffered in thirty home internationals at this level.

Despite that, Scotland's youngsters had cause to feel confident as they travelled to Newcastle. Their most recent match, in November 1966, had yielded a 6–0 demolition of Wales, Jim McCalliog and Eddie Gray each scoring twice, with John Mitchell and Alex Edwards completing the rout.

Brown made two changes from that side for the clash with England, bringing in Kilmarnock winger Tommy McLean and Aberdeen midfielder Jim Smith for Edwards and Bobby Hope. Smith's clubmate Bobby Clark kept goal, with a back four of Jim Whyte (Aberdeen), Hugh Tinney (Partick Thistle), Tommy McMillan (Aberdeen), and captain Pat Stanton (Hibernian). Smith was joined in midfield by Gray (Leeds United) and Peter Cormack (Hibernian), with McLean joined in a front three by McCalliog (Sheffield Wednesday) and Mitchell (Dundee United).

Whilst the side he picked was undoubtedly strong, Brown was unable to pick players from either Celtic or Rangers, with both halves of the Old Firm in European action the same night: Celtic were in Yugoslavia to face Vojvodina in the first leg of their European Cup quarter-final, with Rangers welcoming Spanish side Real Zaragoza to Ibrox for the first leg of their European Cup Winners' Cup last-eight tie.

Similarly, Sir Alf Ramsey had selection issues of his own, with several of his presumed starters – Mick Jones, Len Badger and Allan Clarke – withdrawn by their clubs for Sheffield United's FA Cup replay with Fulham the same evening, whilst Ralph Coates of Burnley missed out due to an ankle injury.

All told, the England boss was forced into making eight changes to the team that had hammered Wales 8–0 in Wolverhampton the previous October. Sunderland's Jimmy Montgomery was chosen in goal, with a back four of Cyril Knowles (Tottenham Hotspur), Chris Lawler (Liverpool), Paul Reaney (Leeds United) and Tommy Smith (Liverpool). Colin Harvey (Everton) and John Hollins (Chelsea) did the grunt work in midfield, with Ian Storey-Moore (Nottingham Forest), David Ford (Sheffield Wednesday) and Bryan Robson (Newcastle United) combining in a front four with David Sadler (Manchester United). Of those eleven players, four – Sadler, Robson, Harvey and Storey-Moore – were making their England debuts.

A frenzied start to the match saw the Scots break the deadlock after a quarter of an hour. Cormack floated a long cross beyond Reaney and Lawler to McCalliog, who controlled well and flashed a fine strike across Montgomery and inside the far post.

England 0–1 Scotland.

The goal spurred the hosts into action and after Whyte blocked a goal-bound effort from Ford, his Aberdeen clubmate Clark was called into action to tip a header over the bar as England pushed for an equaliser.

Early in the second half, Smith squandered a great opportunity to double the Scots' advantage, stumbling in front of Montgomery after great work by McLean. Just before the hour, Robson was temporarily forced out of the game after suffering a bad blow to the head, leaving England a man short and chasing the game for a quarter of an hour. McCalliog should have made it 2–0 after a blunder by centre-half Lawler left him one-on-one with Montgomery. However, the young forward shot straight at the Sunderland keeper.

Ten minutes from time, England were awarded a dubious penalty when Ford stumbled into a tackle with McMillan. Despite the Scots' protests, the spot kick was given and duly dispatched by wing-half Smith.

No sooner had they surrendered their lead than the Scots were back in front. Another mistake by Lawler allowed Cormack to pounce on a loose ball and flash a shot beyond Montgomery. Aberdeen man Smith then settled matters five minutes from time, whipping the ball high into the net after a cross from McLean broke to him inside the penalty area.

Full time: England 1–3 Scotland.

It was just a second victory for Scotland over England at this level, and it was as emphatic as it was deserved.

The following morning, the English tabloids poured as much scorn on their players as their Scottish counterparts had been subjected to after the first Under-23 international in 1955. Under the headline 'ENGLAND FLOP – NO EXCUSES, PLEASE!', the *Daily Mirror*'s Frank McGhee wrote: 'If England want to make excuses for their first home defeat in six years, it won't be difficult. Neither will it be honest.'

That verdict was largely echoed north of the border. 'The Scots deserved their victory,' wrote *The Press & Journal*'s Norman MacDonald. 'They played more skilfully and more cohesively than their rivals and could find their man with considerably more regularity. Ramsey's automatons were speedy and industrious but they lacked the guile of the Scots youngsters and the forwards were shockingly lacking in scoring ideas.'

In Glasgow's *Evening Times,* Shearer Borthwick noted: 'One swallow does not make a summer but if Scotland can keep the nucleus of this team together – allowing for the see-saw of form and fortune – then the future prospect must be rosy.'

Ramsey was magnanimous in defeat, admitting that Scotland were 'by far the better team and thoroughly deserved their success', whilst his opposite number Brown was left to revel in what he described as 'a fine win'.

'It was a braw night for us,' he added. 'I'm very proud of the players. They fought very well, played as we had planned and came back magnificently after that soft England penalty which had brushed out our lead. They really kept their heads. We had a plan and played to it throughout. I think it must be agreed that these lads from the frozen north are not such soccer peasants.'

Caution would serve Brown well. With another game against England just two weeks away, there was little opportunity for much else.

* * *

INTER-LEAGUE MATCHES BETWEEN Scotland and England dated back to the late 19th century. Soon after establishing the Scottish Football League in 1890, the SFA's office-bearers identified a collective desire to test themselves against the English Football League, which had been created two years earlier.

The inaugural match between sides representing the best of each league took place in April 1892 at Pike's Lane. The home ground of Bolton Wanderers, it was an appropriate choice for such a landmark occasion. It was there, at 3.47 p.m. on 8 September 1888, that the first-ever goal in league football anywhere in the world was scored, Bolton winger Kenny Davenport making history after two minutes of his side's 6–3 defeat to Derby County.

Scotland and England shared the spoils in that inaugural match, a 2–2 draw. A return match took place the following year at Celtic Park in Glasgow, where a crowd of more than 31,000 saw England win 4–3. The matches subsequently became a popular and established part of the calendar, even if they did, occasionally, throw up the peculiar anomaly of players facing their own country. Indeed, the English side that contested the first match in Bolton fielded no fewer than four Scots by dint of the fact they were contracted to club sides in England.

It was in the years immediately following the Second World War that the inter-league fixtures exploded in popularity. The first match to be played following the hostilities saw Scotland lose 3–1 to an English side that boasted the great Stanley Matthews and Wilf Mannion. Despite heavy snow, more than 84,000 fans packed into Hampden Park to watch the action unfold. In 1949, the visit of an Irish League XI drew a crowd of around 62,000 to Ibrox, the home of Glasgow Rangers. Six years later, the Scots faced opposition from outside the British Isles for the first time when they defeated a Danish League XI 4–0 in Copenhagen. The finest hour for the Scottish League XI came in 1961 when an Italian League XI – featuring John Charles and Denis Law – was held to a 1–1 draw at Hampden.

Fixture congestion, brought about by increased commitments both domestically on UEFA's new European stages, engendered the gradual decline of the inter-league matches in the early 1960s. Clubs routinely withdrew their players from consideration for the games, whilst matches against the League of Ireland – weakened by the exodus of its top players to the English league in particular – often resulted in embarrassing mismatches. In November 1962, for example, the Scottish League thrashed their Irish counterparts 11–0 at Celtic Park.

In response, supporters started to vote with their feet. Broadly speaking, the average football fan wanted to see two things: competitive games and the best players. Increasingly, inter-league matches were incapable of providing either.

Any hopes of that changing when England travelled to Glasgow in the middle of March 1967 were dashed when Sir Alf Ramsey revealed his starting XI. With all eleven players who started the World Cup Final the previous July theoretically at his disposal – by dint of the fact that all played in the English league – Ramsey opted to select only two: captain Bobby Moore and hat-trick hero Geoff Hurst.

Chelsea's Peter Bonetti replaced Gordon Banks in goal. Len Badger and Keith Newton were picked either side of Moore and Everton man Brian Labone in the centre of defence. Ian Callaghan, John Hollins and Peter Thompson were chosen in midfield with

Hurst in a front three alongside Jimmy Greaves and Allan Clarke, the Fulham twenty-year-old who had bagged four goals in the Under-23 match against Wales the previous October.

Ramsey's team selection was a surprise, and not a particularly welcome one – on either side of the border.

Writing in the *Liverpool Daily Post* on the day of the game, Horace Yates outlined his puzzlement at some of Ramsey's selections. 'In general, the scheme appears to be not to give the Scots any real idea of what the [15 April] opposition is likely to be,' he claimed. Noting that the Football League's most recent victory in Scotland was in season 1948/49, he added it was 'a sequence which hardly looks likely to be ended tonight'.

The Scottish League Management Committee was particularly unhappy about the calibre of opposition chosen by Ramsey and threatened to make a formal complaint about it to Alan Hardaker, the secretary of the Football League. By leaving out so many of his World Cup winners and picking a team of players who were mostly unknown north of the border, it was reckoned that Ramsey had likely knocked thousands off the Hampden attendance and, by extension, hit Scottish League bosses in the wallet.

Gair Henderson wrote: 'Apparently, Ramsey has ignored the fact that Scottish football fans are "choosey" these days. They will pay good money any time to see top-class football but they avoid, like the plague, anything that looks second rate. So, if tomorrow's gate is a flop, the blame will rest squarely on the shoulders of Sir Alfred.'

He added: 'I know for a fact that the Scottish League players are also infuriated at the slight to their country. They will play harder than ever before, they will carry out the pre-match orders to the letter, and they will try to humiliate the man and the team that has tried to degrade them before a ball is kicked. The answer is for them to go out and hit this second-rate England team for six.'

Ramsey, naturally, disagreed. 'I think the people who say that my selections are an insult should wait until they know the result of tomorrow's game,' he insisted. 'Obviously, I do not agree that this is an under-strength team. After all, I picked these players. This game is as important as any other game to me. All games of this nature are vital because all of them are part of a build-up to form our full international team. It was this type of build-up we used in the World Cup and we are doing it again. I don't really see that people should make this an issue now.'

His opposite number Brown tried his best to diffuse the controversy. On the morning of the match, he told reporters: 'My players have all been warned of the importance of this occasion. I was most impressed with the way they trained and worked for me yesterday. They are dedicated professionals and they all realise exactly what is wanted tonight.

'The Football League side may not be packed with World Cup players. We would have liked to meet and beat the team that won the Jules Rimet Trophy at Wembley. But nevertheless, Sir Alf has brought with him a formidable line-up and we will have to go all out to win.'

He added: 'We have one objective in mind – victory. Our aim is to score as many goals as we can, and certainly we will not be treating the opposition with anything but the greatest respect.'

Brown's thirst for goals was reflected in the attacking side he picked. Despite the Old Firm being involved in the latter stages of European competition, the Scotland boss was able to choose seven players from the Glasgow giants: four from Celtic and three from Rangers. Kilmarnock's Bobby Ferguson kept goal, with Celtic duo Tommy Gemmell and John Clark operating at full-back. Another Celtic man, Billy McNeill, was at the heart of the defence alongside Rangers' captain John Greig. Hibernian's Peter Cormack was rewarded for a fine performance in the Under-23 international a fortnight earlier with a start in the heart of the midfield alongside Davie Smith of Rangers. Celtic's Jimmy Johnstone was originally chosen as part of the front four but was withdrawn from the side as punishment for ill-discipline against Queen's Park in the previous weekend's Scottish Cup tie. That saw Rangers' Willie Henderson drafted in to play alongside another Celtic man, Stevie Chalmers, as well as Aberdeen's Jimmy Wilson and Alex Ferguson of Dunfermline Athletic.

As it turned out, Ramsey was fully vindicated for his team selection. In miserable conditions, Scotland were no match for their visitors. Clarke opened the scoring inside the first minute of the match, capitalising on some fine build-up play by Callaghan and Hollins. Stevie Chalmers was denied by a brilliant save from Bonetti as he looked to square matters before England doubled their advantage with only a quarter of an hour played. A defensive mix-up allowed Clarke to set up Hurst for the easiest of tap-ins.

Ferguson and Wilson combined to force Bonetti into another fine stop as the Scots went looking for a way back into the game. Soon after, Ferguson was quickest to react when Gemmell's shot crashed back off the post. The Dunfermline man turned the rebound home but saw his effort controversially ruled out for offside.

As half-time approached, Cormack saw his goal-bound shot blocked by an inspired Bonetti before having a shot cleared off the line by full-back Newton.

Not long after the hour mark, England went close to adding a third, when Ferguson turned away a header from Hurst. The West Ham man went close again before another brilliant save from Bonetti prevented Chalmers from getting the Scots back into the game.

Finally, with just a minute to go, the English got the third goal their sharp forward play deserved. Thompson played in Clarke down the left and he fizzed a strike beyond a despairing Ferguson.

Full-time: Scotland 0–3 England.

As they trudged towards the exits, most Scots fans agreed the better side had won. Not only had the hosts' front four failed to click, they lacked the guile and incision required to break down the English defence. Their play was, for the most part, laboured and predictable and missed the wiles of a Law or Baxter. Likewise, at the heart of the defence, Greig and McNeill appeared to be on different wavelengths, whilst there were questions to be asked of Brown's tactics. The 4-2-4 formation he had elected to go with hadn't worked. Was that because of the players he'd picked or the way in which he had asked them to play?

'I think I know where the game was won and lost and, happily, I think I can do something about it before Wembley,' he said afterwards. 'England were a very good side tonight but I did feel we were a bit unlucky to be two down at half-time and I was disappointed that the referee chalked off what appeared to be a good goal by Alex Ferguson.'

Ramsey added: 'I think both teams are to be congratulated on the standard of their play and their enthusiasm under absolutely appalling conditions which were probably the worst any player could encounter. Naturally, I'm delighted with the result.'

Amongst other things, the result was a concentrated dose of reality for a vocal band of jingoistic dissidents who – for reasons best known only to them – maintained that the Scottish international team should comprise only of players playing in Scotland. Such narrow-mindedness had first manifested in the late 19th century when the SFA refused to include players playing outwith Scotland for international selection. That policy was reversed after six games without victory against England and appeared to have been defeated for good following the 'Wembley Wizards' victory of 1928. An *Evening News* match report noted that 'never again should the Anglo-Scot chosen to play for his country be regarded up home as a foreigner; the "interloper" idea must now be dropped completely.'

Easier said.

After the bruising 9–3 defeat at Wembley in 1961, certain scathing sections of the press lobbied for Denis Law to be dropped from the national team. A *Daily Record* editorial claimed: 'The records of post-war football show that, in most cases, the men who have let us down are the Anglos. I suggest we throw them overboard and depend entirely on home-based players. Let us stand or fall by an all-tartan collection.'

In Grant Jarvie and Graham Walker's paper 'Ninety Minute Patriots: Scottish Sport in the Making of the Nation', Richard Holt observed how 'football had become too culturally important to the Scots'. He added: 'To admit that defeat was not the fault of the Anglos, but the logical result of a small nation trying to compete on equal terms with much larger ones who had a bigger pool of top-class players, flew in the face of the footballing myth that sustained the Scots – namely, that top-class players were born, not made, and more of them were born in Scotland than anywhere else.'

Then there was Alan Gilzean. A forward who represented Dundee and Tottenham Hotspur with great distinction throughout the sixties and seventies, he believed so strongly that only players born north of the border should represent Scotland that he disapproved of his son Ian getting a youths call-up because he had been born in London.

Evidently, the twenty-two times capped Gilzean hadn't been one of the 29,066 spectators who shivered in the stands at Hampden on that frigid night in March 1967. More than a win for England, it was a technicolour, three-dimensional advert for why oft-maligned 'Anglos' like Law were critical to the nation's footballing fortunes.

Matt Busby, Law's Manchester United manager, acknowledged as much. 'Denis is doing all the damage for us this season,' he said. 'He is scoring goals, he is making goals, and he has thrown off the niggling injury which troubled him a lot last year. In fact, he is playing as well as he has ever done. I don't think it matters where the players for a Scottish team come from as long as they are Scottish and as long as they are the best players. That's all that counts.'

In West Yorkshire, Leeds United boss Don Revie was waxing every bit as lyrical about one of his star men. He said: 'Billy Bremner is playing so well for us right now that if a "World" team was being chosen, he would walk into it. He is playing tremendously as he always does. Billy doesn't know what defeat means.'

Ken Gallacher, the *Daily Record*'s erstwhile sportswriter, was adamant that Scotland's best chance of winning at Wembley was to embrace, not resist, the English-based contingent.

In a passionate op-ed, headlined 'WHEN THE KIDDING HAS TO STOP', he wrote: 'The men of the English League proved at Hampden that only a completely professional outlook pays off in modern soccer. Apart from a few of our top players here at home, this attitude is demonstrated most clearly by the Anglos. It must be because they face the cruelly demanding challenges of English soccer week after week. We must accept this. And we must accept Anglos in our team. That is the one way to greatness.'

The debate spilled over from the ink on the page into the pint glasses of pubs across the country. When is a Scotsman not a Scotsman? Is working amongst the enemy tantamount to working *for* them? In truth, only one man's opinion counted.

And with Wembley just a month away, Bobby Brown would soon have to share it.

* * *

SANDWICHED BETWEEN THE UNDER-23 and League internationals, a by-election was held in the Glasgow constituency of Pollok. The seat had lain vacant since December 1966 after the incumbent, a forty-three-year-old

Labour politician called Alex Garrow, died from complications following a heart-attack.

Garrow had won the seat in the 1964 general election, edging out Unionist candidate Robert Kernohan by fewer than 300 votes. He increased his majority, albeit only slightly, when the country went to the polls again in 1966, this time defeating Patrick Smollett by around 2,000 votes.

His sudden passing required constituents to return to the ballot box on 9 March 1967, their third such trip in the past four years. On this occasion, the seat fell to the Conservatives, Tory candidate Esmond Wright narrowly defeating Labour's Dick Douglas. It was the first time the Conservatives had gained a seat in Scotland since the 1959 general election and the party's first by-election gain since the Glasgow Camlachie by-election in 1948.

However, of at least equal significance was the performance of a third candidate, the Scottish National Party's George Leslie. The thirty-year-old Glasgow vet garnered an impressive 28.16% of the vote, as compared with 36.92% for Wright and 31.22% for Douglas.

If conceding a seat to the Conservatives wounded Labour, losing so much ground to the SNP – a party from the same side of the political spectrum as them – rubbed salt into it. Harold Wilson's foot soldiers had been almost contemptuous in their dismissal of the nationalists, even going so far as to predict the SNP would lose their deposit in Pollok. Instead, they held them off by only 1,185 votes. In the grand scheme of things, the Tories merely bloodied Labour's nose; it was the SNP that broke it.

The result of the Pollok by-election was a sign that the mood of the nation was shifting, that the country's political fault lines were quivering.

Nationalism, widely considered to be a dormant ideology and largely confined to the margins of both politics and society, was active once again and threatening to erupt.

Former Rangers goalkeeper Bobby Brown took charge of Scotland for the first time against England at Wembley. *Getty*

England's World Cup-winning coach Sir Alf Ramsey. In 12 senior international matches in which he managed England against Scotland, he won six, drew three and lost three. *Getty*

From left to right: Jim McCalliog, Denis Law, Billy Bremner and Bobby Lennox take a breather during training. *PA*

After getting a goal on his debut against Northern Ireland at Hampden in November 1966, Celtic's free-scoring forward Bobby Lennox was picked to face England at Wembley in 1967. *PA*

Captains John Greig and Bobby Moore lead out the teams. *Alamy*

Billy Bremner narrowly fails to connect with a cross in the England penalty box as Jack Charlton and Nobby Stiles look on. *Alamy*

Denis Law reacts quickest to give Scotland the lead. It was the Manchester United man's 27th goal for his country and third against England. *Getty*

Ronnie McKinnon (5) wheels away in delight after Law gives Scotland the lead at Wembley. *Getty*

Bobby Lennox turns away to celebrate after slamming Scotland's second goal past Gordon Banks as England captain Bobby Moore watches on. *Getty*

Ronnie Simpson and Billy Bremner combine to clear an England attack. *Getty*

Willie Wallace (7) and Jim Baxter (6) celebrate with Lennox after his goal made it 2-0 to Scotland. *Getty*

Jim Baxter, with his socks around his ankles, celebrates with Jim McCalliog (9) as the Scots take control. *Mirrorpix*

John Greig stops another England attack, with Tottenham Hotspur forward Jimmy Greaves (8) lurking. *Getty*

Bobby Moore slides in on Willie Wallace. The Scot was an 11th hour addition to the side following Celtic teammate Jimmy Johnstone's injury. *Alamy*

Alan Ball is thwarted as John Greig (4), Ronnie McKinnon, Ronnie Simpson and Billy Bremner – with the ball at his feet – repel another England attack. *Alamy*

Acting as a makeshift centre-forward, the injured Jack Charlton sweeps the ball past a lunging Ronnie McKinnon to pull a goal back for England. *Alamy*

Alan Ball (7) claims for an England goal as the hosts press for an equaliser. *Mirrorpix*

(Above and below) Jim McCalliog slides Scotland's decisive third goal underneath Gordon Banks, before rushing away to celebrate. *Getty*

(Overleaf) Scottish fans lay siege to the Wembley turf after seeing their side defeat England, just nine months after the hosts had won the World Cup on the same pitch. *Mirrorpix*

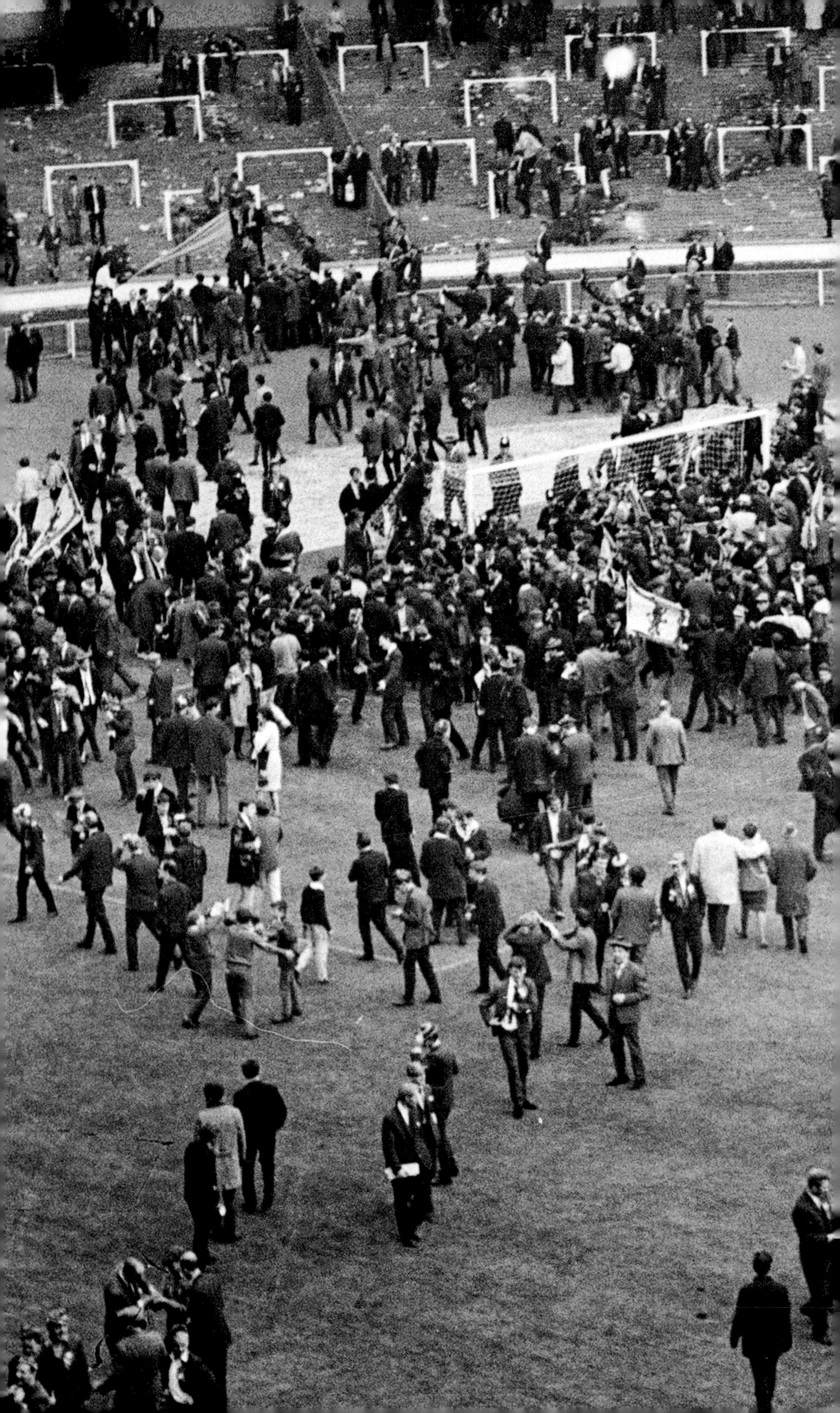

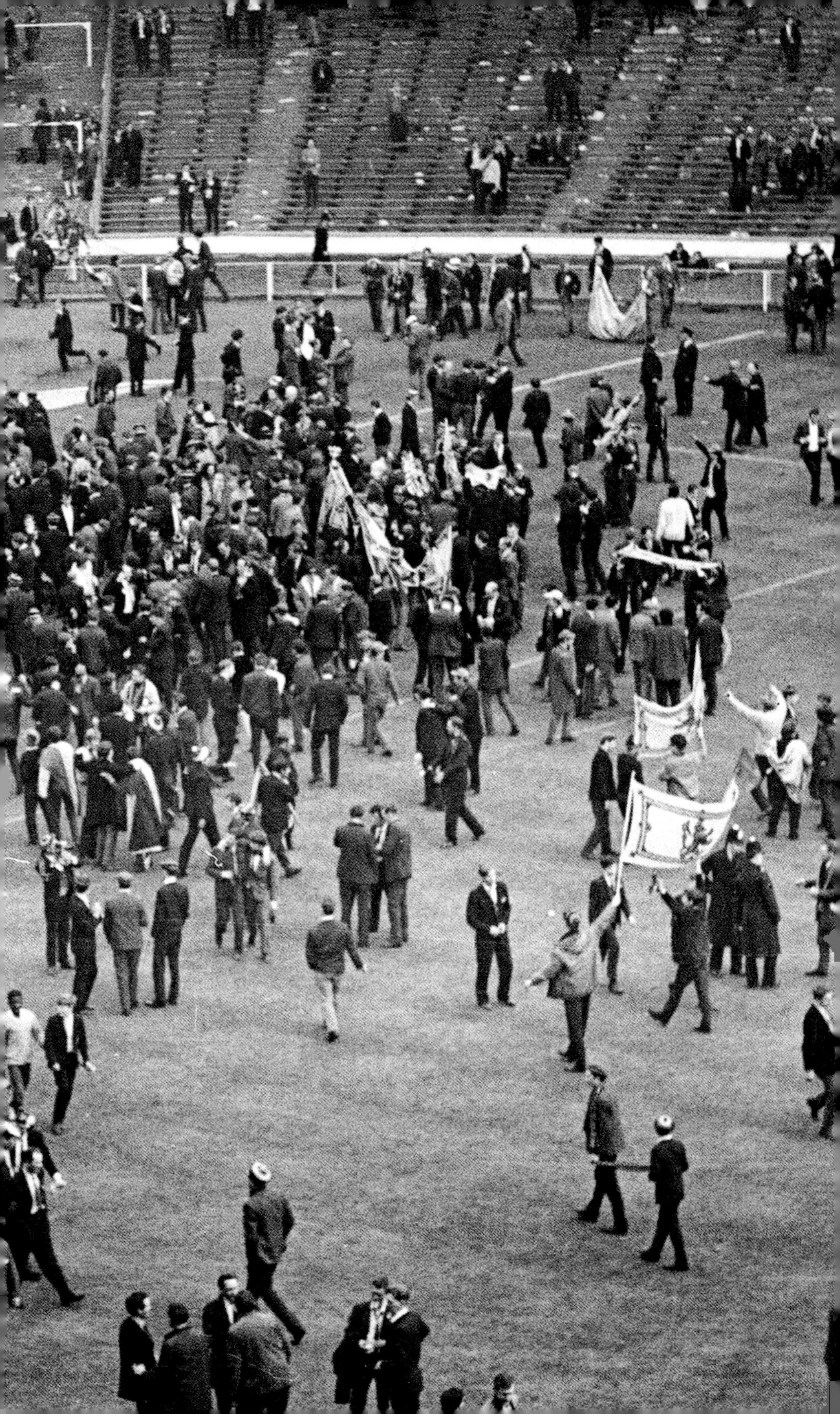

(Above and right) Jubilant Scotland fans pounce on Jim Baxter and Denis Law at full-time. *Alamy*

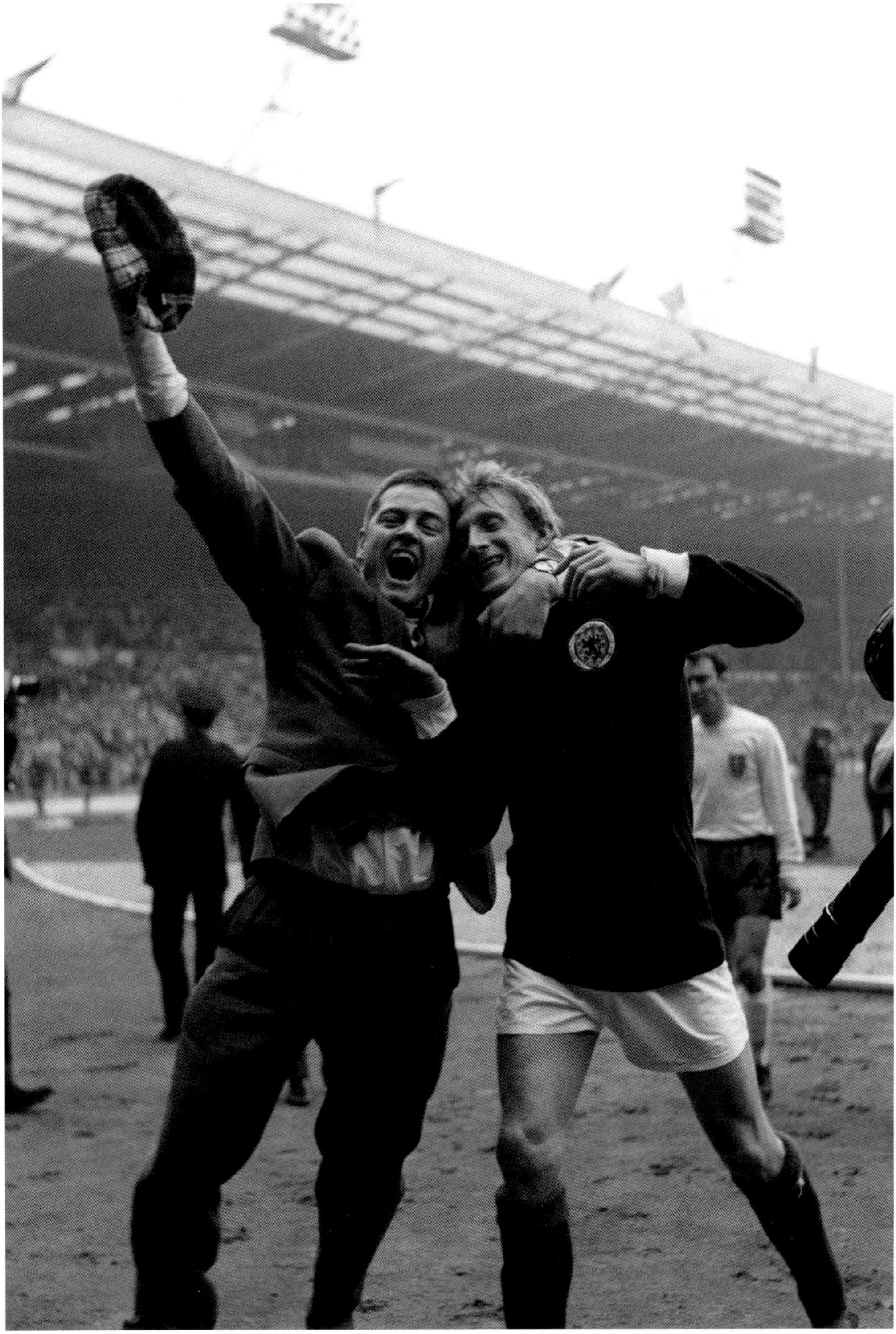

(Right) A dejected Jimmy Greaves and Gordon Banks trudge off the pitch. *Mirrorpix*

(Below) Debutants Simpson and McCalliog celebrate Scotland's victory. *Mirrorpix*

ELEVEN

THE PROMISED LAND

THE ADVENT OF MODERN SCOTTISH NATIONALISM can be traced back to the very moment designed to defeat it: the signing of the Treaty of Union in the early 18th century. A historic agreement which led to the creation of the new state of 'Great Britain', the Treaty of Union resulted in the Parliament of Scotland being adjourned on 25 March 1707 and, in effect, absorbed by the Parliament of England. The new unified 'Kingdom of Great Britain' came into being on 1 May 1707.

The decision to unify form one centralised government was far from unanimous. Many Scots feared becoming another region of England. Likewise, a significant number in England viewed the Scots with an understandable degree of mistrust after decades – indeed, centuries – of fighting.

Still, the English government wanted Scotland – if for no other reason than to assuage any chance of the so-called 'Auld Alliance' being rekindled. Dating back to 1295, the Auld Alliance was a military and diplomatic partnership drawn up by John Balliol of

Scotland and Philip IV of France in order to control what they viewed as England's aggressive expansion plans.

The alliance enjoyed its *heure de gloire* in 1421 when, at the Battle of Baugé, the French – bolstered by 12,000 Scots who had set sail for western France – defeated the English army, killing the Duke of Clarence, the brother of the incumbent King Henry V, in the process.

In the years that followed, the Scots continued to align politically and militarily with France. Some joined Joan of Arc in her relief of Orléans. Others formed the Gardes Écossaises, the personal bodyguards of the French monarchy.

However, the Reformation, which swept across Europe in the 16th century and which saw Scotland abandon its predominantly Roman Catholic heritage in favour of developing a predominantly Calvinist national church, unsettled the Auld Alliance. Indeed, with the exception of wine, nearly all trade between Scotland and France was dramatically reduced and, though it took until 1903 for the original alliance between the two countries to be formally revoked by the French government, the treaty was, to all intents and purposes, redundant by the time the 16th century gave way to the 17th.

Nonetheless, the English aristocracy couldn't risk its revival and so they looked to strengthen ties with Scotland. Uniting under one flag seemed like the most obvious way to achieve that. Their efforts were broadly resisted until William Paterson, a Scottish trader and banker who had been one of the founders of the Bank of England, proposed the Darién scheme.

Born in Dumfriesshire in 1658, Paterson travelled extensively throughout the Americas and West Indies, amassing a substantial personal fortune in the process. Returning to Scotland, he believed he had identified an opportunity to breathe fresh life into the struggling Scottish economy and put the country back on a stronger footing both domestically and abroad.

Paterson's ambition was to garner international wealth and influence for Scotland by establishing 'New Caledonia', a colony on the Isthmus of Panama (the narrow strip of land that lies between the Caribbean Sea and the Pacific Ocean), in the 1690s. This, he reasoned, would provide Scottish-born entrepreneurs with an opportunity to create – and monopolise – trading links with the world.

Through the Company of Scotland Trading to Africa and the Indies, which he helped to establish in Edinburgh in 1693, Paterson sold his vision to his fellow Scots. They, in turn, bought into it to the tune of almost half a million pounds – approximately 20% of the national capital that was available at the time. Virtually every Scot with money to spare invested in the Darién scheme.

On 12 July 1698, around 1,200 Scottish pioneers set sail from Leith Harbour bound for the 'Promised Land'. Three months later, they arrived depleted and divided. Many did not survive the journey, Paterson's wife amongst them. Those who did found themselves embroiled in quarrels as the elected councillors struggled for power. The colonisation itself was an abject disaster. Malaria and other tropical diseases spread through the camp, killing up to ten settlers per day. A lack of demand for traded goods – masterminded by a collaboration between the English East India Company and the English government – left the colonists penniless and impoverished. Completing the tragic trifecta was the Spanish Empire's hostile military response to the subjugation of its land, which could surely have been anticipated by the Scots.

Within twelve months of their arrival, more than 80% of the initial band of settlers were dead and the scheme was abandoned. However, news of the failed attempts to colonise Darién failed to make it back to Scotland. Six more ships set sail for Leith in November. A third fleet of five more ships soon followed.

Out of sixteen ships that left Scotland, just one – carrying nothing more than a handful of survivors – returned. More than 2,000 Scottish lives were lost. The £500,000 national investment was never recovered. At its best, the Darién scheme was a brave attempt to introduce fiscal innovation into a mercantilist world. At its worst, it was a reckless, feckless scheme that delivered manslaughter on a monstrous scale and almost bankrupted an entire country.

As Scottish nobles scrambled to recover what money they could, they did so against a backdrop of widespread famine and the 'Seven Lean Years'. Estimates vary but it is reckoned that up to 15% of the total Scottish population died as a consequence of famine brought about by failed harvests in 1695, 1696, 1698 and 1699. An economic slump caused by the Nine Years' War – a conflict between France and a European coalition which encompassed the Williamite war in Ireland and the Jacobite risings in Scotland – also contributed to the death toll.

Bluntly, Scotland, as both a country and an idea, was on the ropes and taking a relentless volley of haymakers from all angles. The country's establishment finally threw in the towel early in the 18th century. With no respite forthcoming, they had little alternative but to conclude the country's best prospects lay in a union with England. Not only would that see Scottish national debt eliminated at a stroke, it would also give them the opportunity to share in England's burgeoning international trade and overseas possessions. It meant sacrificing their independence but what alternative did they have?

Cap in hand, they put a proposal to the English parliament. Scotland would retain its independence insofar as it would continue to have its own legal and religious systems. However, coinage, taxation, sovereignty, trade, parliament and flag would all be unified.

Deal? Deal.

On 16 January 1707, the Act of Union was signed. Four months later, the Parliament of Great Britain, based in the Palace of Westminster in London, the former home of the English Parliament, came into being.

Before long, old tensions resurfaced and, by the middle of the 18th century, there was a distinct north-south divide in Scotland. Those in the south had started to align more with their English neighbours in terms of cultural identity and as champions of progressive modernity. Those in the north were still largely tethered to the ancient and fiercely independent traditions of clan culture, which prioritised family and fealty above all else. The south viewed the north as backwards and out of step. The north viewed the south as traitors who had betrayed them by signing the Act of Union. They wanted a return of the Stuart monarchy and viewed, with suspicion, the construction of English-manned garrisons that had started to appear all over the Highlands – notably at Fort George in Inverness – from 1725 onwards. It was a nakedly hostile move by the English ruling classes. They wanted to suppress Scottish opposition to the King and, at the same time, remind the highland clans just who was in charge.

However, far from silencing the clans, it prompted another Jacobite rebellion. In 1745, with the majority of the British Army fighting in mainland Europe in the War of the Austrian Succession, Charles Edward Stuart – 'Bonnie' Prince Charlie – led an army into England in an attempt to reclaim the British throne for his father, James Francis Edward Stuart. It didn't last long. When the support he had been promised failed to materialise, Stuart was forced to retreat back into Scotland and, despite winning the Battle of Falkirk Muir in January 1746, they were ultimately defeated on the open fields of Culloden, near Inverness, three months later. Massively outnumbered, the Jacobites were no match for the Duke of Cumberland and his

English redcoats. In a battle that lasted only an hour, more than 1,200 Scots were killed with several hundred wounded. The English casualties were significantly lower: only fifty killed and around 250 wounded. It was a bloody mismatch that effectively signalled the end of Scottish clan culture.

Within months, Westminster had passed the Act of Proscription, which, amongst other things, banned the wearing of tartan, the playing of the bagpipes and the teaching of Gaelic. It was a ferocious and unapologetic clampdown on highland culture and was followed, in 1747, by the Heritable Jurisdictions Act, which stated that anyone who did not submit to English rule automatically forfeited their land.

Worse was to follow. The so-called century-long Highland Clearances resulted in peasant families and communities in the northernmost parts of Scotland being evicted from their homes so that their landowners could capitalise on the Scottish Agricultural and Industrial Revolutions by repurposing the land for sheep and cattle farming. Whilst some of the displacement was done voluntarily, particularly in the early years of the Clearances, the vast majority occurred as a result of significant coercion, with homes frequently set alight to ensure former residents could not return. Initially, the displaced communities migrated to the mainland coast – in particular from Ardnamurchan to Cape Wrath – which, due to overcrowding, soon succumbed to destitution. Subsequently, there was a mass movement into Scotland's rapidly industrialising Lowland towns. Others left Scotland altogether. Towards the end of the Clearances in the middle of the 1800s, there was a massive Scottish diaspora into Canada, the USA, Australia and New Zealand.

Combined with the Highland potato famine and various nationalist revolts that took place in Europe throughout the 1840s, the Clearances prompted the creation of the National Association for the Vindication of Scottish Rights in 1853.

Perturbed by what its members perceived to be disproportionately generous treatment of Ireland by Westminster, it lobbied for a sharper focus on Scottish problems and called for more Scottish MPs in Parliament. It attracted influential support from the likes of Lord Eglinton – a Scottish nobleman and member of the House of Lords – and Professor William Aytoun of the University of Edinburgh. Whilst a short-lived endeavour which was wound up in 1856, the Association was, however, an important preliminary step in the campaign for Scottish independence and ruffled feathers sufficiently enough to convince the UK Government to establish the Scottish Office in 1885.

As the 19th century gave way to the 20th, clamour for independence continued to grow, quietly but steadily, in the margins of Scottish politics. In 1921, the Scots National League (SNL) was formed in London. Its sole purpose? Campaigning for Scottish independence. It knew about so-called Home Rule and the possibility of Westminster devolving certain powers to a Scottish Parliament but it wasn't interested in that. Inspired by the traditions of Gaelic independence and self-determination, it wanted Scotland to be a 'free' nation once more. Influenced by the abstentionist tactics of the Irish republican and democratic socialist political party Sinn Féin, the SNL decided to start contesting elections, hoping to persuade a majority of Scottish MPs to withdraw from the Westminster Parliament to convene an independent Scottish Parliament in Edinburgh. The group also launched its own newspaper in 1926, the *Scots Independent*, to further its cause.

Around the same time, in 1927, a group of students at the University of Glasgow formed a new pro-independence movement called the Glasgow University Scottish Nationalist Association (GUSNA). In 1928, just weeks after Scotland recorded a famous victory over England at Wembley, one of the group's founder members, John MacCormick, convened a meeting of all those in favour of establishing an organised political party favouring Scottish Home Rule. MacCormick recognised that there were too many competing factions who all, in the broadest sense, wanted the same thing: greater political autonomy for Scotland.

Presided over by Robert Bontine Cunninghame Graham, the meeting ended with the amalgamation of the SNL, GUSNA, the Scottish Home Rule Association and Lewis Spence's Scots National Movement into one single political body – the National Party of Scotland (NPS). Its politics skewing slightly left of centre, the NPS contested the 1929 and 1931 UK general elections, as well as a number of by-elections, but failed to return any MPs.

It was following the 1931 UK general election that a group of members of the Unionist Party broke away to form the Scottish Party. Led by Glasgow solicitor John Kevan McDowell and Andrew Dewar Gibb, the faction favoured establishing a Dominion Scottish Parliament within the British Empire. Unlike the NPS, the Scottish Party leaned to the right of centre and consisted mainly of lairds, provosts and business people, as well as several distinguished figures in Scottish public life, such as John Bannerman, Sir Henry Keith and Sir Daniel Stevenson.

Sensing that two parties representing (mostly) the same objective was neither necessary nor conducive towards achieving that goal, NPS secretary MacCormick reached out to McDowell and Gibb to negotiate a merger that would consolidate the Scottish independence movement. After much deliberation and discussion, an agreement was reached and on 7 April 1934 a new, single entity was established.

The Scottish National Party. SNP for short.

To say that the SNP got off to a slow start at the ballot box would be a terrific understatement. It wasn't until 1945 that the party returned its first MP to Westminster and, even then, it did so under peculiar circumstances. Following the death of the incumbent James Walker, who was knocked down and killed by an army lorry in Brighton, the seat for Motherwell was lying vacant. With the four major UK parties – Labour, the Conservatives, the Liberal Party and the National Liberal Party – having called a war-time truce, it was expected that Labour would retain the seat. However, smaller parties and independents had not been part of any truce agreement and so the SNP stood party secretary Robert McIntyre against Labour's Alexander Anderson. On election day, only 54% of the electorate went to the polls, with McIntyre securing an unlikely and narrow win over Anderson. With 11,417 votes, he polled 51.4% for a 2.8% majority.

McIntyre's stint at Westminster was, however, short-lived. Three months after the Motherwell by-election, the whole country went to ballot box in the 1945 UK general election. This time, more than 72% of the electorate turned out and Anderson won at a canter, polling 52.7% of the vote for a 26% majority over McIntyre, with a Unionist candidate, J.H. Hamilton polling 20.6%.

The SNP stood eight candidates in the 1945 election, winning zero seats and collecting a little under 27,000 votes to finish sixteenth in terms of overall votes and well behind the likes of the Common Wealth Party (110,634 votes) and the Communist Party (97,945). Frustrated by a lack of electoral progress, the SNP suffered a significant split in 1955. A faction of younger and predominantly Edinburgh-based members began a coordinated campaign of internal dissent. Calling themselves the '55 Group', they were unapologetically anti-English, even going so far as to publish a radical leaflet headlined: 'THE ENGLISH: ARE THEY HUMAN?'

As schismatic behaviour goes, the chaos caused by the '55 Group' didn't have any material impact on the SNP. Senior figures moved swiftly and decisively to expel them from the party. What it did do, however, was expose flaws in the nationalists' ambitions. Whilst everybody understood that the SNP represented the interests of Scotland and the Scottish people, nobody really knew what that meant. Was achieving independence written in red ink at the top of their manifesto or would they settle for devolution? Were they as radical as their younger, fringe element suggested or was there a moderate core to the party's politics? Which side of the UK's political spectrum did they occupy? Where did they stand on healthcare, education, the economy, Europe, welfare? There were so many unanswered questions which, in turn, made the SNP an unknown quantity. And the worst thing any ambitious political party can be is an unknown quantity. The public was largely apathetic towards them. That much was obvious from the results of UK general elections. In 1950, they stood three candidates, won zero seats and polled less than 10,000 votes. In 1951, two candidates, zero seats, just over 7,000 votes. In 1955, two candidates, zero seats, 12,000 votes. They were operating on the periphery of politics and unsuccessfully so. More pressure group than party.

Then, in the 1959 UK general election, something changed. Not in terms of seats. They continued to win none of those despite standing five candidates. Rather, their share of the vote skyrocketed. A grand total of 21,738 were marked in favour of the SNP – the party's best performance to date. Their Welsh equivalent Plaid Cymru also performed impressively, polling more than 77,000 votes, up from just over 10,000 in 1951. As the 1960s began, minds and moods were changing in the UK and, as far as nationalist groups were concerned, for the better.

In a by-election for Glasgow Bridgeton in 1961, the SNP's Ian Macdonald achieved almost a 19% share of the vote and was only narrowly beaten to second place by the Unionist candidate Malcolm McNeill. The following year, in the West Lothian by-election prompted by the death of sitting MP John Taylor, nationalist candidate William Wolfe finished a comfortable second with almost a quarter of the vote. Tam Dalyell retained the seat for Labour with 50.8% of the vote but that was down considerably on the 75% others in his party had predicted on the eve of the election. The Conservatives' William Ian Stewart, meantime, was a distant third with only 11.4% the vote. Whilst neither by-election yielded a seat in Parliament for the SNP, each was a sure sign of progress.

They rode that momentum into the 1964 general election where, again, they won zero seats but managed to poll a remarkable 64,044 votes. That made them the fifth-biggest party in Westminster behind Harold Wilson's Labour, who narrowly defeated the Conservatives, with the Liberal Party third and Plaid Cymru only narrowly ahead of the SNP (by some five-thousand votes) in fourth. Considering the Scottish nationalists stood only fifteen candidates (as compared to Labour's 628, the Conservatives' 630, the Liberals' 365, and the Welsh nationalists' twenty-three) such an impressive performance at the polls was rightly celebrated at party HQ.

To take the next step, it needed to galvanise nationalist sentiment in Scotland in a way that hadn't been done in centuries. It needed something for the people to unite behind with confidence and conviction, an event or a moment in time to serve – even subliminally – as a vehicle for change. A sociological disruptor with the capacity to activate fresh or forgotten pride in what it means to be 'from Scotland'.

Something like, say, England winning the World Cup?

TWELVE

RUNNERS AND RIDERS

ON 8 APRIL 1967, as 100/1 rank outsider Foinavon was galloping to an improbable victory in the Grand National, Bobby Brown was hard at work masterminding an upset of his own. The big game was now only seven days away and the Scotland boss had so far resisted the temptation to name his team. Instead, he waited to let Sir Alf Ramsey show his hand first. The English coach duly obliged. Condemned for fielding an understrength side in the League international weeks earlier, there would be no such accusations levelled at the England boss this time. He picked a starting XI that was as fierce as it was formidable.

The last line of the defence was **Gordon Banks**, Leicester City's gregarious goalie. Having taken over from Ron Springett in the wake of England's disappointing performance at the 1962 World Cup in Chile, the Sheffield-born shot-stopper had played every minute of England's win in 1966. Despite having been dropped by his club to make way for rising star Peter Shilton, and being on the brink of a move to Stoke City, Ramsey kept faith with the thirty-year-old and handed him his thirty-seventh cap.

Fulham's **George Cohen** was picked at right-back. Like Banks, he profited from Alf Ramsey's appointment following the 1962 World Cup, taking over from Blackpool's Jimmy Armfield. He was given his first cap in May 1964 in a 2–1 win over Uruguay and when Armfield was side-lined through injury, the tenacious Cohen made the position his own. He played in twenty-one of England's next twenty-three matches and was first choice throughout the 1966 World Cup. The twenty-seven-year-old's stamina and willingness to attack made him a nightmare for opposition defences.

On the opposite side of the backline was **Ray Wilson**. A former apprentice railwayman, he traded the tracks for the pitch after being spotted playing amateur football by a scout from Huddersfield Town. Under the supervision of then manager Bill Shankly, he developed into a strong, pacy left-back before joining Everton in 1964. By then, he'd already made thirty appearances for his country, the first of those coming in a 1–1 draw with Scotland in 1960. He was one of the few players to keep his place after the 1962 World Cup, seeing off the challenge of Liverpool's Gerry Byrne for the jersey. His fiftieth England start came in the World Cup semi against Portugal and, at thirty-two, he had the distinction – if that is indeed the word – of being the oldest member of the England team that beat West Germany in the final.

Leeds United's **Jack Charlton** was picked at centre-half. The nephew of the iconic Milburn brothers – Jack, George, Jim and Stan – Jack was all set to join the police force until Leeds secured his services in 1952. Despite his impressive form for the Elland Road outfit, he was three weeks shy of his thirtieth birthday when he earned his first England call-up for the 1965 match with Scotland at Wembley. Ramsey regarded his conservative, no-nonsense approach as the perfect foil for the more adventurous, more skilful **Bobby Moore**. The pair's partnership proved to be critical in England's World Cup success.

Indeed, Moore was once again named alongside Charlton at the heart of the defence for the visit of the Scots. It was the West Ham United man's fifty-first appearance for his country and his thirty-fourth as skipper. He had first assumed the armband in 1964, aged just twenty-three. Renowned for his almost ethereal ability to read the game, he was widely regarded as the 'golden boy' of English football. Ramsey trusted him implicitly, describing him as 'the spirit and the heartbeat of the team, a cool, calculating footballer and the supreme professional, the best I ever worked with'. Former Scotland manager Jock Stein once famously observed: 'There should be a law against him; he knows what's happening twenty minutes before everyone else.' Alex Ferguson, Pelé, Franz Beckenbauer – according to all three, Moore was the best defender who ever lived.

Playing just in front of the back four, **Nobby Stiles** was the team's enforcer, a tough-tackling dynamo who revelled in the parts of the game most other players ran from. Born in the cellar of his family's north Manchester home during an air raid, his tenacity had been forged in the fire of other people's doubt. They said he was too small to be a footballer, that his short-sightedness would hold him back. He didn't listen. With his gap-toothed smile and a dramatic comb-over barely concealing the fact he'd gone bald at a young age, he defiantly reached the very top of the game. He played every minute of England's victorious World Cup campaign and his post-match dance on the Wembley pitch – Jules Rimet Trophy in one hand, false teeth in the other – was beamed around the world.

At twenty-one, **Alan Ball** was the baby of the team. Having made his name at Blackpool, he swapped Lancashire for Merseyside when he joined Everton in 1966 shortly after the World Cup. The £112,000 fee was, at the time, a record transfer paid to an English club. Fast, fearless and nifty, the diminutive redhead was precisely the kind of versatile midfielder Ramsey liked. His all-action style was on display for all to see in the World Cup Final against West Germany, where he had a hand in three of England's four goals. His tireless endeavour – socks hanging around his ankles – was one of the keys that unlocked English football's greatest-ever day.

The equally industrious **Martin Peters** was picked alongside Ball in the heart of the midfield. The scorer of England's second goal in the World Cup final against the Germans, Peters was a West Ham clubmate of Moore and was widely regarded as the 'complete midfielder'. Two-footed, good in the air, difficult to mark and something of a free-kick specialist, the visit of the Scots was only his twelfth England cap.

Also making his twelfth appearance was another West Ham man, **Geoff Hurst**. The son of former Bristol Rovers, Oldham Athletic and Rochdale centre-half Charlie Hurst, the lanky forward was always destined to become a footballer. As a teenager, he was given a £1 fine and cautioned for disturbing the peace after persistently kicking a ball into his neighbour's garden. Capped at youth, Under-23 and League level, Hurst made his senior England debut in February 1966 against West Germany. Five months later, he helped himself to a hat-trick against the same opposition in the World Cup final, becoming the first – and until Kylian Mbappé in 2022, the only – player to find the net three times in football's biggest game.

Playing alongside Hurst was **Bobby Charlton**. The younger brother of Jack, the Manchester United forward was the most experienced player in Ramsey's starting XI, the visit of Scotland yielding his 78th cap for England. The reigning Ballon d'Or holder, Charlton survived the Munich air disaster of 1958 after being rescued by Manchester United teammate Harry Gregg and became a linchpin of the Old Trafford side's rebuild in the wake of the tragedy. He played in their 1963 FA Cup victory and scored ten goals in their league title win two years later. As a key part of England's World Cup success, he scored the opener in the 2–0 win over Mexico in the second group match, before helping himself to both goals in the semi-final victory against Portugal.

The one and only change from the eleven men that started the World Cup final saw Tottenham Hotspur's **Jimmy Greaves** picked ahead of Roger Hunt of Liverpool. It was a switch that, if anything, made the English even stronger. In fifty-four games for his country, the predatory Greaves had scored forty-three goals, which included six hat-tricks. One of those had come in the 9–3 win over Scotland in 1961. He had also netted the last time the two sides had faced each other at Wembley in 1965. Composure, confidence, pace, skill – he was the full package. The danger man's danger man. Keeping him quiet would be both central to Scotland's prospects of getting a positive result and easier said than done.

With almost 400 caps between them, Ramsey's men lacked nothing in experience. Throw in home advantage, an inspirational, newly knighted manager, and an embarrassment of riches in reserve – Hunt was named in the squad as cover for the forwards, with Keith Newton of Blackburn Rovers doing likewise for the defence and Chelsea goalkeeper Peter Bonetti deputising for Banks – it was little wonder the English media were supremely optimistic of prolonging their winning run.

The *Mirror*'s Brian James was particularly confident. 'The Scots have no chance,' he wrote. 'They have not learned as much about football as England.' Desmond Hackett of the *Daily Express* was equally bullish, insisting: 'England will firmly relegate Scotland to their minor role in international football.'

Whilst the rest of Scotland harrumphed and tut-tutted at the haughty expectation blowing northwards, Brown continued to plot and scheme. His diligence went largely unnoticed but, as Foinavon and his jockey John Buckingham were galloping through the finish line at Aintree, Brown was watching his twenty-fourth football match in just six weeks. His scouting of prospective players was as assiduous as it was comprehensive.

That Saturday – less than twenty-four hours after he had been in London watching Arsenal's game with Charlton Athletic – he travelled to Ibrox to see European Cup Winners' Cup semi-finalists Rangers take on relegation-threatened Stirling Albion. Another selector, Jimmy Aitken, was dispatched to Fife for Dunfermline vs Kilmarnock, with Charlie Forbes taking in Celtic's trip to Motherwell and Bob Thyne in London for Chelsea's FA Cup sixth round clash with Sheffield Wednesday.

With competition for places across the park, Brown's biggest challenge was fitting all of his pieces together. Take the goalkeeper position, for example. Bobby Ferguson appeared to have made the number one jersey his own, having started the last six full internationals, plus the March loss to the Football League. Bill Brown had been the first choice until the end of the 1966 World Cup qualifying campaign but, at thirty-five, his best days were behind him. If age ruled the former Dundee and Tottenham shot-stopper out, it almost certainly counted against Ronnie Simpson who, despite being in the middle of a remarkable season with Celtic, was a year older than Brown and had never been capped. Burnley's Adam Blacklaw had done little in his three starts for his country to justify a call-up and had lost his place in the starting XI at Turf Moor, whilst Aberdeen youngster Bobby Clark had impressed in the Under-23s' win at St James' Park but was still uncapped at senior level. That appeared to make Ferguson the most likely starter. He was in good form for a Kilmarnock side that was through to the quarter-finals of the Inter-Cities Fairs Cup, and yet some doubts remained over his ability to inspire confidence on the big occasions.

It was a similar story at the opposite end of the pitch. Only Denis Law seemed assured of his place on the team sheet. Celtic's Joe McBride most likely would have joined him had his free-scoring start to the season not been halted by a knee injury. Sustained just before Christmas, the problem had flared up again early in March and was subsequently diagnosed as a torn cartilage. It required an operation which was expected to rule him out for the rest of the season.

His Celtic teammates Bobby Lennox, Stevie Chalmers, Jimmy Johnstone and Willie Wallace were all in the frame for a Wembley call-up. So, too, were Rangers' Willie Henderson, Tommy McLean of Kilmarnock and Chelsea's Charlie Cooke, whilst the uncapped trio of Jim McCalliog (Sheffield Wednesday), Jim Wilson (Aberdeen) and Alex Ferguson (Dunfermline Athletic) were others under serious consideration.

At full-back, it was widely expected to be any two from four: Tommy Gemmell (Celtic), Eddie McCreadie (Chelsea), Willie Callaghan (Dunfermline Athletic) and Hugh Tinney (Bury). Under-23 captain Pat Stanton and Leeds United's Willie Bell, who had shackled the great Jairzinho on just his second Scotland start in a 1–1 draw with Brazil at Hampden a year earlier, were also touted in various quarters.

The heart of the defence posed no end to the headaches. Rangers' John Greig had been an ever-present for Scotland since making his debut in a 1–0 win over England at Hampden in 1964 and, as captain of the side, was assured of a start. But who to play alongside him? He appeared to have a good understanding with Billy McNeill based on the few occasions they had played together but the Celtic skipper had been frozen out of the international side since making the most recent of his nineteen starts in a 2–1 defeat at home to Poland in October 1965. Greig's Rangers teammate Ron McKinnon had taken McNeill's place for the home loss to Italy weeks later and had missed only one of the eight games since. Moreover, Brown's decision to play Greig and McNeill together in the League international had backfired, so, despite the recent good form of Arsenal pair Ian Ure and Frank

McLintock, the smart money was on Glasgow-born McKinnon starting at Wembley.

That just left the engine room of the team – the midfield. It was widely expected that Brown would set out his side in a 4-2-4 formation. In that event, Leeds United's tenacious, terrier-like Billy Bremner was a shoo-in for one of the two midfield jerseys. Flame-haired and only 5ft 5in, the Stirling man was Scotland's own Nobby Stiles: a combative, tough-tackling, uncompromising workhorse, with boundless stamina and a keen eye for goal. Leeds fans adored him and worked his name into their popular terrace refrain, 'Glory, Glory Leeds United'.

> *'Little Billy Bremner is the captain of the crew*
> *For the sake of Leeds United, he would break himself in two*
> *His hair is red and fuzzy and his body's black and blue*
> *But the Leeds go marching on!'*

Once described as 'ten-stone of barbed wire', he made his Scotland debut in a goalless draw at home to Spain in May 1965 and, a year later, winning just his seventh cap, marked the great Pelé out of the game in Scotland's Hampden friendly with Brazil. The pair's feisty duel made headlines afterwards and earned Bremner the grudging respect of one of the greatest ever to play the game.

Drop him for England? Not a chance. That just left Brown to ponder who to pick as his midfield partner. There was a litany of options. Hibs' Peter Cormack was only twenty and had played just once previously for Scotland but, despite being built like a whippet, was hard as nails. Then there was Dave Mackay, the heartbeat of the Tottenham side that won the League and Cup double in 1961, the FA Cup in 1962 and the European Cup Winners' Cup in 1963. George Best called him 'the hardest man I have ever played against and certainly the bravest' but he had been out of the international picture for over a year since winning the most recent of his twenty-two caps in October 1965. Bobby Murdoch and Bertie Auld were having phenomenal seasons as part of the all-conquering Celtic side and, if Brown's intention was to use some of their clubmates in attack, who better to do the link-up work behind them than one of their Parkhead teammates? Dave Smith had impressed for Rangers since moving from Aberdeen in a £50,000 deal in August 1966 but his international appearances had been limited to a 3–0 defeat at the hands of the Netherlands in May 1966. Arsenal's uncapped twenty-one-year-old George Graham was tipped as an outside bet for a call-up, as was Jim Townsend, who was back impressing for St Johnstone after a brief spell at Middlesbrough.

There was, of course, one other man to consider.

Trouble personified. The embodiment of genius.

'Big Slim'.

James Curran Baxter. Jim, for short.

THIRTEEN

THE BIRDS OF THE COWDENBEATH PALAIS

THE INK WAS STILL DRYING on the £22-a-week contract he'd signed following his transfer from Raith Rovers to Rangers but Jim Baxter was in no mood to hang around. The idea of patience being a virtue was as lost on him as the final panels of the Bayeux Tapestry. So, he gathered his things, went straight to a local car dealership and bought himself a Jaguar. It would, he reasoned, attract the ladies.

When you're a newly minted, twenty-year-old footballing maverick playing for one of the biggest clubs in the country, women are what matter most, right? Slim Jim certainly thought so.

Forget Paul Gascoigne, Diego Maradona, Eric Cantona or even George Best. Baxter was the original flawed genius, a man endowed with a seemingly extraterrestrial talent that was matched only by a tragic predisposition for self-sabotage. He played with dream-like abandon on the pitch but was his own worst nightmare off it. As Aristotle once proclaimed: 'No great mind has ever existed without a touch of madness.' Baxter didn't have much time for ancient Greek philosophy – his reading habits didn't extend far beyond a daily flick through the *Racing Post* – but he could surely have related.

Born in September 1939 in Hill of Beath, a small village just outside Dunfermline, Baxter was football daft. He was good at it, too. The local primary school declared him 'Our Wizard', such was his deftness of touch with the heavy leather balls of the 1940s. He went on to Queen Anne's Secondary Modern School in Dunfermline where another of his gifts – that of the gab – earned him a new nickname: 'Stanley', as in Stanley Baxter, the acclaimed Scottish comedian and actor who had become a fixture on the boards of Glasgow's Citizens' Theatre.

After leaving school in his mid-teens, Baxter spent nine months as an apprentice cabinet maker before following his father, Robert, into the mines. He earned £7 per week chipping away at the coalface of the Fordell Colliery. His mother, Agnes, was dismayed. She had always imagined better for her only son than the lightless soot and stour of the coalmines. But as Baxter said himself, 'Going down the pit in my village was as natural as a boy from Peterhead going to sea.'

Jock Stein had followed a similar path, taking the cage into the pits of Lanarkshire whilst playing part-time for Blantyre Victoria and Albion Rovers. 'There's nothing as dark as the darkness down a pit,' he once said. 'The blackness that closes in on you if your lamp goes out. You'd think you would see some shapes but you can see nothing, nothing but the inside of your head. I think everybody should go down the pit at least once to learn what darkness is.'

Through time and circumstance, Scottish coalmining has assumed a romantic, almost glamourised identity. Good, honest work by good honest men. That sort of thing. Baxter had no time for such idealism. 'Someone once said it must have been character forming,' he remarked. 'These are the kinds of clowns who embarrass miners by calling them the "salt of the earth".

They've never had a co-op number, they always have dinner in the evening, and they think drinking half-pints is daring.

'It could be that a mining village childhood is character forming – but if you go down the pit often enough, it also forms black bits on your lungs.'

At weekends, black coal dust sprinkled through his mop of brown hair, Baxter would play football in the park with other boys from the village. His former school headmaster James Carmichael spotted his potential and arranged for him to play for Halbeath Juniors. In 1955, he joined Crossgates Primrose, managed by Bill Buckard and George Ferrier, two tough Fifers also from the coal yards. Baxter used his £50 signing-on fee – paid out in used one-pound notes – to buy his mother a new washing machine.

Two years later, Raith Rovers came calling. The Kirkcaldy outfit had finished fourth in Scotland's top flight in 1956/57 and were looking to strengthen a squad that already boasted the likes of the free-scoring Bernie Kelly, dependable Willie Polland and the fearsome half-back axis of Andy Young, Willie McNaught and Andy Leigh. Baxter, they reasoned, would provide some attacking élan to an otherwise steely outfit and so the Stark's Park club's hierarchy – led by manager Bert Herdsman – invited him for a trial.

Just one problem. Baxter was still working in the coalmines. At the time, that was a five-and-a-half days a week gig. Knocking off time on a Saturday was 1.30 p.m. but he needed to leave at noon to be ready for kick-off and that meant going to formidable pit boss Mick Johnson for an early finish. 'Asking him for a favour was like patting a crocodile,' Baxter would later reflect.

True to form, Johnson was incredulous that anybody would want this wiry, skin-and-bone slip of a boy for the rough and tumble of football. 'You? A trial for Raith Rovers?' he boomed. 'It's a good feed you're needing.'

Nonetheless, he agreed. Baxter made it in time for kick-off and turned in a polished performance. This was no lump of coal, thought Herdsman. Maybe, just maybe, he'd unearthed a diamond. He wasted no time in signing Baxter to a £3-per-week, part-time deal – his first contract in senior football.

He spent three years with Raith where 'Iron Man' McNaught took him under his wing and helped him add guile to his gift. Instead of running thirty yards to play a five-yard pass, for example, why not run five yards to play a thirty-yard pass? Conserve your energy, play smarter. That was the message and Baxter paid heed.

In November 1959, Rovers travelled to Ibrox to play reigning champions Rangers. Despite a handful of hiccups, the Glasgow side had started the season in fine fashion and were strongly fancied to win the title for the fourth time in five years. Just days earlier, meanwhile, they had disposed of Red Star Bratislava to advance to the quarter-finals of the European Cup. In short, few people gave Rovers much hope and so when Rangers raced into an early two-goal lead, most assumed that was that.

Herdsman's men had other ideas and rallied to win 3–2, Baxter scoring the second and pulling all the strings from the left side of the midfield. It was a virtuoso performance from the twenty-year-old, an accomplished, mature display that dazzled all inside the ground that day – Rangers boss Scot Symon amongst them.

For the remainder of the season, he kept tabs on Baxter's progress. Sure, there were things he didn't much like. The youngster's tackling was suspect and his burgeoning reputation for being a bit of a loudmouth and a rebel was 180 degrees from the values Symon stood for and the way he observed them. Even so, he knew he had to have him.

In June 1960, Rangers swooped to sign Baxter from Raith in a £17,500 deal – a Scottish transfer record. And yes, almost immediately, he went car shopping in order to impress the ladies.

'One day, I was a Raith Rovers player who couldnae pull the birds at the Cowdenbeath Palais,' he said. 'The next day I was in Glasgow and the girls were throwing themselves at me. It was certainly a change and I wasn't letting it go by.'

Around the same time, the Army came knocking at Baxter's door. He was required for National Service – one of the very last of the conscripts – and, thanks to some nimble chicanery from his new club, he would be assigned to the Black Watch.

To say military life didn't suit Baxter would be an understatement. 'A lot of people will tell you that conscription and the Army makes a man of you and all that sort of bull,' he reflected. 'Personally, I found it was almost a total waste of time.'

Nonetheless, he was a more-than-capable recruit, as his old platoon sergeant Bob Ritchie observed. 'There's no doubt Jim would've made a good soldier,' he said. 'He got a prize for "most improved recruit for shooting" as I remember. But National Service was in his road. He was only interested in his fitba and Glasgow Rangers.'

It was during his compulsory stint with the army that Baxter's flair for bedevilment really ran amok. After completing the initial ten weeks of recruit training, he was given an office job at Stirling Castle. But rather take his turn doing the nightly guard stints, he paid a fellow Jock five pounds to do it for him.

'He was always doing funny things and getting away with it,' added Ritchie. 'Going missing and not being on parade when he should've been, for example. Jim was a comedian.'

On more than one occasion, Baxter parked his green Jag next to the commanding officer's 'poxy' Austin, just to get a rise out of him. He wasn't a particularly good driver, though. The Jag was soon written off, as was a car belonging to his Ibrox teammate Ralph Brand, and another for good measure.

'Scot Symon phoned me up one day and told me not to let him travel to Ibrox in a car but to put him on the train,' added

Ritchie. 'He told me, "You jump in the train with him and we'll give you the full service at Ibrox."'

Ritchie wasn't the only one to take a call from Ibrox during Baxter's service. Rangers bribed the company sergeant major with a crate of whisky and tickets for the directors' box to ensure their star man came and went as he pleased. In return, he was made to turn out for the Scottish Command football team, as well as the British army and unit side, in addition to his games for Rangers.

'They moan now about having to play sixty games a season,' Baxter said. 'I played 108.'

Despite his misgivings about the need for National Service – which was abolished soon after he was conscripted – Baxter did see some good in it. 'What I learned about the Army was the fact that you couldn't mess them about,' he said. 'If they said, "Back by eight," they weren't talking about a minute past eight.'

Make no mistake, he understood discipline and, to some extent, the need for it. But by God did he challenge it.

He made his Rangers debut in a League Cup tie against Partick Thistle in August 1960 and, in November, scored his first goal for the club in a 3–1 win away to Clyde. The following week, he made his full Scotland debut in a 5–2 win over Northern Ireland. In a hugely successful first season, Baxter and Rangers won a league and cup double and finished runners-up to Fiorentina in the European Cup Winners' Cup final. The 1961/62 campaign yielded a League Cup title defence as well as a Scottish Cup victory. It was in Baxter's third year, however, that things started to go wrong.

Whilst Rangers started the 1962/63 season in imperious fashion, losing only once in their first thirteen league matches, Baxter's own form had dipped dramatically, prompting Symon to drop him in December. Rumours about his star man's wild ways off the pitch had been steadily intensifying and the Ibrox boss had

had enough. In response, Baxter promptly submitted a transfer request which was accepted. He claimed to be unhappy with what Rangers were paying him. 'I only wanted a few quid more than the less gifted,' he said. 'We were all paid equally, which was like paying Frank Sinatra the same as the Alexander Brothers.'

He decided that his considerable talents would be better compensated south of the border and, in April 1963, after scoring twice in a 2–1 win over England at Wembley, issued a very literal come-and-get-me plea to prospective English suitors. 'What more must I do to get an English club to sign me?' he asked afterwards.

A group of Arsenal fans responded to Baxter's match-winning performance at the national stadium by organising a petition urging their club to sign him but to no avail. Baxter's reputation preceded him and seldom well. It was reported that he had held talks with Leeds United. Their coach Don Revie was a huge fan of Baxter's but, like others, was concerned by some of the stories he'd heard about him. In a bid to establish the facts, he invited the Scot to Elland Road for a frank, honest conversation.

'I'm told,' Revie said, 'that you drink everything that's brewed and distilled, that there aren't enough women for you to chase, and that you're not averse to the odd brawl.'

'Aye,' replied Baxter. 'You're very well informed.'

Negotiations ended there.

In May 1967, after five months on the transfer list, Baxter agreed to an interview with the *Daily Express* in which he attempted to repair some of the damage done by his hellraising. 'It's not true that Rangers have to bail me out before every match,' he insisted. 'I sink a few bevvies on Saturday nights, and maybe one night early mid-week. The rest of the week, I stay home with my parents and watch television.

'Any time I have a bad spell, and I have one every season, they say it's because I'm steamed. It got so that even the club began believing the gossip. I was called before the manager and told to get a grip on myself but I hadn't been doing anything out of line except starting the season in poor form.'

Finally, in August 1963 and with no concrete interest forthcoming, Baxter agreed to a new deal with Rangers but insisted on remaining on the transfer list. Stoke City made an approach for him that same month but it was rejected.

His struggles continued into the 1963/64 season. He was left out of the Scotland team to play Northern Ireland in a British Home Championship match in October of that year but, to the surprise of many, was selected for a 'Rest of the World' side that faced England later that month as part of the Football Association's celebrations to mark 100 years of association football. Taking his place alongside the likes of Alfredo Di Stefano, Eusébio, Ferenc Puskás and iconic Soviet goalkeeper Lev Yashin, as well as fellow Scot Denis Law, there was only one thing on Baxter's mind: money. 'I was on £35 at Rangers, Denis maybe £50 at Manchester United. We knew it was chickenfeed. We looked at all those great players and we wondered what they were getting.' England ran out 2–1 winners.

Nottingham Forest, Tottenham Hotspur and Italian champions Inter Milan all made inquiries for Baxter in the months that followed but none could persuade Rangers to do business. In the end, Baxter stayed at the club into the 1964/65 season. That December, he finally rediscovered his best form, tormenting Rapid Vienna as the Ibrox side advanced to the quarter-finals of the European Cup. Leading 1–0 from the first leg, a Baxter-inspired Rangers won 2–0 in Austria – but the win came at a cost.

Baxter had tormented full-back Walter Skocik throughout the match, nutmegging him repeatedly, mercilessly, provocatively. Finally, Skocik snapped. He flew into a tackle from behind, breaking Baxter's shin in the process.

'Jim was in sensational form that night and all he had to show for it was a broken leg,' recalled teammate Ronnie McKinnon. 'It was sad and we all lamented the fact he was carried off the field injured.

'He was taking the mickey out of the guy Skocik who was one of Rapid's star players. Baxter could do that to anybody. Skocik got annoyed and frustrated. Baxter put the ball through the guy's legs for the umpteenth time and walked round him and the player chased him and kicked him and broke his leg. The Rapid player just couldn't take any more punishment.'

Baxter subsequently spent four months on the side-lines – and during that time, his drinking and gambling problems deepened. When he finally returned to the first-team fold, it was clear to all – not least his manager, Symon – that Baxter was neither the player nor the man that he had been before Skocik's tackle. In May 1965, when Sunderland made a £72,500 bid for him, Baxter's Rangers career – the first chapter of it, at least – was over.

Immediately, speculation began as to whether this fabulously talented but equally flawed twenty-six-year-old could cut it in English football. For his former Rangers teammates, there was mainly relief. Having arrived almost straight from the pits of a small village, Baxter was seduced by the size, sights and sounds of Glasgow, and with plenty of money in his pocket, he indulged in all that the city had to offer. Game tomorrow? Sure, but that's tomorrow. There's a whole night to come before then. As he would later admit: 'Friday night was always Saturday night to me.'

In Tom Miller's definitive biography of Baxter, former Ibrox man Harold Davis recalled: 'Jim would come in and the smell of drink on his breath was obvious, even only a couple of hours before a match. You just knew he had been out all night on another bender. How did he get away with it? Well, he was Symon's blue-eyed boy.'

Huge bills for caviar, smoked salmon, Havana cigars, Bacardi, champagne and more routinely passed from the St Enoch Hotel – Baxter's favourite haunt – to Ibrox. On more than one occasion, Baxter even forged the signature of a teammate in an inventive attempt to allay his employers' suspicions. One of those belonged to outside-left Davie Wilson, who was horrified when a club official presented him with a bill and informed him that the amount would be deducted from his next wage packet.

'I didn't drink and everybody knew who the real culprit was but it took a bit of convincing before Symon told me to have a word with Jim,' he recalled.

His gambling had also become the stuff of club legend. A habit honed in the Institute card room back in Hill of Beath was suddenly exposed to the likes of the Queens Club and Chevalier Casino – and, unfortunately for Baxter, he didn't know his limits. In October 1963, he was part of the Rangers side that lost 6–0 to Real Madrid in the European Cup. Afterwards, he went to the casino in the team's hotel and, before long, found himself £5,000 to the good. When bosses announced that they were closing the casino for the night, Baxter wagered the whole lot on the final spin of the roulette wheel. He lost.

His belligerent ways knew no bounds. He would routinely show up for training in a casual sports shirt and slacks in open defiance of the club's strict dress code that required players to report for all club's duties in a shirt and tie. When he was sent home as punishment, he would head straight into town for yet more hijinks.

As mercurial a talent as he was, Baxter was also a liability and everybody at Rangers knew it. Sunderland? Well, they would soon find out. Weeks after making the move to Wearside, Baxter married Glasgow hairdresser Jean Ferguson. It was, he claimed, their nuptials that prompted him to accept the offer from Sunderland, which included a reported £12,000 signing-on fee.

'I wanted to get married but I didn't have a penny to my name,' he said. 'I'd gambled or drunk most of it.'

Any hopes that he might settle into a better domestic routine were short-lived. He was out of shape and out of form when he made his debut for his new club, a 5–0 pre-season friendly defeat to, of all clubs, Celtic. Throughout his first season at Sunderland, his drinking continued to attract negative headlines. During the summer that followed, as England were building towards World Cup glory, Baxter was part of the Scotland squad that hosted Portugal – Eusébio, José Augusto and Jaime Graça et al. – at Hampden. The night before the match, he hit the town, eventually returning to the team hotel at 4 a.m. where he was made to do press-ups until he vomited.

He did similar in March 1967 as Sunderland prepared to face bitter rivals Newcastle in a Tyne-Wear derby. A bouncer called Barry Robson recalled seeing a 'comatose' Baxter being carried out of a nightclub at 2.30 a.m. the night before the game. 'Twelve hours later, from 3 p.m. that afternoon,' added Robson, 'I was privileged to witness the destruction of Newcastle United, aided and abetted by the revived corpse. It was nearly a one-man show, with Baxter mesmerising the Newcastle players.' Sunderland won 3–0.

News of Baxter's performance that day filtered back to Scotland coach Bobby Brown. The clash with England was only weeks away and much was riding on it. From a personal standpoint, of course Brown wanted to get off to a winning start in his first game as Scotland manager. Of far greater significance, however, was the chance to qualify for the European Nations Cup and the Wembley result would likely go some way to determining which of the home nations did so.

Could he really gamble on a man who gambled on everything, a man of whom his great friend, Celtic captain Billy McNeill, once said 'didn't do "wee nights" out', only full-scale, riotous benders? Then again, could he honestly and in good conscience overlook Baxter's immense, indisputable talent, a talent that often only fully revealed itself on big occasions such as this?

The difference between winning and losing could very well hinge on Baxter's ability to indulge his wand of a left foot at the expense of his drinking arm, and Brown knew it.

He had a decision to make.

FOURTEEN

MR BROWN'S BOYS

BOBBY BROWN FINALLY NAMED the eleven men he was entrusting with the task of beating the world champions on their own patch on Monday, 10 April 1967. Sir Alf's side was undeniably strong. Stronger, perhaps, than the team he had picked for the World Cup final. However, it was also predictable. Even the most contrary clairvoyant could have foreseen the players he'd thrust into this battle. Despite the infrequency of international competition, England had come to operate with the efficiency, consistency, and familiarity of the very best club sides. They played with an easy, almost telepathic understanding of each other's abilities and responsibilities; a straightforward alchemy that was notoriously difficult to bottle and coveted by other international sides the world over.

The same could not have been said of Brown and his line-up. It was a divining rod's nightmare and left even the most informed pundits both stunned and red-faced.

With only 121 caps between them, the Scots had vastly less experience at this level than their hosts. Eight of Brown's men had played fewer games for Scotland to that point than the least capped players in the English line-up. Only six had made more than five appearances. Two, quite remarkably, were chosen to make their debuts in the formidable, cauldron-like playground of their biggest rivals. And yet for all that, all but three of them had started the 4–3 defeat to England at Hampden twelve months earlier.

Of even greater significance was the trust Brown showed in the Anglos. He picked five of them – almost half of his team – with the remainder of his line-up comprised of players from either side of Glasgow's Old Firm divide.

As was widely expected, Rangers' **John Greig** was picked to captain the side. It would be the recently married centre-half's twenty-first appearance for his country and his eighth in a row wearing the armband – a far cry from his humble beginnings with the United Crossroads Boys Club. He combined an engineering apprenticeship with turning out for the Edinburgh youth side. A string of impressive displays caught the eye of Rangers, who swooped to sign him in 1959. Despite his initial reservations about joining the Glasgow giants, the Hearts-supporting Greig was finally sold on the move after seeing them thrash Hibernian 6–1 at Easter Road in a Scottish League Cup tie.

Originally signed as a forward, Greig soon dropped into a deeper role with the Ibrox side and, in 1964, he made his Scotland debut in a 1–0 win over England at Hampden. Alan Gilzean scored the only goal of the game but Greig's assured performance in silencing Roger Hunt, Terry Paine and Johnny Byrne in the English attack attracted a considerable share of the plaudits. He hadn't missed a Scotland game since then.

Picked alongside Greig at the heart of the defence was his clubmate **Ron McKinnon**. The twenty-six-year-old had started out as a winger during his days with junior sides Benburb and Dunipace but was converted into a centre-half when he signed for Rangers. 'I was 5ft 10½in at sixteen or seventeen but going to Rangers made me taller,' he recalled. 'My muscles and my legs just sprouted.' Famously debonair off the pitch, with an eye for the ladies that wouldn't have looked out of place in Jim Baxter's sockets, McKinnon developed an unflappable, uncompromising demeanour on it. He was a solid, reliable, and proven foil for Greig.

His inclusion meant no place for Billy McNeill, the totemic, twenty-seven-year-old captain of a Celtic side that was still competing on all fronts and in with a legitimate chance of completing an unprecedented quintuple of trophy victories that season. It was a decision that Brown agonised over. In the end, he listened to his gut.

Either side of Greig and McKinnon were the full-backs, **Tommy Gemmell** and **Eddie McCreadie**. At twenty-three, Gemmell had already established himself as one of the best full-backs in the country, a phenomenal athlete with a remarkable engine and the heart of a lion. However, he was more accustomed to playing on the left side of the defence and Brown had picked him to play on the right. Moreover, he had made only three prior appearances for Scotland. McCreadie, meantime, was only marginally more experienced. The England match would yield a tenth cap for the Chelsea man. The London club's boss, Tommy Docherty, had spotted him playing for East Stirlingshire during a trip to scout one of his teammates. 'This left-back,' Docherty later recalled. 'I thought, 'Why the hell are you playing here?' He was great in the air, he was quick, his control was magic. I didn't know if he was a left-back or an outside-left.' A £5,000 fee was quickly agreed and the Glasgow-born McCreadie was off to Stamford Bridge. He made his Scotland debut the last time they travelled to Wembley, in 1965, and was regarded by Brown as being 'ahead of his time'.

In midfield, Leeds United's **Billy Bremner** was picked to win his tenth cap. Pugnacious, tenacious and absolutely fearless, he was the heartbeat of the side both on and off the pitch. Maybe it was on account of his diminutive stature that Bremner developed an aversion to people challenging him, a cast iron will and determination to prove them wrong.

His Elland Road clubmate and fellow Scot Eddie Gray recalled one such occasion during training with Leeds. 'We were training down at Fullerton Park behind the West Stand,' he explained. 'A supporter, who looked drunk even though it was only 11 a.m., had come down to watch.

'We had drawn the previous weekend and this fan was determined to make his point, shouting things like, "Bremner, you're useless, I'm a better player than you." He told us all that we were crap.

'Billy had heard enough and marched over to where this supporter was stood and said, "So, you're better than us are you? Prove it then."

'With that, he walked off towards the little gymnasium that used to be under the main stand and the fan followed. We did the same, as we could clearly see Billy was up to something.

'Anyway, they got into the gym and Billy said, "Come on then, show me what your heading ability is like." Billy then tossed him the ball and this guy headed it as powerfully as he could.

'Unfortunately for him, Billy had deliberately picked up a medicine ball and it knocked the guy clean out. Eventually, the fan came round and, as he did, Billy walked off with a smile and said, "Well, you're crap at heading for a start."'

Bremner's only previous experience of playing England had been in the 4–3 defeat at Hampden a year earlier. That just wouldn't do. Not for a man with an instinctive hatred of losing. Had Brown, for whatever reason, not picked him, he likely would have turned up anyway.

Alongside him in the engine room? **Jim Baxter**. Despite his unpredictability, his penchant for self-sabotage, his recent inconsistent form and his predisposition for being a bit of a rascal, Baxter checked more pros than cons in Brown's book. 'There was no doubt that he was no longer the player he had been at Rangers,' the boss would later observe. 'But he still had bags of ability and great belief in himself.' That much was certainly true. For all of his questionable proclivities, Baxter was lavishly, prodigiously talented – and yes, he knew it.

'I remember we played Brazil in 1966 – with Pelé – in Glasgow,' McKinnon recalled. 'I was teasing Baxter the day before saying, "It's Pelé tomorrow, Jim, the big test." Jim said to me, "Pelé? Who's he? You watch me tomorrow, big man." The next day, Baxter went out and ruled the show.'

A big man for the big occasion, Baxter was also the yin to Bremner's yang. Bremner was industry; Baxter was artistry. As far as many in Scotland were concerned, they were at least the equal of anything that England had to offer, both as individuals and as a partnership.

Scotland's four-pronged attack was led by Manchester United forward **Denis Law**. The most experienced man on Brown's team sheet, the twenty-seven-year-old was about to win his thirty-seventh cap on his fourth trip to Wembley (on international duty, at least). Law had experienced football's gamut across his previous three visits: he was the sole survivor of the 9–3 humiliation in 1961, had featured in the 2–1 redemption in 1963, and scored in a 2–2 draw in 1965. What's more, he was in devastating, free-scoring form for a Manchester United side that was closing in on a seventh First Division title and a second in three seasons. Not only that, Brown knew that Law would bring something extra to his attack, something intangible that statisticians couldn't measure: vengeance.

England winning the World Cup had wounded him on a personal level. Unable to escape the gloating and constant celebration that followed it by dint of playing in Manchester and alongside several of the winning team, Law's envy was aggravated by a gnawing and resolute belief that, had Scotland qualified for the tournament, they could have lifted the trophy. 'That was even more annoying than England winning,' he admitted.

Still, he loved Wembley. 'It was, quite rightly, a famous stadium and a beautiful pitch to play on,' he said. 'If you couldn't do your stuff on the Wembley turf, you couldn't play on anything.'

If Brown's charges were to have any chance of winning, much would hinge on the performance of Law.

On Law's left was Celtic's **Bobby Lennox**. Since scoring on his international debut against Northern Ireland the previous November, the tricky forward had grown in stature and importance for Jock Stein's Celtic, filling much of the goalscoring void created by a Christmas-time injury to teammate Joe McBride. His goals in both legs against French side Nantes had helped Celtic progress to the last eight of the European Cup in December and, since the turn of the year, he had chipped in with nine goals in all competitions, including the opener in a 2–0 Scottish Cup semi-final replay win over Clyde less than a week prior to Brown naming his team for Wembley. It was thought that his pace and skill would trouble England's right-back George Cohen and stifle the Fulham man's forward advances.

Another Celtic man, **Jimmy Johnstone**, was picked on the opposite side of the front line. Brown loved 'Jinky'. Everybody did. Hugh McIlvanney once wrote that no other player 'besieged opponents with such a complex, concentrated swirl of deceptive manoeuvres or ever conveyed a more exhilarating sense of joy in working wonders with the ball.' With his bright red curls and slender frame, the Lilliputian 'Lord of the Wing' was a maverick who thrived on the big occasion. 'The pitch was my stage,' he once remarked, 'and the whistle meant it was showtime.'

A former ball boy at Celtic Park, Johnstone combined natural talent with an insatiable thirst for self-improvement. Growing up in the family home in Viewpark, North Lanarkshire, he would dribble milk bottles up and down the hallway for hours at a time to perfect his skills. After finding out that English great Stanley Matthews – a player of similar stature and who played in the same position as him – used to walk to Blackpool's ground wearing heavy boots in order strengthen his leg muscles, Johnstone reportedly started wearing pit boots and regularly played football in them. That, he reckoned, added about three yards to his blistering pace.

Johnstone signed youth terms with Celtic on the same day as Gemmell and, after a spell with junior side Blantyre Celtic, made his first-team debut for the Glasgow giants on 27 March 1963. Just eighteen months later, he was a Scottish internationalist, starring in a 3–2 defeat away to Wales. He scored his first goals for his country in the 4–3 defeat to England at Hampden in April 1966. The opportunity to avenge that defeat would yield his fifth cap.

That left two positions to be filled – and both went to debutants at opposite ends of their respective careers.

Sheffield Wednesday's twenty-year-old forward **Jim McCalliog** was rewarded for his standout performance in the Under-23 victory at St James' Park at the beginning of March, whilst, in goal, Celtic's well-travelled thirty-six-year-old stopper **Ronnie Simpson** was chosen ahead of Kilmarnock's Bobby Ferguson.

'I had to decide who would best combine with Bremner and Baxter and offer some fluidity in the formation by being able to go forward as an attacker and also cover back when required,' reasoned Brown. With his boundless stamina, terrific skill and boyish enthusiasm, McCalliog was perfect man for the job. He had also been playing in England since he was fifteen, so knew what it was like to play with and against the best the Auld Enemy had to offer. For good measure, he had big game experience of Wembley, too, having played and scored there in the 1966 FA Cup Final.

The decision to parachute McCalliog into the team for his Scotland debut, particularly in a match of such significance, surprised many but not his club boss. 'Jim is a boy of high integrity,' said Alan Brown. 'There is none better in the game. He applies himself all the time to playing real football. He is a credit to the game.

'He has an old head on very young shoulders and has developed very quickly since coming to Sheffield Wednesday. I can use him as a midfield player, or I can play him as a striker. The role I allocate to him depends on the opposition. He has not scored many goals for us this term but those he had were vital. He is a great goal-pincher.'

Simpson, meantime, made his senior football debut before McCalliog had even been born. He was well-known to Brown, having been his understudy at Queen's Park for several years. 'I felt confident about him,' said Brown. 'He was playing well for Celtic in big games at home and in Europe, was used to appearing in front of big crowds, and has previous experience of Wembley.

'The other main candidate for the position was Bobby Ferguson but I felt he was not at his best for the Scottish league against the English league.' Nonetheless, he was picked as travelling reserve, along with Arsenal's Glasgow-born centre-half Frank McLintock and Celtic forward Stevie Chalmers. The latter might have felt aggrieved to have been overlooked for a place in the starting eleven. In five previous appearances for his country, he had scored three times – including a first-minute opener in the 1–1 draw with Brazil the previous summer – and had notched thirty-six goals in all competitions for the Parkhead side so far in the 1966/67 season.

Bobby Brown knew better. Or at least, he hoped he did.

And so did all of Scotland.

FIFTEEN

FAITHER

RONNIE SIMPSON WAS WALKING up the seventh fairway at West Kilbride Golf Club in Ayrshire when a breathless runner caught up with him. The thirty-six-year-old goalkeeper was staying at the nearby Seamill Hydro hotel with his Celtic teammates ahead of their European Cup semi-final with Czech champions Dukla Prague later that week.

A consummate professional, Simpson had a tunnel-like focus on that game and how he might keep Dukla's attacking threats – Stanislav Štrunc and Josef Masopust, for example – at bay. Celtic were not so much on course for a season of unprecedented success as hurtling towards it like a green-and-white-striped juggernaut. The League Cup and Glasgow Cup had already been secured; a last-four replay victory over Clyde had put them into the final of the Scottish Cup where Aberdeen awaited at the end of April; and they were only four games shy of a first successful league title defence in half a century.

The prospect of a clean sweep of trophies was tantalisingly close for Jock Stein's men and, as far as Simpson was concerned, that was all that mattered.

Scotland's match with England, he figured, would be somebody else's responsibility. Bobby Ferguson, most likely. The Kilmarnock keeper had been in goal for seven of the last eight internationals, including the 4–3 defeat to England at Hampden a year earlier, the 1–1 draw with Brazil in June 1966 and the previous two matches with Wales and Northern Ireland. Despite some competition from Tottenham Hotspur's Bill Brown, Adam Blacklaw of Burnley and, most significantly, Bobby Clark of Aberdeen, twenty-one-year-old Ferguson appeared to have made Scotland's number one jersey his own.

Simpson had all but abandoned any hopes he'd once harboured of playing for his country. For one thing, he was fifteen years Ferguson's senior. In Simpson's mind, that was no big deal. The great Lev Yashin was pushing forty yet he was still, by some measure, the best goalkeeper in the Soviet Union. Then there was his mind. 'Experience can teach you a lot,' he once said, 'but the great thing is to keep one's mental reactions sharp all the time.' As his Celtic teammates, particularly centre-halves Billy McNeill and John Clark, would have confirmed had anybody asked, Simpson's reactions could have split the atom.

Even so, it was widely assumed that his career was winding down, not least by Simpson himself.

'I felt, though I was playing as well as ever, that I had had my chance,' he later recalled. 'At the age of thirty-six, you could hardly expect to begin a new career as an international player.'

Goalkeeping had been in Simpson's blood for as long as he could remember. As a young boy running around the garden with his father, the former Rangers centre-half Jimmy Simpson, his instincts had been to dive at the ball and grab it rather than to kick it. His mother instinctively knitted him goalkeeper's sweaters to play in and, when he was lifted over the turnstiles to watch his dad in action, his attention was fixed on the lone individual playing behind him.

'I used to have childish fantasies about growing up and becoming a man in a big yellow sweater,' he admitted.

In kick-arounds with friends in the King's Park neighbourhood of Glasgow where he grew up, Simpson would not so much volunteer as demand that he be put in goal, a position usually reserved for the worst footballers of the group. 'You can imagine how popular that made me,' he acknowledged. 'Nobody else wanted the position.'

In 1945, aged just fourteen years and 304 days, he became the youngest player to feature for a club side when he kept goal for Queen's Park during a Summer Cup match at Hampden. He spent five seasons with the 'Spiders', during which time he also represented the Scotland Youth side in a match with England in Doncaster in 1947 and was picked by the great Matt Busby as part of the Great Britain squad for the 1948 Olympics in London. The team narrowly missed out on a medal, losing first in the semi-finals to Yugoslavia and then to Sweden in the bronze medal match.

Still just a teen, Simpson soon became a man in demand. A trial with Rangers amounted to nothing and so, after completing National Service in the Royal Armoured Corps, he moved to Third Lanark.

'They were a great crowd of players at Cathkin Park,' he remarked. 'Everyone was a character. Matt Balunas, Norman Christie, wee Harry Mooney, the flying Pole Felix Staroscik or "Starry" as the fans called him, and the brilliant, bewildering Jimmy Mason. They made me feel at home right away.'

Not that he was there long. Six months after joining Thirds, Simpson was on the move again, this time south of the border – just – to Newcastle United. After displacing the Magpies' regular goalkeeper Jack Fairbrother, he won the FA Cup twice in nine successful seasons on Tyneside. Simpson returned to Scotland in 1960 when he joined Hibernian and, in 1962, he was praised for a string of impressive performances that, ultimately, helped the capital club stave off relegation. He subsequently fell out of favour at Hibs following Walter Galbraith's resignation as manager and, as the 1963/64 season ended, he was seriously contemplating retirement. Life outside of football was going great. He had a good job as an industrial representative of an oil company and had been bitten hard by the golf bug. Training all week just to sit on the bench for ninety minutes every Saturday just didn't appeal.

'I saw the end of the season out and stopped training. Frankly, I lost all interest. The only time I called at Easter Road was to get my weekly wage packet. For the first time in my life, professional football was no longer of real interest to me. I wasn't drifting out of the game, I was galloping.

'At thirty-three years of age, I had had a fair run. It seemed to be the end of the road.'

Such was Simpson's disillusionment with the game, he even accepted the offer of a trial run as a football reporter for a Sunday newspaper. Around the same time, Berwick Rangers' manager Ian Spence doorstepped him at his home in Glasgow to see if he could persuade him to sign with the Borderers. Simpson refused. He was, he insisted, done with playing.

That was until Sean Fallon picked up the phone.

The Celtic great had been tasked with finding out if Simpson would be interested in joining the Parkhead outfit. A £3,000 transfer and personal terms were agreed in short order and so it went that, a month before his thirty-fourth birthday, Simpson became a Celtic player.

The assumption was that he had been snapped up by the Glasgow giants as cover for first-choice goalkeeper John Fallon. His first-team opportunities appeared to suffer a further blow when Stein, the same man who had sanctioned his departure from Hibs, was appointed Celtic manager in March 1965. By then, Simpson had made only a handful of starts, including the two Fairs Cup matches with Barcelona. Fallon, though, was proving difficult to dislodge and Simpson sat out the rest of the season on the bench.

He started the following campaign, 1965/66, in the same vein before finally getting his chance at home to Aberdeen in late September. A 7–1 win over the Dons saw Simpson keep his place for the European Cup Winners' Cup tie with Dutch side Go Ahead four days later. Celtic won 6–0. Five days later, Simpson was lining up in goal for Celtic against former side Hibs in the League Cup semi-final at Ibrox. After seeing them off – albeit only after a replay – Celtic, with Simpson in goal, defeated Rangers in the final of the competition at Hampden Park.

For Simpson, the match was significant on two fronts. One, it was his first Scottish medal. Two, and arguably more importantly, it cemented his place as the Hoops' first-choice goalie.

'It completed my comeback as a First Division player,' he acknowledged. 'I had proved that I was far from finished. I could still do a job in goal. I felt that there was a new career opening up for me.'

At club level, perhaps, but international recognition continued to elude him. The closest Simpson had ever come to a Scottish call-up had been during his time at Newcastle when international selectors travelled to watch him in action away to Liverpool.

'I played so badly they never came back,' he would later laugh.

Despite his Indian summer with Celtic and, in 1966/67, the side's dominance on all fronts, Simpson had long since reached the inevitable conclusion that the two 'B' caps he had received in the mid-1950s would have to suffice as far as international recognition went.

As several newspaper columnists began to tout his name as a potential starter for the England match, Simpson resisted the notion. Not even the backing of his club colleagues – who affectionately referred to him as 'Faither' on account of his years

– could convince him that maybe, just maybe, he still had a chance.

'My Celtic teammates kept telling me, "You're a certainty, Ronnie. They must cap you at Wembley." It's nice to play with fellows who have such confidence in you but I thought we had such a good sprinkling of fine young keepers in Scotland that they would hardly come for an old man like me.'

And so, as the morning of the team announcement dawned, Simpson grabbed his golf clubs and nipped across to West Kilbride where he pegged it up with teammate Stevie Chalmers. They were deep into their front nine when an out-of-breath club assistant caught up with them.

'Ronnie, you're in,' he told him. 'You're in the Scotland team. You're playing against England.'

Simpson refused to believe him. It had to be a wind-up. Had to be. He and Chalmers played out the rest of their round. As they walked up the eighteenth fairway, they saw photographers from the main Scottish newspapers all camped behind the green.

'That's when I knew something was going on,' said Simpson. 'They stated their business. I was in the Wembley side and they wanted a picture. Well, they could have a dozen!'

Catching up with the rest of his Celtic teammates back in the hotel, Simpson was showered with congratulations, not to mention a few wisecracks.

Jock Stein told him: 'I hear Jerry Dawson is making a comeback for Falkirk.' Formerly of Rangers, goalkeeper Dawson, the so-called 'Prince in the Yellow Jersey', was in his forties when he made his final competitive appearance in 1949.

Bobby Lennox, one of three other Celtic players picked to face England, added: 'Ronnie's only had one card of congratulations. His friends are more stunned than he is.'

Every taunt landed with a smile. Nobody, least of all his clubmates, doubted that Simpson deserved his chance.

He told reporters that it was his 'happiest day in twenty-two years of football'.

'It is the ambition of every red-blooded Scotsman who kicks a ball around for a living to play for his country at Wembley,' he later added. 'Even the fitba-daft Scot, who never had the ability to kick the ball with any great control or accuracy – and few will admit to this – feels his life is incomplete unless he has made a pilgrimage to the Wembley ground to see Scotland beat the Auld Enemy.'

For the first time since Newcastle United's FA Cup victory over Manchester City in 1955, and just three years after he had assumed his career was ending in capless ignominy amongst the Hibernian reserves, Ronnie Simpson was returning to arguably the most famous football ground of them all.

He was going there with his country and, at the age of thirty-six, as the oldest man ever to play for them.

Methuselah, be damned.

But first, Dukla.

* * *

BACK IN GOVAN, on the south-side of Glasgow, the pints were flowing in Simpson's Bar, the pub owned by Ronnie's former footballer father Jimmy.

In fourteen hugely successful seasons with Rangers, Jimmy was an integral part of the side that dominated Scottish football throughout the 1930s. When he left Ibrox in 1941, he did so with six league and four Scottish Cup winners' medals.

He also had fourteen Scottish caps, three of them coming against England. Not once did he suffer the agony of defeat to the Scots' most bitter rivals. Indeed, he had captained his country for the 1936 visit to Wembley, where a young Tommy Walker scored a late penalty to salvage a 1–1 draw.

'My father talked often about the wonderful atmosphere in and around London during such a game,' said Simpson Jnr. 'The tartan tammies, flags, banners, scarves, bagpipes, singing and tippling. An occasion one doesn't readily forget! He used to say: "I don't think England had any supporters at all."'

Jimmy had always dreamed that his son would follow him into football, which he did, and represent Scotland, which, to that point, he had not.

Before the week was out, that would change. The front pages of the evening newspapers carried the good news from the streets to the bar. Happy hour indeed.

'I am always Ronnie's most severe critic,' he told reporters. 'However, this season he's played as well as he has ever done and I'm not saying that from any personal outlook. I think he fully deserves his cap.

'There is no prouder dad in Scotland today. This is wonderful news.'

SIXTEEN

A BOY AND THE DOC

IT WAS THE MORNING AFTER THE NIGHT BEFORE and Jim McCalliog was hurting. The slender twenty-year-old, barely the width of a touchline but with a canny knack for scoring goals, had spent the previous day in London where he and his Sheffield Wednesday teammates played Chelsea in the quarter-finals of the FA Cup.

The Yorkshiremen had reached the final of the competition the previous season, McCalliog scoring in a 3–2 defeat to Everton, and so they were determined to go one better this time around. Chelsea had other ideas.

Losing to a last-minute goal had been bad enough but compounding matters was the fact that McCalliog had swapped Stamford Bridge for Wednesday just eighteen months earlier. It was a sore one alright and so when the phone rang as he sat down for breakfast with his family that Sunday morning, he was in no mood to talk to anybody. His mother, Mary, answered it instead.

'Jim,' she called out. 'It's for you. It's Tommy Docherty.'

Docherty? thought McCalliog. *As in Chelsea manager Tommy Docherty? My former gaffer Tommy Docherty? What could he possibly want?*

He took he receiver and pressed it to his ear.

'Hello?'

'Hello, son.'

There was no mistaking that voice. It was him alright.

'Hi boss,' replied McCalliog. It might have been a year and a half since he'd played for him but, well, old habits and all that.

'I just wanted to be the first to say congratulations.'

'Congratulations?' He was confused before but now McCalliog was downright non-plussed.

'Aye, congratulations,' repeated Docherty. 'You're in the Scotland team for the game next week.'

In the split-second that followed, McCalliog's head started spinning. He knew he'd been playing well and that selectors had been looking at him. The Sunday papers he'd managed to glance at that morning seemed to rate his chances quite highly, too. One reporter had managed to grab a word with one of the SFA men who'd been watching the game on Saturday, and he had apparently praised McCalliog's bravery. The Chelsea defenders – the notorious Ron 'Chopper' Harris amongst them – had kicked lumps out of the young forward for the whole ninety minutes but he'd held his own and done well.

This, though, was different. Papers were supposed to talk but Tommy Docherty calling him to say he was in before he'd heard anything official from the SFA themselves? He started to wonder if it was a wind-up. Perhaps his pals were pranking him. Nah, surely not. Plenty of them had a wicked sense of humour but that would be going too far. Besides, if any of them could do that good an impression of The Doc, he figured he'd have heard it before now.

No, this had to be legit. The real deal.

'Eddie McCreadie's in as well,' added the familiar voice on the other end of the line. 'You'll be getting official word soon enough.'

'No problem, boss,' said McCalliog. He thanked him for the call and hung up. The whole exchange was bizarre and left him a little bit stunned and, yes, a little bit sceptical. His parents appeared in the doorway.

'What was all that about?' asked his dad.

'That was Tommy Docherty,' he replied. 'He says I'm in the Scotland team for the game next week.' Saying the words aloud only made the whole thing more surreal.

'Well, just you stay calm,' said his mum. 'Nothing's official yet. Best thing to do is go out today, try to take your mind off it and don't talk to anybody. Let's just wait and see what happens.'

Mothers always know best and so McCalliog took his girlfriend to the cinema that afternoon. He can't remember what they saw. His eyes were on the screen but his head was elsewhere. Wembley, truth be told.

The following morning, he showed up for training as usual. Never mind England and a possible Scotland debut; Wednesday had a midweek match with Manchester United to take care of. He was changing into his training gear when one of the coaches approached him.

'Jim,' he said. 'The boss wants a word.'

The dressing room immediately cracked up. *Oh yeah? What did you get up to at the weekend, McCalliog? Somebody's in bother! The usual stuff.*

He laughed it off and made his way to the manager's office. As he walked in, he saw Alan Brown stand up from behind his desk and extend his hand.

'Congratulations,' he told his young forward. 'You're in the Scotland team to play England at Wembley on Saturday.'

Recalling that moment fifty-five years later, McCalliog chokes back tears. 'I'll never forget what he told me. He said, "Just do what you do here and you'll be okay. Don't be flashy. Just be yourself. Enjoy it. And good luck.'"

Born in September 1946 to Irish immigrant parents, McCalliog grew up in Glasgow's infamous Gorbals neighbourhood, on Caledonia Road, just around the corner from Celtic and Manchester United legend Paddy Crerand. Originally intended to be a southern extension of the city centre when tenement buildings sprouted throughout the community during the 1840s, it didn't take long for the Gorbals to become run-down, over-crowded and filthy. During the 1930s, the number of people living there had shot up to 90,000, giving it a population density of 40,000 square-kilometres. To put that into perspective, the city of Glasgow today has a population density of around 3,400 square-kilometres – and it is Scotland's most densely populated city. In the period immediately following the Second World War, residents of the Gorbals sometimes lived ten to a room with one toilet per thirty people.

To ease the congestion indoors, children were encouraged to spend most of the day playing outside. Amongst them were McCalliog and his brothers, Freddie and Danny. In time, they'd be joined by a sister, Ann, and another brother, Eddie. Their mother, Mary, kept house whilst their father, James, worked long hours as a mechanic.

'We didn't have any money,' said Jim, 'but we didn't go without, either. We always had food on the table. My dad would come home on a Friday, and I remember he would always put his wages on the table. That wasn't as common as you'd think at that time. Other guys would get their wages, go straight to the pub and drink half of them away. My dad never did that. Plus, we took in a couple of lodgers – Irish guys who came over to work on the roads – and so that helped, too. But honestly, I didn't pay too much attention. As long as I could get a kick-about, I was happy.'

McCalliog was a typical Gorbals kid: football daft. Any time he didn't have a ball at his feet, he was thinking about the game, watching the game, obsessing over the game.

'I remember a reporter asking me some years later, when I first got picked for Scotland, if I thought that growing up where I did had held me back. I didn't really understand the question. From where we lived, it was only a twenty-minute walk to get to Shawfield to see my team, Clyde; it was half an hour to Celtic Park; about forty minutes to Ibrox; Firhill, depending on buses, was around the same. And of course, Third Lanark were still going at that time and their ground, Cathkin Park, was right next to my school, Holyrood Secondary. I could even go and see international matches because, at that time, they were played mostly on a Wednesday afternoon and, like Cathkin, Hampden was just around the corner from the school. As soon as the bell went at the end of the day, we'd be right up there if there was a game on in time to catch the whole of the second half.

'So, it was never a disadvantage to grow up in the Gorbals. If anything, it was an advantage. I could see Tommy Ring, Archie Robertson and Harry Haddock at Clyde; Paddy Crerand and Willie Fernie at Celtic; Ian McMillan, wee Willie Henderson and Davie Wilson at Rangers. It was incredible, really.'

Despite all the domestic talent available to watch, it was in 1960, when the European Cup final was staged at Hampden, that McCalliog first started to dream about becoming a footballer. Real Madrid and Eintracht Frankfurt played out a ten-goal thriller in front of a record crowd of 127,000 just under two miles from his front door. Alfredo di Stefano scored a hat-trick, only to be outdone by his Hungarian teammate Ferenc Puskás who grabbed four as the Spanish giants won 7–3 to continue their record of being the only side to win the continent's premier club competition. It was, indeed, their fifth successive victory. The match has passed into legend as one of the greatest games of football ever played and it remains the highest-scoring final in the history of the competition. Like so many, McCalliog was transfixed by what he saw that night.

'I don't know where she got it, but my mum managed to get a telly for us to watch it on,' he recalled. 'It was black-and-white, and the screen couldn't have been much more than twelve or fifteen inches wide, but I sat and watched the whole thing. I didn't move for ninety minutes. Honest, the building could have fallen down around me and I wouldn't have noticed. My eyes were glued to the screen watching these incredible players and that huge crowd. All I could think was, "Oh my God. Imagine what it would be like to play in a game like that." It fired me up.'

It helped that Frankfurt had secured their place in the final by knocking out Rangers in the semis. It didn't matter that they'd battered the Glasgow giants 12–4 on aggregate. To McCalliog, the fact that a team from his city had come so close to European glory made what had previously seemed like an impossible dream suddenly possible.

'Up until then, I'd planned on becoming a boxer,' he said. 'That's what my dad wanted for me, too, but football gradually took over.'

A string of impressive performances for Holyrood led to a Glasgow schoolboys call-up. Suddenly, his weekends comprised of football and little else. The goals started to flow, too. 'I was two-footed, which helped,' he said. 'I really worked hard on my finishing.'

His performances led to a Scotland schoolboys cap, and it was around this time that scouts started to take notice. Small and slight, McCalliog still had plenty of growing to do but the raw materials were there.

He was fifteen years old when Leeds United came calling. After impressing during a three-day trial, he signed for Don Revie's side as an amateur.

'Years later, my mum said to me, "You know, Jim, there's something I never told you." I said, "What's that?" She said, "I never told you how many clubs were in for you back then." Turns out there had been twenty-two of them.'

What Leeds United and their iconic manager Revie had that those other clubs didn't was a man with a keen eye on the Glasgow and Scotland schoolboys' set-up. John Barr had spotted Billy Bremner, Eddie Gray, Jimmy Lumsden and Tommy Henderson, so when he gave glowing reports about McCalliog and Peter Lorimer, Revie took notice.

'They moved my whole family down there,' added McCalliog. 'They got us a house, got my dad a job, and gave me a £9,000 signing-on fee and £14 a week. It was life-changing, it really was.'

At that time, there was an obscure rule preventing players who weren't from England from signing as apprentices with English teams, so Revie – ever the wily tactician – devised a clever ploy to get around it. 'I remember he told Lorimer and I to get in his car one day after training,' said McCalliog. 'He never really said what we were doing or where we were going, and we never asked. Finally, we arrived at this printer shop where he introduced us to the guy that owned it. We shook his hand, exchanged a few pleasantries and left. As we made our way back to the car, Revie was walking in front of us. Lorimer nudged me and said, "What the hell was all that about?" I said, "Well, looks to me like that's our job." He said, "What?" I said, "How the bloody hell do you think we're going to live in England without any wages?" That's how it went. As far as the Football Association was concerned, we were amateur footballers who worked for a local printing firm. It was sneaky but clever.'

For a while after that, things were great. With each day that passed, McCalliog got a step closer to fulfilling his dream of becoming a professional footballer. The carrot on the stick was a promise Revie made him when he joined Leeds that, if he continued to develop, he would sign him on professional terms when he turned seventeen. The terms were juicy, too. There was nothing concrete. Just a gentleman's agreement.

A few months shy of his seventeenth birthday, McCalliog got a lift home with the manager. It was a regular arrangement given that they lived close to one another. This particular day, McCalliog decided to chance his arm.

'So boss,' he ventured. 'How am I doing?'

'You're doing great, son,' replied Revie. 'We knew that you would struggle for a bit at first because you're only slight but you're getting stronger all the time and we all know how much ability you've got, so we're all delighted with how things are going.'

McCalliog knew an open goal when he saw one.

'Does that mean you're going to sign me as a professional when I turn seventeen?'

'Oh yeah. No doubt about that.'

'And are you still going to give me what you promised?'

There was an awkward silence.

'What was that again, son?'

McCalliog reminded him of the agreement and Revie let out a snort.

'Son,' he said. 'Bobby Collins doesn't even get that.' Collins was the Leeds United captain and a Scotland international.

McCalliog barely spoke a word for the rest of the journey and when Revie dropped him off and said something about seeing him at training the next day, he continued to blank him.

'I was fuming,' he said. 'I'd been brought up in a family where your word is your bond. I figured that if Revie would go back on a promise about this, it wouldn't be the only time he'd do it. He would continue to do it again and again and again. Don't get me wrong, it wasn't about the money. It was the principle of it. He'd broken my trust and, for me, when somebody does that, there's no way back.'

He trudged into the house, grabbed a ball and went straight out into the garden. Before long, his mum appeared.

'Is everything alright?' she asked, even though she knew the answer.

'No,' replied McCalliog. 'Let's talk when dad comes home.'

Later that night, the three of them sat down and McCalliog filled his parents in on the conversation with Revie. His mum had been present when the original offer had been made, so she knew that what her eldest was saying was true.

'Okay then,' said his dad. 'What do you want to do about it?'

'I'm getting the train back to Glasgow first thing in the morning,' said McCalliog.

Sure enough, with his parents' blessing and with arrangements having been made for him to stay with his aunt and uncle, McCalliog got up the next day, hopped on a bus into Leeds city centre and boarded a train. His plan was to meet with two reporters he knew well: Jim Rodger of the *Scottish Daily Express* and the *Daily Record*'s Ken Gallacher. He figured that if he told them his version of events and they covered it then that might spark some interest amongst clubs in Scotland.

The plan worked. Two days after their stories ran, Celtic and Chelsea got in touch. The latter were particularly keen. Their manager, Tommy Docherty, had tried to sign McCalliog shortly before he joined Leeds. In the meantime, perhaps recognising his mistake, Revie dashed to Glasgow with multi-millionaire Leeds chairman Harry Reynolds in a last-ditch attempt to persuade him to stay.

'He offered me what he'd originally promised plus a little extra for the inconvenience, but it didn't matter. He'd tried it on, and I couldn't just forget that.'

Chelsea made their move and flew McCalliog and his mother to London for talks in September 1963. They didn't take long.

'I liked Docherty straight away,' he recalled. 'He was quite different to Revie in that he wasn't as wrapped-up in football. He was tough and ran the club with a real ruthless streak, but he was also a very funny man with a helluva personality.'

He was shrewd, too, assembling a squad capable of contending on all fronts for next to nothing. When it came to talented footballers, Docherty could spot a bargain at a thousand paces.

'It reminds me a little bit of Manchester United and the "Class of 92" that Alex Ferguson had,' said McCalliog. 'Look at the team we had that year. Peter Bonetti cost nothing. Ken Shellito, nothing. Eddie McCreadie, £8,000. John Hollins, nothing. Marvin Hinton, £30,000. Ron Harris, nothing. Bert Murray, nothing. George Graham, £5,000. Barry Bridges, nothing. Terry Venables, nothing. Bobby Tambling, nothing. Myself, nothing. That's all the money The Doc spent. We were all young guys, too. There were only three players in our squad in 1963 who were over twenty-three. So, we had an incredible team spirit, we really did.'

It showed. In the 1964/65 season, Chelsea could – and perhaps should – have won the domestic treble. They finished third in the league, reached the semis of the FA Cup and won the League Cup. They might well have won the league had it not been for an incident that has since entered club folklore for all the wrong reasons.

Challenging Manchester United and, by grim irony, Leeds for the title, Chelsea's final three games were away to Liverpool, Burnley and Blackpool. With each of the fixtures taking place in the north-west of England, Docherty decided to set up camp in Blackpool rather than commute back and forward three times in seven days. What seemed like a perfectly sensible plan backfired in the most spectacular way. After losing 2–0 to Liverpool on the Monday, Chelsea had five days to kill until facing Burnley on the Saturday. Docherty allowed his players to let their hair down on the Monday night and Tuesday night but set a strict curfew of 11 p.m. for the Wednesday night.

'I was rooming with John Boyle and, if I remember correctly, we were both in bed by half-ten,' recalled McCalliog. 'We got up the next morning and went downstairs for breakfast. It was pretty much empty apart from a bunch of photographers all clicking away and TV cameras pointing at us. John and I looked at each other thinking, "Jesus Christ, what's happened?"'

'We went into the breakfast room. Again, nobody to be seen. We spotted Harry Meadows, our trainer, walking towards us. I said, "Harry, where are all the boys? Is nobody up yet?" He shot me a look, said "stop taking the fucking piss" and walked right past me.'

As it turned out, eight of the players who had been out on the town that Wednesday night – Venables, McCreadie, Hinton, Murray, Graham, Hollins and Bridges, along with squad player Joe Fascione – made it back in time for the curfew . . . then promptly left through a fire escape and went back into Blackpool. They finally returned deep into the early hours of the morning. A night porter reported the incident to a furious Docherty who sent all eight back to London on the next train.

'All hell broke loose,' sighed McCalliog. 'It made national headlines. Suddenly, it wasn't the sports reporters who were covering us but the main news guys. It broke the spirit in the dressing room.'

Worse, it ended any hopes Chelsea harboured of winning a second league title. Missing several of their key men, they were thrashed 6–2 by Burnley before going down 3–2 to Blackpool. A season that had promised so much ended on an abject, miserable note. Worse, the issues spilled over into the next campaign. Docherty tightened his grip on the squad, which only fostered resentment, and McCalliog found himself piggy-in-the-middle of an enduring enmity between the boss and some of his key players.

'One week, I found myself playing alongside Graham in place of Venables. The next, I was playing alongside Venables in place of Graham. It was a pretty horrible position to be in.'

Finally, he requested a meeting with The Doc.

'I remember going into his office and him asking me what the trouble was,' he recalled. 'I said, "You're not going to like what I have to say, boss." He said, "All right, go ahead." I said, "I want a transfer." Well, he was furious. He said, "Get the fuck out of here. You're not leaving as long as I'm in charge. Get out!"'

McCalliog persisted. A second transfer request was again dismissed before finally, at the third time of asking, he got his wish.

'It was in October '65 that I got summoned to the boss's office,' he said. 'He told me, "There's a club in for you and we've accepted their offer so you're to go to this hotel – I can't remember what it was called – and have talks with them." I said, "Can't you tell me who it is?" He said, "No. You'll find out when you get there." So, I did as I was told and, when I arrived in the hotel reception, I spotted this figure walking towards me. I knew who it was straight away. It was Alan Brown, the manager of Sheffield Wednesday.'

The talks went well, Brown even offering to go back to McCalliog's family home to meet his parents and reassure them that their eldest would be well looked after at the Hillsborough club. An offer was made and McCalliog asked to sleep on it, promising to give Brown a decision the following day.

The next morning, he reported for training at Chelsea as normal. Docherty was keen to hear how the talks had gone. 'Aye boss, they went well,' said McCalliog. 'By the way, what's the fee they're paying for me?'

'The fee?' said Docherty. 'It's £37,500.'

It was a new British transfer record for a teenager. McCalliog was taken aback, and he was far from the only one. Reporters lined up to question Brown's judgement. That was an extraordinary amount of money to pay for a nineteen-year-old who, whilst talented and full of potential, had played only a handful of league games. Many speculated that the pressure of living up to such a huge fee would be too heavy a burden for the young Scot to bear.

How wrong they were.

Far from being crushed by the weight of expectation, McCalliog thrived. In a superb first season, he scored the goal that sent the 'Owls' into their first FA Cup final in more than thirty years. He then opened the scoring against Everton in the Wembley showpiece as Wednesday raced into a 2–0 lead, only for Harry Catterick's Merseysiders to hit back and win 3–2. The memory of being on the wrong side of one of the greatest comebacks in FA Cup history makes McCalliog wince to this day.

'I was shattered by that result,' he admitted. 'I mean, the idea that any team could put two goals, never mind three, past our keeper Ron Springett was just so unlikely. Ron was a fantastic goalie. He was England's undisputed number one until Gordon Banks came along. So, aye, three goals. I still can't believe they did that.'

More Wembley drama unfolded in the weeks that followed as England brushed aside all comers to win the World Cup. Uruguay, Mexico, France, Argentina, Portugal and finally West Germany – none could derail Alf Ramsey's juggernaut. McCalliog was on holiday in Marbella at the time of the final and so missed much of the bedlam that ensued and by the time Sheffield Wednesday returned from a pre-season training camp in Bulgaria, it was time for a new season to begin.

McCalliog scored his first goal of the campaign in a 2–2 draw with city rivals Sheffield United in September and added another in a 1–1 home draw with Fulham the following month. Even more impressive, however, were the performances he was putting in and, by the time he scored in a 6–1 thrashing of former club Chelsea on Hogmanay, talk of him receiving an international call-up was beginning to intensify.

He had been the subject of such scrutiny a couple of years earlier when, during his time at Chelsea, the Irish Football Association came calling.

'I remember The Doc sitting me down in his office and saying, "I've just had an interesting phone call,"' he remembered. 'He said, "I've had the Irish FA. They are interested in you and want you to go and play for Ireland. What do you think?" Well, I just looked at him. I didn't know what to say. Finally, he said, "Right, what we'll do is this. Don't decide just now. Instead, take the night to think it over and come in tomorrow and let me know what your decision is."'

'I remember thinking what an honour it was to have to decide between two countries. One, the country I was born in; the other, the country my parents were born in. It was a helluva thing.'

Despite having been capped at Scotland schoolboys and youths level, McCalliog hadn't yet been called up for either the Under-23s or the full side by that point and so, such were the rules of international eligibility at that time, he was entitled to play for the Republic of Ireland if he so wanted. And they certainly wanted him.

'My big concern was being seen to slight the Irish people by turning down the offer,' he added. 'They were my dad's people, my mum's people, and I didn't want to offend them. So, I turned to my dad for advice.'

It couldn't have been better.

'He told me, "The only thing that matters here is you. It's your career. Just you do what you think is best and what your manager thinks is best." Hearing that was a huge relief because, if I'm honest, in my heart of hearts, I considered myself Scottish. It was where I was born and brought up. All I wanted to do was play for Scotland and, if I had a chance of doing that, even if it meant waiting a little longer, then that's what I was willing to do.'

Naturally, The Doc was pleased.

'He told me, "I knew you'd come to that conclusion,"' laughed McCalliog. 'He said, "You're a good Gorbals boy, right enough." So, that was that. It was then just a matter of working hard, staying patient and hoping that my time would come.'

Little did he know that, when it did, it would be The Doc who would break the good news.

SEVENTEEN

ORIGINAL WIZARDS

IF THE SCOTLAND CLASS OF 1967 WERE SO INCLINED as to look to the past for inspiration, there were five Scottish victories at Wembley they could draw from. Of those, the British Home Championship match in 1963 was the most recent. The most impressive? A competitive field, for sure, but the 1928 win probably edged it.

That day, 31 March, was arguably the greatest in the history of Scottish football, if not Scottish sport.

Twenty-four hours earlier and two hundred miles north-west, a little-known amateur jockey Bill Dutton pulled off perhaps the greatest upset in the eighty-seven-year history of the Grand National when he rode 100/1 shot Tipperary Tim to glory at Aintree.

'Billy boy,' a voice from the crowd shouted to him as the riders took their starting positions, 'you'll only win if all the others fall.'

They did, and he did.

A ten-year-old boy was amongst the few to back Tipperary Tim. It was Peter O'Sullevan's first-ever wager and, when it came in, a lifelong love for horses, that would see him ultimately become the 'Voice of Racing', was born.

Winston Churchill, the then Chancellor of the Exchequer, sent a congratulatory telegram to the horse's trainer, Joseph Dodd. Cigarette boxes soon started carrying Tipperary Tim's photograph. Newspaper columnists waxed lyrical about the most remarkable edition of the world's most famous steeplechase.

En route to Wembley, Scotland captain Jimmy McMullan and his side were fixated on causing an upset of their own, as were the eleven trainloads of fans who followed them south from Glasgow.

The circumstances of the match were quite unusual. Both Scotland and England badly needed a positive result. The Scots had lost 1–0 to Ireland at Hampden Park in the opening match of the 1928 British Home Championship, followed by a 2–2 draw away to Wales. England, meantime, had lost each of their first two matches. Compounding matters for the hosts was an abject recent record against Scotland. Only once in the 1920s had they beaten their old rivals. That, though, had come courtesy of a 2–1 triumph in their most recent clash in Glasgow in 1927.

As the day of the match drew ever closer, the mood in Scotland was less than optimistic. A large crowd had gathered outside of the SFA offices to hear the official announcement of the team to face England – and few left satisfied. Regular starters Davie Meiklejohn, Jimmy McGrory, Bob McPhail and Willie McStay were all left out, with eight of the eleven jerseys taken by the so-called Anglo-Scots who plied their trade in the English Football League. One of those was Tom Bradshaw. The Bishopton-born Bury wing-half was handed his Scotland debut and, for good measure, the unenviable task of marking the free-scoring forward Dixie Dean. The Everton man was approaching the end of his sixty-goal league season, a record haul that stands to this day.

Also selected was Newcastle United centre-forward Hughie Gallacher. It was the Bellshill man's first start for two months after serving a suspension for pushing a referee into a bath.

The Scottish side averaged just seven caps between them, their inexperience exacerbated by a physical disadvantage. Of the forward line of Alex Jackson, James Dunn, Gallacher, Alex James and Alan Morton, Jackson was the tallest at just 5ft 7in. The *Daily Record*, one of Scotland's biggest-selling newspapers, was left to bemoan what it witheringly described as 'not a great side'.

By contrast, England had picked four players from the all-conquering Huddersfield Town: Roy Goodall, Thomas Wilson, Bob Kelly and Billy Smith. They were, in the estimation of most observers either side of the border, overwhelming favourites to win.

In the Regent Palace Hotel the night before the match, Scotland captain McMullan bid his teammates goodnight and told them: 'Put your head on the pillow and pray for rain.' A heavy pitch, he reasoned, would mitigate England's advantage and better suit Scotland's petite forwards.

His prayers were answered.

As dawn broke the next morning, it revealed dark clouds and an incessant downpour. Throngs of Scottish supporters emerged from their hotels into the deluge and made their way to Wembley, much to the chagrin of some local observers.

'It is rather startling to find such douce buddies as Kirk elders and bank tellers flaunting garish tartan tammies and flying Scottish favours in the Strand on a Saturday morning and possibly going gyte in the afternoon if Gallacher scores a goal at Wembley,' read an editorial in the *Weekly News*. 'In the minds of the public there seems to be some association between putting a tammy over one's head and straw in it.'

Undeterred by the disapproving glances and tut-tutting, the Tartan Army soldiered on, some lugging their own ladders. If they weren't going to make it through the Wembley turnstiles, they'd scale the walls of the ground instead.

Mingling with the visiting support were ten of the Scottish side that thrashed England 4–1 in the same fixture in 1900, their expenses having been covered by their old teammate Robert Smyth McColl. He had scored a hat-trick that day and later put his name to the popular Scottish newsagents, RS McColl.

They weren't the only 'celebrity' guests to take their place amongst the 80,000-capacity crowd inside Wembley that day. The King and Queen of Afghanistan were also there to bear witness.

England were dealt a significant blow in the build-up to kick-off when their captain, Leicester left-half Sid Bishop, was forced to withdraw from the starting line-up after falling ill overnight.

However, any suggestion that the loss of such an influential player might impact the hosts' preparations was dispelled in the opening minute of the match. Straight from kick-off, Billy Smith ghosted past Scottish full-back James Nelson and struck a shot that beat Jack Harkness in goal only for the post to come to the Scots' rescue.

Minutes later, the visitors were ahead. Rangers winger Morton collected the ball on the left and crossed for Jackson to head past Ted Hufton. It stayed that way until just before half-time when Alex James beat two men and slammed a left-footed shot beyond Hufton.

England nil, Scotland two.

The unthinkable, the impossible, the downright remarkable was happening.

Any hopes of an England comeback were quashed on sixty-five minutes. Another perfect delivery was converted by Jackson for his second and Scotland's third. James made it four after some good build-up play by the returning, ref-shoving Gallacher, before Jackson completed his hat-trick, yet another Morton cross being forced home by the Huddersfield Town hitman. Five goals to the good with five minutes left to play. The Scottish supporters were in dreamland.

Not even a late consolation by Jackson's clubmate Kelly – who, at thirty-four years and 136 days, became his country's oldest goalscorer – could take the shine off the celebrations. Against all odds and predictions, Scotland had not only defeated England but inflicted their heaviest defeat since the 6–1 hammering at the hands of the Scots at the Kennington Oval in 1881.

The 'Wembley Wizards' were born. A new chapter of Scottish sporting folklore had been written.

In his match report for the *Athletic News*, former player Ivan Sharpe observed: 'England were not merely beaten. They were bewildered, run to a standstill, made to appear utterly inferior by a team whose play was as cultured and beautiful as I ever expect to see.'

The *Glasgow Herald* noted that 'want of height was looked upon as a handicap to the Scots' attack, but the Scottish forwards had the ability and skill of such high degree as to make their physical shortcomings of little consequence'.

Scottish captain McMullan praised his forwards for being 'inherently clever' but added that the English tactics were wrong.

'The Saxon wing-halves paid more attention to the wingers than the inside forwards, therefore the latter were given a lot of space,' he observed. 'It is a common thing in England to let wing halves, and not fullbacks, mark the wingers. It doesn't pay and I don't know why they pursue it.'

Preston North End forward James was every bit as succinct. 'We could have had ten,' he said, a cheeky grin stretched wide across his face.

Somewhat surprisingly, that was about as good as it got for the Wizards. The eleven players who humbled their greatest rivals on their own turf never played together again. For 'Tiny' Tom

Bradshaw, imperious in restricting the talisman Dixie Dean to the role of mere bystander, the match proved to be his one and only appearance for Scotland.

That win also had the unfortunate consequence of elevating the expectations of Scottish supporters beyond the realms of realism. The so-called 'Cult of Wembley' spread across the nation with 'Wembley Clubs' formed to help working men afford the biennial trip to London. Approximately 45,000 travelled south in both 1930 and 1932 only to suffer the agony of 5–2 and 3–0 defeats, respectively.

These may be the first recorded instances of that agonisingly exquisite Scottish football and cultural phenomenon: death by hope.

Indeed, it wasn't until 1938 that Scotland would again savour victory at Wembley, an early strike from Heart of Midlothian forward Tommy Walker settling matters. By then, most of the Wizards had long since hung up their boots.

Hat-trick hero Jackson traded Huddersfield for Chelsea in 1930, in part because of his desire to forge a living away from football. Soon after he made the switch, he snapped up a pub in Covent Garden, was involved in another hotel in Leicester Square and wrote a weekly newspaper column.

The bright lights, though, also proved to be his downfall. He was suspended, transfer-listed and told he would never play for Chelsea again after it emerged he had treated the entire squad to a round of drinks the night before a crucial match with Manchester City. He subsequently made a handful of appearances for non-league outfits Ashton National and Margate before joining French outfit Nice.

After his Wembley heroics, he scored only two more goals for Scotland, bagging a brace in a 7–3 win over Ireland at Windsor Park in February 1929. An SFA ban on English-based players representing Scotland ended his international career somewhat prematurely. He died in a traffic accident whilst serving with the army in Egypt in 1946.

James, meantime, also served in the Second World War before succumbing to cancer in 1953. Four years later, his old international colleague and fellow Wizard Hughie Gallacher – by then bankrupt and an alcoholic – took his own life. He was only fifty-four.

As it turned out, Bradshaw was the last surviving member of the side. He passed away in February 1986 at the age of eighty-two, just four months after goalkeeper Harkness.

You see, for all their magical moments, their tantalising trickery and their bewitching brilliance, wizards are no less vulnerable to the unpredictable whims of mortality than the rest of us.

In time, the class of 1967 would become further object examples of that fact.

Before then, there was a match to be won.

EIGHTEEN

'WE CAN DO IT!'

THE WEEKEND BEFORE WEMBLEY, the *Daily Record*'s Ken Gallacher secured an exclusive interview with two fiercely patriotic, English-based Scottish managers – Liverpool boss Bill Shankly and Tommy Docherty of Chelsea – to get their thoughts on the game and Scotland's prospects.

Born in Ayrshire, Shankly had represented Scotland twelve times during a career spent, primarily, with Preston North End. He was in his ninth year in charge of Liverpool and had transformed them from Second Division fodder into two-time – and reigning – champions of England, adding an FA Cup for good measure. A shrewd and meticulous manager, he revolutionised the fortunes of the Anfield side, laying the foundations for the powerhouse they have since become.

Docherty, meanwhile, joined Preston from Celtic just months after Shankly departed Deepdale. He spent nine years there before signing for Arsenal. After three years at Highbury, The Doc moved across London to become player-coach of Chelsea. Despite his best efforts, he was unable to prevent the Blues from being relegated but led them straight back up to the First Division the following year. In 1964/65, he masterminded League Cup glory over Leicester City and, the following season, led Chelsea to the semis of the FA Cup and Inter-Cities Fairs Cup.

He was preparing for an FA quarter-final with Jim McCalliog's Sheffield Wednesday when he and Shankly sat down for an extensive, two-part interview with Gallacher . . .

Gallacher: *Obviously, this is going to be one of the toughest internationals Scotland has ever played at Wembley. What do you think of our chances?*

Docherty: We can win this game all right. But we must realise that this is a very, very strong England side we are up against.

Shankly: When you assess the English team, they must be assessed as a club side because that's what they are. One of the greatest international teams for many, many years.

Docherty: Exactly right, Bill. They haven't got individual stars as good as other English teams before them. But they do have this team spirit that until now only a really great club side has developed. This is what will make them difficult to upset. Yet I don't for one minute consider them unbeatable.

Shankly: Nor do I. There is no team in the world that you can say cannot be beaten. There never has been and there never will be. But remember, this is a machine that Scotland will be facing. Ramsey has built an efficient machine and it's a machine that has grown even better since it won the World Cup. I didn't expect to see any changes in the English team. There is one, Jimmy Greaves for my player, Roger Hunt. But Ramsey has stuck to the men who did the job for him in the World Cup. Some of them haven't been having a great season. But that victory has made them giants. That one victory has made all of them grow until they're like mountains whenever they are asked to play for England.

Docherty: Some of the players, in fact, have had right bad seasons. But what Bill says is true. Every man connected with the World Cup squad has become a more confident player. It's been amazing to see some of them. These English players are world champions and they believe now that they are the best players in the world. The only good thing for us is that they're not all playing that way.

Gallacher: *How do you think we should play against them at Wembley next week?*

Shankly: There's only one way to play against them and that's to play them at their own game. Play it tight, as tight as we can, and be patient. Make them come out and make a game of it. Because make no mistake, it's a defensive machine that Ramsey has. They're not an adventurous team. Other teams were criticised for being defensive during the World Cup but England are as defensive as any.

Docherty: There were times when they were more defensive. We'll probably be blamed if this isn't a good game and if we decide to play it a bit tight, but we shouldn't worry about it. This game counts for the European Nations Cup, doesn't it? Well, then it's got to be looked upon as a first leg European game to a certain extent. We've got them coming to Hampden in the decider, or what should be the decider. And it's important to us to get into the last stages of this Nations Cup. We need that as a build-up to the next World Cup.

Shankly: This could be the worst international for a long time as far as the fans are concerned but if Scotland get a result, that's what counts. If we draw with them or if we snatch a win then the team have been a success. Only the result counts. The way the game is going, it's getting more and more defensive. We're getting like the Italians. No one wants to lose. And if that idea is good enough to win the World Cup, then it's good enough for Scotland to take to Wembley.

Docherty: I'm like Bill. Results count. Nothing else. Look at West Ham. Ron Greenwood has been trying out attacking football. He's scored a helluva lot of goals but he's lost a helluva lot too and he's in the middle of the table. I asked him the other week if the fans would stick with the new idea if it took them into the Second Division. They wouldn't, you know, no matter how attractive it was.

Shankly: Anyway, to get back to the original question, I think Bobby's Brown's team has to be picked to win this game. This isn't the time to build because a result here is vital. The best players have got to be fielded even though some of them might not be around in 1970. And we've got to be defensive and make England go a bit. It's the only way.

Docherty: Aye, they haven't got very many weaknesses. But I feel that if we played on this right back a little bit then they could be in trouble. If anyone in the team is weak then it's Cohen. And this boy Martin Peters has not been doing a lot for West Ham. These things can help.

Gallacher: Was that Inter-League result a disaster for us?

Docherty: No, not a bit of it. It was a good thing because it seems to have killed the idea of all-tartan teams once and for all. It doesn't matter where a man is playing. If he's the man for the job, then he has to go in. If he's a right-half with Tranmere Rovers but he's the best right-half, then he must be picked.

Shankly: I couldn't agree more. There are great players playing down here and they should not be ignored because they aren't playing up in Scotland. We need all our good players for this game so let's pick them and give them the chance of beating the World Cup holders.

Gallacher: I reckon that we do need players such as Billy Bremner and Denis Law, for instance. What do you think?

Shankly: If I had them, they would never be out of my team. That Bremner, there should be a golden crown above his head. He's a driving little player who never knows defeat. And Denis, too. There's some player for you! He is always threatening your defence, always forcing your men into making mistakes and then being able to punish these mistakes. That's how he gets half his goals for Manchester United.

Docherty: Neither of the two players you mentioned wants to think about defeat and that's always an attitude of mind you want among your players. Denis is the type of player who can conjure goals out of nothing. There seems no danger, then he strikes and it's a goal. He would be ideal in this match. And wee Billy goes all the time. He's been having this tremendous experience against Continental players, too, which I feel is important for every player today. It helps anyone.

Shankly: Och, I don't know so much about this playing against Continentals. You're either a good player or you're not a good player and playing against foreign teams won't change you very much because they have been capped. They're not picked for the clever things. They're picked to do a job.

Docherty: I think Ramsey has the English players doing this. Doing a job, not trying to impress. They are playing for each other and I think it's a great thing. Most of the Scottish teams I played in, there were too many people playing for themselves. That won't pay off today.

Gallacher: What's going to be the big danger for us?

Docherty: That's easy: Geoff Hurst. This boy gets better all the time. He's the most dangerous forward in Britain, maybe in Europe, and he's so good at scoring goals. If you want to stop him, then you've got to have someone shadow him all the time. I put Ron Harris on to him when we played West Ham. It's the one sure way of holding him.

Shankly: Aye, but still the main problem is that this is a tremendous club team. A super club side if you like. That's where their success has come from. But we still have players with the individual flair and the greatness that can upset them. Don't forget that.

Gallacher: You've both emphasised how hard it will be to beat England. If we lose, will that be a personal disaster for Bobby Brown?

Shankly: Not for a minute. If we lose, then we can learn. It's in defeat that you learn most about this game. We beat Notts Forest and we thrashed Leeds early in the season. Since then, they've hardly been beaten because they learned from losing to us. I always maintain that it's when defeat comes that you see mistakes and you are ready to remedy them. At Liverpool, we haven't been learning as much over the past few years because we have been winning most of the time. It hasn't been good for us.

Docherty: Losing doesn't mean it's a tragedy. As long as we learn from it, then it's okay. I am hoping that Bobby Brown will establish a pattern for the team and that he'll be ready to stick to that pattern to give them a real test. If he does this then we will be able to see a real build-up to 1970 and Mexico.

Gallacher: *An English sportswriter suggested to me recently that Scotland should forget all about the World Cup, that we had no chance of ever winning it. What do you feel about that?*

Shankly: It's nonsense. Scotland is still one of the greatest producers of players in the world and it always will be. It's a wonderful nursery for players, and every manager in England knows that. If we have the right policy, then we can win the World Cup.

Docherty: When any country has players with the imagination and brilliance of Jimmy Johnstone, or Denis Law, or Billy Bremner, then they can win anything. If we had been in that North East section last year, we might have won it. Let's not forget that. And this is our chance to show people that. That's another reason why I'm sure our players will be giving everything they've got next week.

Shankly: When I was playing, I know I felt confident going on against England. And now that they're world champions, I'd feel it even more. I'd be out there to win. That's the way the Scots have got to feel. They've got to hold them and then strike.

Docherty: As Bill said, play them at their own game, then use our brilliant individuals to beat them. We can do it.

NINETEEN

AND SO IT BEGINS

THEY SAY THAT NOTHING worth having ever comes easy. As he awoke on the Tuesday before the match, Bobby Brown understood that sentiment for perhaps the first time.

He received word that Denis Law, his totemic forward, the linchpin of the side he had picked to face England, was facing up to the very real possibility of having to withdraw from the weekend's game.

The twenty-seven-year-old had been in the Manchester United team that had played out a 2–2 with Jim McCalliog's Sheffield Wednesday the night before. Law, indeed, had gone out of his way to introduce himself to his young soon-to-be international teammate ahead of the match at Hillsborough.

By full-time, however, the picture was decidedly less rosy. Law felt a twinge in a thigh muscle after overstretching to intercept a pass and reported at Old Trafford the following morning for further treatment.

United boss Matt Busby was initially pessimistic about his star man's prospects of leading the line at Wembley. 'It's quite a bad strain,' he said, 'and we can only hope that there will be sufficient improvement for Denis to join the Scotland team on Thursday.'

One of Busby's first actions was to call Scotland team boss Brown, who was understandably concerned by the development. 'It's a worrying situation,' he conceded. 'I thought everyone had come through the games all right when I didn't hear anything last night – then this!'

Compounding matters was the fact that several more of his side were expected to play for Celtic in their European Cup semi-final with Dukla Prague on the Wednesday night. Such was the fixture congestion caused by having sides competing on all fronts – both domestically and in Europe – the prospect of postponing games was simply not an option. All Brown could do was wait and hope for a clean bill of health.

'The big worry is that what happened to Law might happen with Celtic,' he admitted. 'Still, let's hope the Law injury clears up and that the Celtic players come through okay. Then I can start breathing again.

'They have every facility at Old Trafford to give Denis the kind of treatment he will need. If there is a chance of him being fully fit for the game, then we could leave him there for a day or two.'

Law himself was bullish on prospects of playing. 'I'll have to have a bit of a run at the ground to make certain everything's okay but I'm sure it's only a slight strain. I'm ninety-nine per cent certain that I'll play at Wembley.'

England, meantime, had their own issues to worry about. Jack Charlton, their towering centre-half, reported a sore throat and a high temperature whilst travelling to Leicester with his Leeds United teammates on Monday. On arrival at the ground, he was immediately dismissed to a nearby hotel where he was ordered to remain overnight. Club officials suspected he had come down with a very poorly timed bout of tonsilitis.

'A doctor will examine him again in the morning,' said Leeds boss Don Revie. 'Then we will notify Sir Alf Ramsey of his condition.'

Losing Charlton would be a blow for England, no doubt. But no Law? That had the potential to completely derail Scotland's prospects. The pride of a nation potentially hinged on the extent of the damage done to his thigh.

Brown endured an anxious twenty-four hours, fretting and drafting contingencies. The consensus was that nothing less than Plan A would suffice but it made sense to prepare a Plan B just in case.

Finally, as he prepared to travel to the Queen's Hotel in Largs to meet with his squad's Scottish-based contingent, Brown got the news he was hoping for from Busby.

Law was good to go.

'The leg is a great deal easier now and there are no worries about Denis being ready for Saturday,' Busby told reporters.

Brown added: 'Denis will be joining us at the training HQ tomorrow with the rest of the Anglo players. Walter McCrae [the team trainer] will be able to give him any treatment for the strain if it is needed, but I don't think it will be.'

The collective sighs of relief stretched from Wick to Wigtown. News that Jack Charlton had declared himself fit to play barely registered north of the border. It wasn't important. Law was fit and that was all that mattered.

Fears over his star man having been allayed, Brown's focus returned to the task at hand. After the home-based players converged upon Largs, he, McCrae and physio-cum-masseur Tom McNiven led a light training session at the nearby Inverclyde Sports Centre. However, the bulk of the work that day was done indoors. Brown made a point of spending as much time as he could with each of the players, getting to know them and letting them get to know him. This was his first proper match as Scotland head coach and he was determined to start on a sure footing. He wanted to foster a sense of camaraderie and team spirit within the group. *Victoria concordia crescit.* Victory comes from harmony.

In McCrae and McNiven, he had two able deputies. Like Brown, McCrae had been a goalkeeper but only ever in the junior ranks. A qualified physiotherapist, he had completed his National Service in the Royal Marines. Respect for him came easy. Crucially, he also had international experience, having worked alongside Brown's predecessors Ian McColl, Jock Stein and Malky Macdonald. His links to his hometown team Kilmarnock had already proven useful, as he had been able to negotiate use of the Ayrshire side's Rugby Park ground for an individual training session the weekend prior with Jim Baxter. Apparently, Baxter had volunteered for the session and had thoroughly impressed.

McNiven, meantime, had spent several years working as trainer and physio at Hibernian where he had attained cult status amongst the Easter Road faithful for his ubiquitous white bunnet. Whenever a player lay stricken on the pitch, McNiven could be easily identified running to their aid from the back row of the terraces. His own playing career went no further than a spell in the junior ranks with Stonehouse Violet. Preferring to pursue a career away from the pitch, he studied at Tom McClurg Anderson's Scottish School of Physiotherapy in the 1950s and upon completing his studies, at the age of twenty-four, joined Third Lanark as the Glasgow outfit's trainer. Ahead of the 1963/64 season, he joined Hibs, replacing Eddie Turnbull. The emphasis he placed on the importance of physical conditioning was legendary around the Edinburgh club. Many considered him to be a man several years ahead of his time.

'Have you ever seen a cat after it has been out chasing mice?' he would ask the players. 'Or maybe a lion on the television? They are always stretching, always trying to relax their muscles. That's why you never see a cat with cramp.'

Most importantly, the players loved him. His dry humour was one thing – he got a kick out of persuading new recruits that the athletics medals he had won in his younger days had, in fact, been earned fighting in the Korean War – but it was his fidelity to the team that set him apart.

'If Tom saw you burning down the Main Stand,' explained Pat Stanton, 'he wouldn't tell the manager.'

Between them, Brown, McCrae and McNiven made for a formidable trio and, as the sun set over Ayrshire that night, the boss was a man at peace with the world. Tomorrow, he and his squad would be joined by the contingent from Celtic and travel south to London. He had been thrown a curveball by the injury to Law but had batted it beyond the fences. The biggest week of his career had got off to a good start.

'Things are going well for us so far,' he told reporters. 'Let's hope they stay that way.'

TWENTY

WILLIAM WALLACE

IT WAS JUST AFTER MIDDAY ON THURSDAY, 13 April, and a little more than forty-eight hours until kick-off at Wembley. With fears about the fitness of Law having finally been allayed and the journey to London about to begin, Bobby Brown should have been putting the finishing touches to his team to face England. Instead, he was fretting over the health of another of his key men – winger Jimmy Johnstone.

The flame-haired attacker had been at his wily best the night before as Celtic took another huge stride towards European Cup glory. His first-half goal set Jock Stein's men on their way to a 3–1 victory over Dukla Prague in the first leg of their semi-final in Glasgow's east end.

Johnstone's jinking heroics, however, had come at a cost. A thigh injury sustained during the match had put his involvement in the England match in serious doubt. He still was limping heavily when he arrived at Celtic Park on Thursday morning. Celtic physio Bob Rooney worked on him intensively for almost five hours, stopping only briefly for lunch, before finally conceding defeat shortly after 3 p.m.

'It was hopeless,' Johnstone admitted. 'I was in pain every time I started sprinting. The more I tried, the more I knew I wouldn't make it. It is a heartbreak, but the club has done all they can.' With that, he got into his car, his beloved collie in the passenger seat next to him, and drove away.

It was a significant blow to Brown's preparations. Only twenty-two years of age, Johnstone was well on his way to establishing himself as one of Scotland's most important creative players and had scored twice against England in a 4–3 defeat at Hampden Park a year earlier.

'With his close dribbling, Johnstone would have caused a great deal of trouble to England, I'm sure of that,' said the boss, who was given the bad news after a short training session at the home of Hendon Amateurs. 'He was playing so well. I said in the stand at the Dukla game just how well he was going and I hoped he would repeat this against England. I felt he would have caused a great deal of trouble in the England defence.

'Obviously, I must rethink certain things for the game now. So much was going to hinge around Johnstone. We will miss him. There is no doubting that.'

Fortunately, there was a ready-made and in-form replacement for the Scotland boss to call on – Johnstone's Celtic teammate, William 'Willie' Wallace. Dubbed the 'Hammer of Dukla' by the Scottish media, the man with the most famous name in Scotland had scored Celtic's other two goals in their emphatic defeat of the Prague side. That earned him the nod ahead of more orthodox wingers, such as Rangers' Willie Henderson – capped twenty-three times by Scotland but struggling for his best form at club level – and Tommy McLean of Kilmarnock.

'Willie is the man of the moment,' added Brown. 'He showed that with his two European Cup goals. I picked him because he is playing with fire and with confidence. However, because he is a different type of player, I will have to rethink my tactics. I must think of something to suit the more direct style of Wallace. But I am confident he can do a job for me. If he plays as well as he is playing for Celtic, then he can help us win this game.'

Born in Kirkintilloch in June 1940, Wallace began his career with junior outfit Kilsyth Rangers before breaking into the senior ranks with Stenhousemuir. After a year at Ochilview, he moved to Raith Rovers where he scored twenty-three goals in just over fifty appearances. His predatory instincts in front of goal in Kirkcaldy earned him a transfer to Hearts in 1961 where he spent five years before joining Celtic in December 1966 for a club record £30,000.

Whilst he continued his free-scoring form after joining the Hoops, Wallace had failed to add to the three Scotland caps he had earned during his time at Tynecastle. Crucially, though, he did have experience of facing England on two previous occasions.

The first was as a member of the Scottish League XI that had beaten their FA contemporaries 3–1 in Newcastle in 1966. That day, England had fielded the Charlton brothers, Alan Ball and Nobby Stiles – who, months later, would go on to lift the World Cup on home soil – not to mention the prolific Jimmy Greaves. It was Greaves, indeed, who opened the scoring for England, only for Dundee's Andy Penman to equalise within a minute of the second half. A double from Celtic's Joe McBride sealed a famous win but it was his clubmate Wallace who stole the show, leading the line with an inspired performance.

That earned him another crack at the same opponent in the British Home Championship match at Hampden a fortnight later. Stung by the backlash from their League loss – a result that prompted one critic to dismiss their World Cup prospects as 'ridiculous and unsupportable' – Alf Ramsey's men ran out 4–3 winners. It assured England of a third successive Home Championship title and saw John Prentice's brief stint as Scotland boss start with a defeat. It might all have been so different had Wallace's goal-bound effort not been cleared off the line by Nobby Stiles in the final minute with goalkeeper Gordon Banks well beaten.

By his own admission, joining Celtic had helped Wallace rediscover both his best form and his confidence. Little wonder he was 'absolutely thrilled' to get the call from Brown, albeit at the expense of his Celtic clubmate.

'I was told to phone the boss, Mr Stein, at the ground at 3.30 p.m.,' said the then twenty-six-year-old. 'That's when he told me that Jimmy was out and that I would travel. It was all a bit hectic. I never imagined when I was congratulating all the boys on their call-ups at the Seamill Hydro on Monday that I would be joining them at Wembley.

'I don't know yet what job Bobby Brown will want me to do but I'm pretty versatile and I'm not worrying about it. Though I play mostly in the middle, I'm no stranger to the outside right position, having played there for Stenhousemuir, Raith and Hearts.

'I'm absolutely thrilled about getting this chance to play at Wembley but, at the same time, I'm sorry that it has to be in these circumstances. I can appreciate how Jimmy must feel.'

After speaking with Stein at half-three, Wallace was en route to Abbotsinch Airport at 4 p.m., the boots that had downed Dukla the previous night carefully stowed amongst his luggage. At 6.15 p.m., he waved goodbye to his wife, Olive, and baby daughter Lynn and boarded the plane bound for London. He relaxed into his seat at thirty thousand feet and smiled wryly to himself as he shook his head.

What a crazy twenty-four hours.

The decision to send for Wallace came as a surprise to some, not least another of his Celtic clubmates, Stevie Chalmers. Alongside Frank McLintock, Chalmers had been named as one of Brown's two outfield travelling reserves. Arsenal man

McLintock was there to cover any last-minute defensive call-offs or mishaps, with Chalmers on stand-by for the forwards.

From the moment Johnstone got injured against Dukla, Chalmers had been psychologically preparing himself to fill the void. So, whilst happy for Wallace, he quietly seethed at having been overlooked.

'I felt as though the Scottish FA had not played fair with me,' he later admitted. 'It rankled with me then and it still lingers today. Nobody came to me and told why and how it had happened. I was very late in knowing they had sent for "Wispy". I think it was Ronnie Simpson who told me. None of the officials said to me they were leaving me out and wanting Willie to come in. Bobby Brown didn't even discuss it with me. They should have had the gumption to come up to me and explain the whole thing.

'Willie had been hit with a big present overnight and I did not grudge him that at all, but it would have been nice for someone to have explained it all to me, not least what the point had been of me travelling down to England in the first place.'

Chalmers added: 'I just didn't like the way it had happened. I had been picked as twelfth man because I could play anywhere across the forward line, so if someone called off late or was injured, I could slot into the team very easily. I should have been automatically in the team.'

Wallace arrived at the team's base, the swanky Brent Bridge Hotel in Hendon, late on Thursday evening. As he checked in, Bobby Brown was doing what Bobby Brown did – poring over the tactical options available to him.

If Scotland were going to lose, as so many reporters kept telling him they would, then it wouldn't be through poor preparation.

* * *

A FEW MILES AWAY, Sir Alf Ramsey and his English squad were in characteristically relaxed mood. After having taken in Tottenham's FA Cup quarter-final replay with Birmingham at White Hart Lane the night before – a game which Jimmy Greaves had not only come through unscathed but had scored twice in – the world champions had a light training session on the Thursday.

Their original plan had been to train on the Wembley Town Amateurs' pitch nearby but, because of the damp and cold weather, they decided to use the indoor facilities at Arsenal instead. 'A few of the boys are a bit sniffy,' explained Ramsey. 'That's why I decided it would be better to work indoors. This means you will not be able to spy on us. Not that I have any objection to that but the restricted space in the indoor gymnasium means that no spectators are allowed.'

Ramsey added that he had no plans to take his players to Wembley for a look at the pitch before Saturday's game, insisting: 'If they don't know it by now, they never will. They have played there often enough.'

Greaves joined the party just before lunch, bouncing into the team's Hendon Hall HQ after his heroics the night before. Having put Birmingham to the sword, Scotland were now firmly and squarely in his crosshairs.

'It's wonderful to be in an England team against Scotland,' he said. 'The atmosphere at Wembley never fails to thrill me. Saturday's game will bring me my fifty-fifth cap for my country and I am looking forward to this match with exactly the same excitement as when I gained my first cap.'

Even if he didn't articulate it quite as resoundingly, Ramsey shared his star striker's determination. Apart from the obvious benefits of beating Scotland – consolidating their position at the top of the European Nations Cup qualifying group and extending their unbeaten record – Ramsey had a very personal reason for wanting to win.

The upcoming game would be the fourth time he had come up against England's noisy neighbours from the north at Wembley. As a player, he lost one game and drew the other. As manager, he lost 2–1 four years earlier and drew 2–2 in 1965. It was a record that gnawed away at him. This was a man who had led his country to World Cup glory and been knighted for his troubles. His legacy had already been fulfilled, his epitaph written, his place amongst the pantheon of England's footballing greats well and truly cemented. And yet this one thing – this one *bloody* thing – continued to haunt him like some kilted spectre. Winning at Hampden? Sure, he had experienced that and enjoyed it. But Wembley was England's patch, *his* patch. Losing there was never acceptable. Losing to Scotland, even less so.

'Alf enjoyed getting beaten by the Scots about as much as he might enjoy root canal work at the dentist's,' explained Bobby Charlton. 'His determination to beat them was all the more powerful because he knew the taste of defeat. The wounds ran very deep.'

As he watched his men train inside Arsenal's Highbury Stadium – trainer Harold Shepherdson putting them through their paces – Ramsey wondered if this would be fifth time lucky.

He hoped so. Oh, how he hoped so.

TWENTY-ONE

SMOKED SALMON AND ROAST BEEF

AS THE DAY OF THE MATCH INCHED EVER CLOSER, demand to be there intensified. Forget the Yukon gold rush. Those Klondike prospectors had nothing on the hundreds of thousands of football fanatics who would have pulled up trees from Lerwick to London if they thought they might find a ticket tangled in the roots.

The stadium's box office manager Fred Jackson suddenly discovered he was the most popular man in the country with friends he never knew he had. 'I feel like a pools winner who has hit the jackpot,' he told reporters. 'I can't figure out whether I am the most popular or unpopular man in the country. My phone hasn't stopped ringing.'

It was a similar story at the Wembley switchboard where call handlers were logging up to 7,000 calls per day from fans desperate for a ticket. Enquiries poured in from across the globe. Canada, New Zealand, even Hong Kong – it seemed that everyone from everywhere wanted to be at the game. The Football Association described the interest as 'completely unprecedented', with bosses convinced they could have sold out the stadium at least ten times over.

Of course, such pent-up demand posed some obvious issues, not least industrious swindlers looking to sneak through the turnstiles. Fortunately, the crew on the ground was well prepared. They'd seen it all before, none more so than Wembley 'maister' Jack Smith. A former Scotland Yard chief inspector, there was no scam he hadn't foiled. From a heavy-set gentleman, who insisted his ticket had been taken at the turnstile 'just around the corner' but he'd been too fat to squeeze through the barrier, to a panic-stricken 'kitman', who once appeared before a big game waving a pair of football boots that he insisted belonged to one of the players, Smith had rumbled every ruse you could think of.

His favourite one was the time a milkman pulled up at the turnstiles complete with can and white overalls and claiming he had been sent by Buckingham Palace to personally deliver the milk for the Queen's tea.

No, Smith was nobody's mug, so when a greyhound meeting took place at Wembley in the days leading up to the football, you better believe he checked and double-checked every toilet cubicle inside the ground, just in case some enterprising fan decided to camp out until kick-off.

In the run-up to matchday, Wembley was a well-oiled machine. Every provision was made, every eventuality accounted for. Take catering manager Arthur Golby, for example. Never mind that he had arranged a four-course lunch of smoked salmon and roast beef for the 300 VIPs expected to attend; he'd also had the foresight to order in 500 bottles of whisky and 4,000 bottles of heavy beer, as well as enough tea to make 20,000 cuppas. His 250 snack-bar attendants, meantime, were put to work preparing 25,000 sandwiches for hungry supporters.

Beyond the catering service, there were also seventy programme sellers, 300 commissionaires, 450 honorary stewards and around 100 first-aiders.

Bottom line: Wembley was ready. All it needed was to be filled. And while that could be almost guaranteed, doing so was not without its problems.

Around 100,000 tickets had been printed for the match, 29,000 of which had been sent to the SFA to distribute amongst clubs, officials and fans. And, as a *Daily Record* exposé demonstrated, the latter were staggeringly under-represented.

Roughly 60% of the SFA's 29,000 tickets went to Scottish League clubs, or 17,503 to be exact. The country's smaller clubs and associations were given the lion's share of the remainder, including a special allocation that was put aside for members of the SFA Council and League Management Committees, each of whom got forty tickets.

By the time the clubs and the blazers had all taken their cut, just over a tenth of all tickets – a measly 3,555 of them – were sold by public ballot. Of those, just over 2,000 were for the terracing.

SFA secretary Willie Allan responded to the *Daily Record* report to say that the organisation always wants supporters to 'get the first chance of a ticket' but acknowledged that there were deficiencies with the current system. President Tom Reid was far less contrite. 'The SFA have always been blamed for bad allocation and it's not fair,' he fumed. 'Once these tickets leave us, it is up to the other organisations to be as fair to their supporters and members.'

Representatives of the member clubs toed the party line. Rangers manager Scot Symon said that tickets for international matches are 'fairly divided out to all branches of our supporters'. Celtic secretary Desmond White added: 'We give our tickets out as we see fit.' Bill Divine, the Heart of Midlothian secretary, pointed out that 'everyone who applied got a ticket'.

The only club to sing from a different hymn sheet was Falkirk. 'The ordinary supporter has virtually no chance of tickets unless he knows someone in the club,' groaned their representative. However, he had better cause than most to cast a shadow of doubt at the door of the SFA. He was, after all, the recently deposed national team manager, John Prentice.

Nonetheless, the lack of transparency from the SFA hierarchy and clubs themselves left many wondering just how many tickets had actually reached the average man on the terrace. The consensus? Not many, and certainly not enough.

Undeterred, eager Scots poured into England, keen to soak up the atmosphere in London more broadly if not Wembley specifically. According to the Automobile Association, more than 600 cars crossed the border on the A74 every hour the day before the game. One patrolman was quoted as saying: 'I've had the same two requests from drivers all day: what's the weather like up ahead, and have you got a ticket. If I did have any tickets, I could have made a fortune!'

The *Sunday Post* subsequently reported upon the exploits of one unnamed Scotland supporter who attempted to hitchhike from Glasgow to London in the hope of picking up a ticket on the road. 'I dropped into my Govan pub for a pint at lunchtime last Monday,' he said. 'The boys were all talking about going to Wembley. I didn't have a ticket. I'd only four quid in my wallet. But there and then, I decided I was going, too.'

He went home, packed a duffle bag, and made a sandwich board out of cardboard and string. He scrawled 'I'M WALKING TO WEMBLEY, CAN YOU SELL ME A TICKET' in crayon, draped the makeshift billboard over his shoulders and started walking. Remarkably, he made it to London with just hours to spare. And yes, he got a ticket.

Elsewhere, British Railways laid on sixteen additional services to London from Aberdeen, Perth, Dundee and Glasgow. These so-called 'Soccer Specials' passed through Carlisle at a rate of one every nineteen minutes. The number of fans aboard two Edinburgh to London overnight trains that departed on the Friday night was conservatively estimated at around one thousand.

Airlines scheduled several extra flights. A group of 132 Rolls-Royce workers from East Kilbride were amongst those to fly out from Glasgow the day before the game having saved for it for two years. Just one problem. Only forty-four of them had tickets. Organiser William Carrick told reporters: 'After saving for so long for the trip, those without tickets just couldn't stay at home. They had to take a chance. They have money with them if it turns out that tickets are available.' Maybe they should have hitch-hiked . . .

A group of fifty fans travelled from Wick – a royal burgh in Caithness, in the far north of Scotland – as part of a delegation from Wick Academy Football Club. Glasgow's Possilpark YMCA team ventured south as the guests of Arsenal FC. The English side even arranged a match for their visitors against their youth team prior to kick-off. And that's to say nothing of the forty supporters from a masonic lodge in Wishaw who, having been held up by traffic, arrived at Glasgow Airport just as their flight to London was preparing to taxi down the runway. Luckily for them, airline officials managed to stop the plane so they could get on board.

It seemed as though every single Scot was trying to get into England for the big match. Those who stayed at home struggled to find any way to follow it. STV had acquired the exclusive television rights to the match but, rather than show the whole thing as it happened, they opted instead to broadcast a forty-minute highlights package almost two hours after the full-time whistle had blown. Unsurprisingly, that didn't go down well with the Tartan Army's armchair regiment. One particularly disgruntled fan, an East Kilbride man called James Lawlor, put his grievance in writing. In a letter to the *Sunday Mail*, he complained that showing the build-up but nothing of the match itself was like 'showing a thirsty man a drink of water then taking it away from him'.

John Finnigan, a fifty-year-old admiralty clerk from West Lothian, went so far as to send a telegram to his local MP, Labour's Tam Dalyell. Mr Finnigan called on Dalyell to take 'personal action' to ensure the match was televised live and in full north of the border, but to no avail. A spokesperson for Associated Television – the company responsible for broadcasting football on independent TV networks throughout Britain – revealed: 'No one will be able to see the international "live" on television – not even in England. Under agreements with the Football Association in England, it will be tele-recorded and then transmitted by local television stations after the match.'

Radio listeners, meantime, were able to hear live commentary of the second half only on either the Home Service or BBC Sports Service. With no internet to share information – far less social media to communicate it – the only way fans could experience the whole match as it unfolded in real time was to be there.

That was an option Mary McCalliog passed up. The mother of twenty-year-old Jim, she decided to stay at home in Glasgow with her other children: seventeen-year-old Fred, fifteen-year-old Danny, eleven-year-old Ann, and Eddie, eight.

'It's a wonderful thing for all of us that Jim has been capped,' said Mary, 'but it's too long a journey for the two youngest children, so I'll be staying at home to look after them.'

She had done the same a year earlier when Jim turned out at Wembley in the white of Sheffield Wednesday for the 1966 FA Cup final. He had scored the opening goal, too, netting after four minutes in front of a capacity crowd that included John Lennon and Paul McCartney. David Ford doubled Wednesday's lead shortly after half-time before a Mike Trebilcock double and a fine finish from Derek Temple gave opponents Everton their third victory in the competition, and a first in thirty-three years.

'We watched that game on television,' added Mary. 'I'll never forget when the team lost that day. I went into the kitchen to cry so that the youngsters wouldn't see me but they knew and they were crying in front of the TV set.

'This time, we'll listen on the radio and hope for a victory. I hope they get it because none of my boys likes to lose.'

As supporters made their way south on the Friday, both teams continued their preparation. Brown took his men to Wembley for a look around the ground. Training on the pitch was forbidden but they were, at least, able to familiarise themselves with their surroundings. It was an impressive place alright. Originally known as the British Empire Exhibition Stadium – or simply, the Empire Stadium – Wembley had opened in 1923. It cost £750,000 (approximately £46 million in modern terms) and was constructed on the site of an old folly called Watkin's Tower. Built for a colonial exhibition that ran throughout 1924 and which was extended into 1925, the ground staged its first football match in 1923 when it played host to the FA Cup Final between Bolton Wanderers and West Ham United. Such was the demand to be there that the actual attendance far outstripped the stadium's capacity. Official records claim that 126,047 people were there to see Bolton win 2–0. The real total has been estimated at anywhere between 240,000 and 300,000.

After surviving the threat of liquidation later in the 1920s, Wembley slowly but surely started to thrive. At international level, it was used exclusively for the biennial visits of Scotland, with other fixtures spread throughout the country. That changed in 1951 when Argentina became the first team other than the Scots to face England there. Twelve years later, in 1963, a raft of ambitious renovations was carried out that saw the installation of an electric scoreboard and an all-encircling roof made from aluminium and translucent glass.

With all of this, plus its trademark 'Twin Towers' framing the approach to the stadium from Wembley Park tube station, the ground proved to be a fitting centrepiece for the 1966 World Cup. It was, all at once, a mesmerising and intimidating place to play. Playing the game and not the ground was critical for any visiting team.

Standing close to the tunnel, full-back Eddie McCreadie turned to Bobby Lennox and pointed up at the giant scoreboard, which read '0–0'.

'If that's the score after the final whistle tomorrow,' he said, 'I'm going to wear my Scotland strip into training at Chelsea next week.' The pair roared with laughter.

After leaving Wembley, the Scots did anything they could think of to pass the time. Some, including Brown, went to Highbury where they joined a crowd of almost 8,000 in watching a friendly between Arsenal and Dunfermline Athletic. Whilst the Londoners ran out narrow winners, it was the Fifers' forward – future Manchester United manager Alex Ferguson – who stole the show with, according to *The Press & Journal*, some 'clever ball-play that often had Arsenal's defence in trouble'.

Others in the squad went to a nearby cinema where, by total coincidence, the England team were watching the same movie! As the credits rolled, the Scots' Anglo continent – chiefly Law, Baxter and Bremner – chatted with their opponents. As Lennox later acknowledged, that close relationship was to Scotland's benefit.

'Denis, Billy and Jim were playing against them every week and told us that we had nothing to fear,' said the Celtic man. 'Their belief in the ability of our team was infectious and their practical knowledge of our opponents was invaluable.

'At training, for example, Billy told us that, at corner kicks, Jack Charlton would stand on the goal-line, in front of the goalkeeper, and that when the ball came across, he would use his height and weight to prevent the goalie getting to the ball. Billy, a teammate of Jackie's at Leeds, said that they had scored several goals that way. As a means of stopping this working, Billy suggested that we should post a player either side of Charlton but Ronnie Simpson quashed that idea immediately. He said that, now that he knew about Charlton's ploy, he would not stand close to him but would instead time his run and jump so that he could get into the air just as the corner was coming over and use his momentum to catch the ball or punch it clear. If there were players standing around Charlton, Ronnie said, it would hamper his efforts and he would be scrambling to get past people to clear the ball. There was a lot of debate about that but eventually we decided that, as Ronnie was the goalkeeper, we should go with his advice.

'Still, one or two other little tips such as that one helped us to get the measure of our English opponents.'

Back on the streets of London, canny bookmakers were taking bets by the dozen. Chalkboards were updated constantly as the odds shifted. Pre-match, England were priced at 4/7 for the win with Scotland trading at 4/1. You could get 5/2 for a draw. If you wanted to bet on Scotland scoring (penalties excluded), you'd have been given odds of 4/5, whilst the prices on individual players scoring was surprisingly generous. Wallace was 5/1, Bremner 7/1, McCalliog 3/1, Lennox 6/1, Law 9/4. There was money to be made for those predisposed to a flutter. Just how much would be determined within the next twenty-four hours.

As the sun set over London that Friday night, anticipation filled the air. This wasn't like the World Cup final. Not at all. But there was a sense of occasion, a sense of importance, a sense of purpose that only the most significant football matches can imbue.

The eighty-fourth international match between England and Scotland lay in wait on the other side of the dawn.

That, and so much more besides.

TWENTY-TWO

JIMMY CLITHEROE'S SON

SATURDAY AT LAST. Bobby Brown awoke in the Brent Bridge Hotel feeling quietly confident. As he came to and pondered the day in prospect, he considered how everything had gone up to this point. First, the negatives. The injury to Johnstone was a blow. Jinky was in great form. But so, too, was Wallace. He would have loved to have had Johnstone in his starting XI but his clubmate was a more than able deputy. Beyond that, things were mostly positive. His players were upbeat, despite the English press insisting that they shouldn't be. The preparation had gone to plan and he had liked what he'd seen in the training sessions, both in Largs and in Hendon. As for himself, Brown was looking forward to getting into the dugout. Sure, this was a few steps up from managing St Johnstone but he had total faith in his players and, having played international football himself, he had a sense of what to expect.

If anybody ought to feel nervous, it was Sir Alf. Not only was his team expected to win, they had a proud unbeaten record to maintain. That's where the pressure lay. Not on Scotland and not on Brown.

After breakfast, the squad assembled for some light ball work before attending to the usual admin. Press photos, last-minute phone calls and the like. A handful of players went for a walk around nearby Golders Green, an upmarket, middle-class neighbourhood that had been created by American property developers at the beginning of the 20th century. Ronnie Simpson was amongst those who went for that wander. If the veteran goalie was feeling any pre-match jitters ahead of his Scotland debut that afternoon, he wasn't showing it. Brown was impressed. 'He looked as if he was just going out for a walk with his dog,' he remarked. When they returned to the hotel, Simpson received a phone call from Rangers goalkeeper Billy Ritchie. Despite the intense rivalry between their two club sides, Ritchie wanted to wish his fellow shot-stopper all the best.

Some players studied the newspapers for a flavour of what the 'experts' were predicting. What they read fired them up. In *The Times*, for example, Geoffrey Green noted: 'Who wouldn't be keen to upend a side beaten but once in their last thirty matches? That, indeed, is England's enviable record. One day, the unbeaten run will end. It may do so this afternoon. But I doubt it.'

'We were wasting our time even bothering to travel,' recalled Lennox. 'The more arrogant and ignorant sections of the media believed England were close to invincible. It was clear that they regarded us as inferior talents who would be crushed by the mighty world champions. That motivated us enormously.'

After a light lunch, it was time to go. The Scots climbed onto the team coach and set off for Wembley. It was just a short journey, no more than six miles, but the bus was guided along the route by police motorcycle outriders. Just as well. Fans spilled out onto the streets and cheered the coach almost every inch of the way. Finally, at around 1.30 p.m., the bus turned onto Wembley Way where it was met by a sea of tartan.

Jim McCalliog had never seen anything like it. 'It was incredible,' he recalled. 'As I sat there on the bus, staring out the window, I realised that I was living my dream. This was why I had spent all those hours kicking a ball about as a kid. This was why I'd left home and moved to England as a teenager. All the sacrifices and the hard knocks along the way. It had all been leading to this.'

The spectacle connected with Brown on a cellular level. 'I think the realisation of the enormity of the fixture began to hit the players as our coach made its way through the masses of our fans,' he said. 'They appreciated they were carrying a nation's hopes with them.'

Amidst the amorphous blob of Glengarry hats, scarves, Scottish standards and Saltires that filled the view, Lennox made a shock discovery. 'As the vehicle got close to the stadium, the driver had to take a sharp left to go through a big wooden gate into the part of the ground nearest the dressing rooms,' he recalled. 'Just as the bus was turning, my eyes were drawn in one direction and, amongst all those other supporters, I found myself looking directly at the figure of my father, sitting on a step outside Wembley in his three-piece suit.' Lennox Snr had been too shy to come and collect the tickets that his son had arranged for him at the team hotel earlier in the day, so his uncle had gone instead. 'Seeing him was a big thrill for me,' he added.

Willie Wallace had a similar experience. 'As we neared the ground, I saw my next-door neighbour Tom Fergus and his mates. They had parked their caravanette just next to the entrance to the dressing rooms. I had managed to get tickets for them for the game but they had left Scotland early on the Friday morning so they didn't know I was involved.

'When I walked over to them, they were surprised to see me. They asked what I was doing at Wembley. You should have seen their faces when I said I was playing! They didn't believe me at first but I managed to convince them. They wished me all the best and I headed inside.'

Brown led his players out for a short stroll on the pitch and to acknowledge the travelling support as the ground filled up fast. 'The atmosphere was electric,' added Wallace. 'There seemed to be more Scots than English and we soaked up their thunderous applause.'

Taking in the sights and sounds around him, Ronnie Simpson's mind drifted to his father, who had seen this all before thirty years earlier. It dawned on him how right his dad had been. Wembley is a wonderful place to play in an international against England, and he was determined to enjoy it.

As the cheers of the crowd boomed around them, the clock continuing its inexorable countdown towards kick-off, the teams sat in their respective changing rooms. While Wembley was undoubtedly impressive – the Brazilian great Pelé once described it as 'the cathedral of football, the capital of football, and the heart of football' – the visiting team's facilities were (perhaps deliberately) basic. They were old-fashioned with high ceilings, slate flooring and the most rudimentary fittings.

The SFA had provided each player with a small booklet of guidelines detailing how they were expected to conduct themselves on international duty. It was stipulated, for example, that shirts had to be tucked into shorts at all times, with the red tops of the navy socks pulled down a specific number of inches. For the most part, the players observed the rules.

Bobby Lennox recalled: 'As the minutes ticked down, Ronnie Simpson said, "I could have done with a wee sip." At Celtic Park, a cup of whisky was kept in the dressing room before matches for anyone who needed something to settle their nerves.

'Stevie Chalmers piped up, "I bought a half-bottle in Golders Green this morning." Next thing you know, Ronnie, Jim Baxter and one or two others had disappeared into the toilet to have a quick gargle of Stevie's whisky. That would almost certainly not have had the approval of those who compiled the SFA's booklet of pre-match advice!

'Thing is, Stevie was a non-drinker but, in his typically considerate way, he had known that one or two of the boys might like a wee nip before the match, so he had come prepared. It definitely got the boys up for it.'

'I was determined to contribute to the cause,' added Chalmers. 'It was not so much the alcoholic kick that players looked for when they took a wee swig pre-match. It was actually to help cope with a dry mouth, by providing them with a bit of moisture and a nice tingling sensation to calm the nerves.'

The Football Association arranged a full programme of pre-match entertainment to help build the atmosphere within the ground. The Band of Her Majesty's Royal Marines (Portsmouth Group) performed an eclectic medley of songs between 1.30 p.m. and 2 p.m., including everything from 'The John F. Kennedy March' and 'The Gathering of the Clans' to 'Bye Bye Birdie' and 'Puppet on a String'. Performed by Sandie Shaw, the latter had won the Eurovision Song Contest just seven days earlier – the first time the United Kingdom had won the annual music competition. One of its writers, a Scottish music impresario called Bill Martin, was at Wembley to hear this unique pre-match cover version. Martin, incidentally, went to school in Glasgow with Scotland centre-half Ron McKinnon.

Between 2.30 p.m. and 2.50 p.m., the *Daily Express* newspaper had arranged for a period of what it called 'Community Singing'. A full song-sheet was provided within copies of the match programme. 'I Belong to Glasgow', 'A Scottish Soldier', 'Yellow Submarine', 'Loch Lomond', 'Tipperary', 'When The Saints Go Marching In' – all featured, and were performed with gusto by an expectant crowd.

As warming up on the pitch was not permitted, the Scottish players had to do their limbering up indoors. They stretched, kicked balls against the wall, some got a light rub-down from the Tom McNiven, whilst Walter McCrae made sure every player had what they needed. Plasters? You got it. Bandages? No bother. Whisky? Ask Stevie.

Suitably hydrated, Baxter sat back down in his seat, pulled a copy of the *Sporting Life* out of his bag and started thumbing through it. Encouraged to get up and get ready instead, he first stretched out his left leg, then stretched out his right. 'That's me warmed up,' he replied, his eyes never leaving the newspaper.

In typically low-key fashion, Brown decided not to address his players with a well-rehearsed battle cry. That wasn't his style. Instead, he went around each player individually, reminding them of their roles and encouraging them to enjoy the experience. *This is what you've trained for your whole life*, and so on.

Jim McCalliog remembers every word of what Brown told him. 'He told me to just do what I had been doing at Sheffield Wednesday and enjoy the game. He said, "You're in here on merit Jim. I have every confidence in you, so enjoy it." Aye, that meant a lot.

'Looking around, I was struck by how confident everybody was. Not in an arrogant way. It wasn't like that. It was more of a "so what if England won the World Cup" kind of attitude. It seemed as though there were no nerves whatsoever.'

Suddenly, perhaps sensing the occasion called for something more, Brown decided to address the group after all. He took his place in the middle of the room and cleared his throat.

'As soon as he started to talk, Baxter started bouncing a ball on the floor and said, "Aye, okay boss, great, come on, lads, let's go,"' added McCalliog. 'I mean, Bobby was actually talking and I was sitting there watching and listening to him. Everybody else gets up and goes with Baxter, so I'm left thinking, "Here, I'd better go with him." It was the first time in my life that I've ever gone with the crowd. All we could hear in the background was poor Bobby shouting, "All the best lads, all the best."'

At 2.50 p.m., the teams emerged from their changing rooms and lined up behind German referee Gerhard Schulenburg and his assistants.

'A lot of verbals were exchanged between the two teams,' said Lennox. 'Although it was often said that the England-Scotland match was more important to the Scots, that wasn't true of players on the English side that day. Alan Ball and Bobby Moore, to name just two, were desperate not to concede their unbeaten record to the "Jocks" of all people!'

Bobby Charlton added: 'It is probably true to say that the balance of competition and respect was never more precarious than on that afternoon. We knew that as champions of the world, we had never before provoked such Scottish determination. It wasn't a match as much as part of a tribal war.'

Baxter cast a sideways glance and saw he was standing next to Alan Ball. A mischievous smile slowly formed at the corners of his mouth as he remembered something Billy Bremner had told him previously. Ball, evidently, was sensitive about his high-pitched voice, which other players had compared – somewhat unkindly – to that of Jimmy Clitheroe, the four-foot-two-inch comedian who was still able to pass for eleven years old well into his forties. Ball didn't like having their similarities pointed out. Not one bit.

Baxter smelled blood. He leaned towards Ball.

'Congratulations on winning the World Cup.'

The Everton midfielder smiled a 'thank you'.

'Is it true, though,' added Baxter, 'that Jimmy Clitheroe's your dad?'

Bang! He'd got him.

'He went fucking spare,' said Baxter. 'Kept trying to kick me the whole game, as though he was confusing my shins with the ball. He couldn't play at all. He was running about, demented, like a fart in a bottle. He wasn't the only Englishman to go daft that day. Jackie Charlton wasn't in the best of moods either, and Nobby Stiles, minus those front teeth, looked as if he could cheerfully have killed us all. But only Ball kept on kicking. Maybe Bremner shouldn't have asked him: "D'you think you'll be a player when your voice breaks?"'

The guttural cheers of more than 99,000 expectant supporters melted into a single cacophonous roar as the two sides emerged.

'The tunnel sloped upwards as you walked along it,' recalled Lennox. 'When we came within sight of the crowd, we were greeted by a sea of lions rampant and an enormous roar from the Scottish supporters. There were so many of them that it seemed almost like a home match.'

Just as he had done in the World Cup final 259 days earlier, Moore led out England, dressed in their familiar white shirts, navy shorts and white socks. John Greig, making his twenty-first appearance for his country, led Scotland, clad in their traditional navy shirts, white shorts and navy-and-red socks.

'Scotland were clearly up for it,' said England keeper Gordon Banks. 'They took to the pitch hyped-up but in control of their emotions. They exuded gritty determination and their will to win was there for all to see.

'As we walked out onto the pitch, I knew we were in for an almighty battle because of one astonishing sight: Denis Law was wearing shinpads. In all the games I had played against Denis, I'd never seen him wearing them. I remember thinking, "If he's tooled up for battle, what can we expect from Billy Bremner, Tommy Gemmell, Eddie McCreadie and John Greig?"'

The players lined up on the pitch, either side of the halfway line, where they were introduced to a team of dignitaries, led by Bernard Fitzalan-Howard, the 16th Duke of Norfolk. Wallace recalls being 'a shade disappointed' by that. 'My favourite royals at the time were Princess Alexandra and Princess Margaret,' he laughed.

Beneath his navy shirt, Eddie McCreadie could feel his heart pounding as though it was trying to escape his chest. 'Like most games, I was very nervous,' he said. 'It was always even more nerve-racking when you were playing for your country. I remember thinking, "Man, I wish they could get this game going, so I can get at it."

'I looked across at England and I could see Bobby Moore, Geoff Hurst and Alan Ball. I remember thinking, "This is going to be tough." Then I looked down the line at our team and I saw Denis, Jim, Bremner, John Greig, and I thought to myself, "What am I worried about?"'

Greig and Moore introduced the royal party to their respective teams. After that, it was time for the talking to stop.

Kick-off was nigh.

TWENTY-THREE

THE RESURRECTION OF HARRY LAUDER

'AND IT'S SCOTLAND IN THE DARK SHIRTS kicking off and attacking the goal to your left,' declared commentator Hugh Johns as Denis Law wheeled away from the centre circle with the ball at his feet. A pilot in the Fleet Air Arm during the Second World War, Johns had designs on becoming an actor when the conflict ended and joined the repertory company at the Castle Theatre in Farnham.

His long and winding road to the commentary booth began when he started writing match reports for his local newspaper, the *Surrey and Hants News*, and later the *Southend Standard*, the *Daily Herald and News Chronicle* and the *Sunday People*. He swapped the pen for the microphone with freelance commentary stints covering Cardiff City for Television Wales and West, an ITV subsidiary. It was when ITV decided to take on the heft of the BBC at the 1966 World Cup that he got his big break. As Kenneth Wolstenholme was delivering his famous line at the climax to the match – 'They think it's all over. It is now!' – Johns was in the adjacent booth, calling the action in his own way.

'Here's Hurst. He might make it three. He has! He has! So that's it!'

Johns brought the same approach to every game he called: 'Homework, identification, no waffle, go-with-the-flow.' It was a credo that served him well.

Alongside him in the booth at Wembley for the 1967 visit of Scotland was former England captain Billy Wright. Capped 105 times, the Wolverhampton Wanderers man had faced Scotland fifteen times and lost just twice. His final appearance against them – a 1–0 win at Wembley in 1959 – had coincided with his 100th match for England. Perhaps unsurprisingly, he fancied his compatriots to get the job done again.

Asked by Johns for his prediction, Wright replied: 'I think England will just about win, Hugh, because they've played together for so long. But I never underestimate the Scots because their fervour and wanting to win should make this a great game.'

After a scrappy opening few minutes in which both sides struggled to hold on to possession, Scotland captain John Greig set a marker with a thundering challenge on Geoff Hurst just inside the Scotland half, drawing boos from the crowd. A couple of minutes later, Scotland won the first corner of the game after Tommy Gemmell dispossessed Alan Ball close to the halfway line and attempted to slide in Denis Law. Jack Charlton, though, was alert to the danger, tracking Law's turn and shepherding the ball behind.

A minute later, there were huge cries from the Scotland players for a penalty after Law's probing pass into the penalty area appeared to bounce off the arm of Charlton. Herr Schulenburg was unmoved and waved play on.

Still, Scotland continued to press, their intensity and movement visibly rattling their hosts in the opening ten minutes. Billy Bremner had two chances in quick succession to open the scoring and grab his first-ever goal in Scottish colours.

First, he lashed high and wide from the edge of the box after good build-up play. Then, moments later, unmarked at the far post, he threw himself at a fantastic cross from Gemmell, only marginally failing to connect.

It took until the eighth minute for England to post any kind of alarm for Scotland, a Jimmy Greaves corner from the left bouncing off the top of the bar and behind for a goal kick.

Wright was both impressed and stunned by the start Brown's men had made. 'Scotland have upset the England rhythm because of their tackling,' he said. 'England are playing too casually.'

Scotland kept up the pressure. An outswinging corner from Bobby Lennox found its way to the feet of Law near the penalty spot. However, the Manchester United man's wild swing never looked like troubling Banks, flying well wide.

It was in the twelfth minute that the game had its first major flashpoint, with an incident that would go on to have a bearing on the remainder of the match. Lennox chased a hopeful ball played into the left-hand channel by Ron McKinnon. Alert to the danger once again, Jack Charlton came flying across and slid into a crunching challenge with the Celtic man. As the ball bounced out of play for a Scotland throw, both players hobbled away, each of them visibly hurting from the collision.

When the ball next went out of play, the two men fell to the turf, their respective trainers waved on to the pitch by the German official. Whilst Lennox was quickly back on his feet, Charlton had to be helped off the pitch by Alf Ramsey's right-hand man Harold Shepherdson for further treatment.

'Here is a tragic sight for England,' said Johns. 'Big Jack Charlton being supported off the field.'

Years later, Lennox gave his version of events. 'He came out of it worse,' he said. 'The story goes that he had a flaw in his stud and that when he made contact with my knee, the stud broke, went up through the sole of his boot and broke his toe. I thought that was fair enough. If his stud hadn't broken, he might have broken my kneecap.

'There was a lot of blood spilled as a result of that challenge and I discovered I had a deep gash in my knee. Both of us were down on the turf for quite a while and I reckoned that he was pretending to be hurt in the hope that the referee would look on him more leniently in light of his over-the-top challenge. At half-time, my knee needed to be cleaned up a bit more but it was fine. The wound wasn't stiffening, but it was a nasty one, nonetheless.'

As substitutions were not allowed in those days – indeed, it wasn't until 1970 that FIFA permitted personnel changes mid-match in the World Cup – England were temporarily reduced to ten men whilst their physios worked frantically on Charlton's foot.

On sixteen minutes, the hosts finally managed their first shot on target. Bobby Charlton gathered the ball in the centre circle and for really the first time in the game, there was space in front of him. His incisive reverse pass found the feet of Greaves who played in strike partner Hurst just inside the Scotland box but his left-foot effort was straight at Simpson.

Moments later, Charlton blazed over from just inside the box before Greig lashed a shot wide at the opposite end of the park after Bremner tapped a free kick into his path from the edge of the England box. From the resultant goal kick, Scotland ought to have taken the lead. A mix-up between Gordon Banks and Ray Wilson allowed Willie Wallace to intercept and swing a hopeful ball across the six-yard box. With Banks out of position and the goal at his mercy, Law slid in at the far post but the ball was fractionally too far in front of him and his outstretched left leg could only divert it into the side-netting.

It was an almighty let-off for England, who were struggling to keep up with the frenetic pace of the Scots. Sensing blood – and not just that pouring from Lennox's knee – the travelling supporters upped the ante. Cries of 'Scotland! Scotland! Scotland!' boomed around the ground.

Gemmell saw his powerful left-foot shot headed behind for another corner by England captain Bobby Moore. Baxter tested Banks with a looping header. A collision between Gemmell and Wilson on the byline led to another Scotland corner. The pressure was relentless.

Finally, after ten minutes of treatment, Charlton returned to the pitch. Clearly struggling with the injury, he was moved up front by Ramsey as part of a tactical reshuffle that saw Nobby Stiles drop back to support Moore in the heart of the defence. Less than ideal but what alternative did they have? With his height, Charlton could be a useful out-ball.

Finally, on twenty-seven minutes, Scotland broke the deadlock, scoring the goal their play had merited. Bremner charged down Martin Peters just inside the Scotland half, winning a free kick from the England man as he raced away down the left. McCreadie tapped inside to Baxter who drove at the England defence. His attempted one-two with Wallace was well read by Moore but he could only divert the ball back into the path of the Celtic forward. His powerful shot was blocked by Banks but Law was there to pounce, lashing the rebound into the net.

'I scored a lot of goals for United that way because of Davie Herd and Bobby Charlton, both of whom had tremendous shots,' said Law. 'I always felt when they had a go there was a fair chance that, if the keeper saved, the ball would rebound because of the power. This time, it was Wallace shooting, Banks didn't get hold of it and it fell for me. In you go. One-nil.'

Wembley erupted as Law wheeled away, one hand in the air.

'It was like Hogmanay, Burns Night and the resurrection of Harry Lauder all rolled into one,' recalled Banks. 'The thousands of Scottish supporters wildly celebrated.'

Up in the commentary booth, Billy Wright added: 'It's been

coming, Hugh. Scotland have been the more impressive side, especially this Law. He has been a terrier this first half. He has worked and worked and worked and got his just reward. I think England are really up against it now.'

As play resumed, Brown's men looked to turn the screw on the shell-shocked world champions, Wallace flashing a left-footed effort just over the bar. With half an hour gone, Scotland could have been two or three goals to the good, and perfectly good value for it, too. Their front three of Law, Lennox and Wallace were causing the England defence all kinds of trouble whilst, at the back, Greig and McKinnon were breezing through the game.

Still, at 1–0, the game hinged on a knife-edge and the precariousness of Scotland's advantage was exposed in the thirty-fifth minute when an immobilised Jack Charlton headed straight at Simpson from ten yards out. He ought to have done better. A yard either side of the Celtic keeper and England would have been level, albeit very much against the run of play.

As half-time approached, Scotland pressed again for a second. Bremner slid a wonderfully weighted pass in behind the defence for Law that brought Banks sprinting out from off his line. He, Stiles and Law all slid in for the ball, leaving the Scottish forward and English goalie both needing treatment. Despite the pair's obvious distress, play raged on down to the other end of the pitch where Simpson sportingly kicked the ball out of play so that the increasingly busy trainers could come rushing on again.

It had been that kind of a first half. Physical, full-blooded, no holds barred. Even Wilson appeared to be carrying a knock following an earlier tackle by Bremner that Greaves subsequently described as 'later than a south-east commuter train'.

After a brief stoppage, both Banks and Law – and Wilson – were able to continue and the play resumed. Interestingly, England didn't return the ball to the Scots, Bobby Charlton preferring to throw to a teammate instead.

Lennox saw a right-footed effort diverted behind for another Scottish corner after excellent build-up play by McCalliog before the Charlton brothers combined again, Bobby crossing for Jack who was unable to direct his header on target.

Having added four minutes for stoppages, Schulenberg blew for half-time.

The world champions, nil; Scotland, one.

'England will have to do a lot to get to back into this game,' remarked Johns.

He wasn't wrong.

* * *

IT WASN'T JUST THE PROSPECT of losing to Scotland, giving up their British Home Championship crown, and conceding ground in the race for the 1968 European Championship that was on the line for England. So, too, was their proud, nineteen-game unbeaten streak. Avoid defeat at Wembley and they would also match their previous unbeaten record of twenty matches.

That had been set back in 1896. No prizes for guessing who ended it. In front of a new world-record attendance of more than 56,000, goals from William Lambie and Jack Bell gave the Scots a 2–1 victory at Celtic Park.

Almost three-quarters of a century later, the venue was different but the lightning bolt looked awfully similar. England were determined not to let it strike.

Just two minutes into the second half, they should have been level. Alan Ball, who had been virtually anonymous in the first half, gathered a pass from Moore on the left touchline. He cut inside Gemmell, danced into the box past Bremner and ghosted beyond a lunging Greig before firing the ball across goal to Jack Charlton on the six-yard line. His first-time effort cannoned back off McKinnon on the line and was prodded goalward again by Charlton.

'Oh yes, it must be . . .' exclaimed Johns.

No goal.

Simpson leapt across his goal, smothering the ball on the line. As play raged down the pitch, Charlton stood in the Scottish penalty area with his hands on his hips. He knew how big a moment that potentially was.

Spurned though it was, the chance seemed to give England renewed belief and, minutes later, Greaves forced Simpson into action once again with a fierce strike on the angle from just inside the box. It wouldn't have counted – he had been flagged for offside – but England appeared to have sparked into life. Suddenly, they seemed be dictating the tempo. They wanted the game played at a fast pace and on their terms. It suited them.

The trouble for Ramsey's men was that Jim Baxter knew it. He might have been a rogue but Slim Jim was no mug. If England wanted to play the game at great speed, well, he would just slow it right down, all the way to walking pace.

Every time he got the ball, the Sunderland midfielder created a yard of space and promptly sucked the intensity out of the game with a lackadaisical sideways pass, or casual flick. Not once did he give the ball away. With every blasé kick of the ball, Baxter made England suffer.

His teammates quickly fell in step. On fifty-five minutes, a low, hopeful cross from Cohen was gathered inside the Scotland penalty area by Greig and his pass to Baxter on the left set in motion a seventeen-pass sequence that had the English supporters inside Wembley audibly agitated.

Baxter, to Bremner, back to Baxter, to McCreadie, inside for McCalliog, to Baxter, back to McCalliog, to Baxter, back again to McCreadie, to Bremner, Baxter again, then McKinnon, all the way back to Simpson, who threw to Greig, out wide to

Gemmell, inside to Wallace. Finally, an England toe diverted the ball, but only as far as – who else – Baxter, whose pass down the left found Bremner. His flick into the box was screened by Stiles, whose clearance cannoned back off Bremner and into the arms of Banks. The whole sequence lasted one minute and fifteen seconds and left England exasperated, exhausted and chasing navy shadows. It was utterly masterful game management.

'England, the world champions, are being taunted by Scotland now,' observed Johns.

Sometime later, Baxter said: 'Deliberately, we kept the game on a razor's edge, staying that wee bit ahead on goals, stroking the ball about, everything designed to indicate that, if we felt like it, we would score a few more. It was so sweet in 1963 when I scored the two goals that gave us victory at Wembley but this was even better. The crowd was fantastic. They kept urging us on all the time. You can't beat a Scottish crowd – and that's why I made the ball talk.'

Despite their confident start to the second half, England found themselves being dictated to once again. In particular, the Scottish full-backs – Gemmell and McCreadie – seemed to be marauding up and down their respective flanks with ease, forcing opposite numbers Wilson and Cohen into a greater degree of defensive duty than either had become accustomed to.

Around the hour mark, the hosts started to accelerate back through the gears and pressed to get back on terms. Bobby Charlton had a shot headed behind for a corner by Baxter. Peters glanced a header over the bar from a Cohen cross. Jack Charlton headed goalward from a Peters cross that Greig cleared off the line. From the corner that followed, Cohen dragged a powerful effort wide of the goal.

Back came Scotland. McCreadie connected sweetly with a right-footed strike from just outside the box after great work by Law on the England right, but the ball whistled past Banks' far post. Lennox and McCalliog then won quick-fire corners as the visitors looked to reimpose themselves on the game.

The ebbs and flows suited the visitors more. Every loose ball seemed to fall to a Scottish boot and, before long, England's frustrations started to show. With seventy minutes on the clock, McCalliog received the ball on the left touchline. As he darted forwards, he was hunted down by Ball, who scythed the Sheffield Wednesday man down as he cut inside. Free kick to Scotland. Minutes later, Ball obstructed Bremner as the Leeds man looked to drive into the box from the left byline. The away supporters howled their derision and chanted 'Off! Off! Off!' as the German official sprinted over to the England man. Schulenberg held up one finger on hand and pointed to the dugout with the other. The message was clear: *one more of those and you'll be off.*

Ball wasn't the only England player getting frustrated. Starved of service, the ineffective Greaves started to drop deeper and deeper looking to get involved, whilst Jack Charlton was, by this point, virtually static.

With just under fifteen minutes to go, Hurst had a fierce shot blocked at close range by the cat-like Simpson after Peters' deflected effort fell at his feet.

Scotland's response? To go down the other end and score a second.

After Law won a free kick thirty-five yards from goal, Baxter played a sideways pass towards the onrushing Gemmell. His ferocious, long-range strike was headed back towards the Celtic man by Moore. Gemmell nodded the ball back down to Wallace on the edge of the penalty area who let the ball run beyond him, wrong-footing the English defence. The ball fell to Lennox just inside the area and he swept a fierce first-time strike low to Banks' left and into the corner of the net.

Two-nil to Scotland.

Lennox later described the moment. 'I knew as soon as I hit

it that the ball was sweeping away from Banks,' he said. 'There was such a feeling of delight to see it hurtle low into the corner of the English net.

'As soon as the ball went in, I thought about how delighted my dad would be. I didn't know that if I had kept on running after scoring the goal, I would have ended up beside him in the stands. I wish I had done exactly that.'

As it was, Lennox – the first-ever Celtic player to score against England at Wembley – jumped into the arms of Baxter. Wallace was next on the scene, followed by Bremner and Law. McCreadie sprinted forty yards to jump on top of his teammates. McKinnon, Greig, Gemmell and McCalliog soon joined in, too. The togetherness of the squad that Brown had spoken about at length in the build-up to the game was there for all to see in that moment.

With twelve minutes to go, Scotland were on the brink of victory.

'That's the one that's put in the nail,' said Billy Wright on commentary. The Scottish supporters all around the stadium started to chant 'Easy! Easy! Easy!'

Cue Baxter.

With his socks now around his ankles, he insouciantly poked passes towards teammates, prompting Johns to remark: 'Scotland are slowing it down, taking the mickey out of this England side.'

Little did he know what was about to follow. With the clock showing eighty-three minutes, McCreadie won the ball back on the left touchline and simply left it there, walking away as Law ran over to collect. The Manchester United man slid a pass down the line to McCalliog, who, as he had been doing all game, cut inside before casually backheeling the ball back to Law. Walking towards the England goal – *walking* – Law then backheeled it himself to Baxter.

Under absolutely no pressure from the English players, he flicked the ball up and juggled it once, twice, three times, four on his wand of a left foot before trapping it under his boot and killing it stone dead as an exhausted Cohen looked on, powerless. With one slick movement, Baxter then slid his foot under the ball and lifted it in behind Cohen, Stiles and Bobby Charlton towards Law. His cut-back finally richoted into the arms of Banks but hardly anybody noticed. They were all struck dumb by Baxter's gallus gambolling.

It required many things to pull that off. Arrogance, swagger, confidence, belief, not to mention a ton of talent. And what a stage to do it on; the same pitch where the same opponents had been crowned the best in the world just nine months earlier. Baxter had hated that and so this was his payback. From Scotland, with love.

Not that everybody saw the funny side. In the dugout, Bobby Brown fumed at his star man's nonchalance and confronted him about it afterwards. He had wanted goals, not to make a fool of Ramsey's men. Baxter saw it differently.

'Why didn't we bury the English under an avalanche of goals?' he later remarked. 'We could have done. No bother. But the choice was ours. By that, I mean the choice was down to Bremner, Law and myself. Naturally, I've had lots of arguments since, with people who didn't like the way we took the mickey. I don't think they understood, I really don't.

'A team and a country can forget big scores against them. Such things can happen if one side has an off-day and the other a good day, or if there's an unusual element of luck.

'Our aim was to show England how easily we could beat them. We wanted to give them no excuses. We wanted the Scottish punters to laugh at the English as well as to enthuse over victory and that's exactly what happened.'

What history hasn't recorded as clearly is the fact that, within a minute of Baxter's infamous ball-juggling, England pulled a goal back. Bobby Charlton surged forward, playing the ball into the feet of Greaves just inside the Scottish half. He knocked it wide to Ball, who played it back into Greaves and then ran in behind Greig to latch on to the Tottenham man's clever flick. As Simpson came rushing, the England youngster prodded the ball across the six-yard line where Jack Charlton was waiting to fire into an open goal.

As the English supporters rejoiced for the first time all game, Charlton limped heavily back to the halfway line.

Game on.

Shocked into life, Scotland went seeking a third goal to restore their two-goal advantage and surely kill the game off. Law drew an acrobatic save from Banks after trying to chip the English goalie from the edge of the area. Moments later, Law again tested the Leicester City shot-stopper, this time with a fierce low strike from just inside the area.

It was in the eighty-eighth minute of the game that Jim McCalliog – outstanding in the heart of the pitch alongside Bremner and Baxter – fully repaid the faith Brown had shown by picking him.

Jimmy Greaves poked a pass towards Jack Charlton but Bremner reacted sharply to intercept and . . . well, let's allow McCalliog to explain it, shall we?

'So, I was in the centre of midfield and my job really was to get the ball off our defenders, back up the forwards and, if I got a chance, get a shot at goal. Anyway, I could see Billy breaking with the ball on the left-hand side. When Leeds were winning towards the end of a game, they would keep the ball and run the clock down like they do in rugby. So, Billy went in the corner with the ball and I thought, well, that's Billy doing what he does naturally at Leeds – but me being me, I was still looking for an opportunity to go forward.

'That's when I saw Bobby Lennox go to support him and I thought I would just go down there as well on the sneak. I started moving and Billy put it to Bobby and, as Bobby got the ball, I was running in behind. Bobby saw me, squared it to me and, as I took the ball, I turned a wee bit to the right and played a one-two off Willie Wallace.

'Suddenly, I was in front of goal. I could see Bobby Moore coming across in an attempt to block me, and I could see Gordon Banks, and in that split-second, I steadied myself.

'I thought, "Just hit it as hard as you can into the bottom corner." And that's what I did.'

Three-one.

'I veered to the left because I knew my dad was up that side of the stand. I don't know where exactly he was but I just had this urge to run towards him. As I turned back around, the first person running towards me was Denis. We just grabbed each other and – ach, it was so special. Denis had been my hero growing up and here we were, celebrating together at Wembley.'

Sitting in his home in Ayrshire, the walls adorned by pictures of his career's exploits, McCalliog's eyes well up at the memory and his voice trembles.

'Brilliant,' he says softly. 'Memories to last a lifetime.'

In the commentary booth, as the Scotland fans again burst into a deafening refrain of 'Easy! Easy!', Billy Wright watched it all with a smile. 'I bet that young man feels like a king today,' he added.

Incredibly, England weren't quite done yet. For almost the first time in the entire game, Baxter misplaced a pass in the midfield, which was pounced upon by Stiles. He knocked it outside to his Manchester United teammate Bobby Charlton, who floated a cross into the box that Hurst met on the six-yard line, flashing a header back across Simpson and into the corner of the net.

Three-two.

Ninety seconds to go. They couldn't, could they?

A breathless Wright struggled to summon the words to

describe what was unfolding. 'What a game,' he gasped. 'What a brilliant, entertaining game. It's had everything. It's the best game of football I've seen between these two sides for many a long time.'

As he spoke, play raged on. The Scottish supporters' cheers had given way to whistles, encouraging the referee to bring proceedings to an end but still England came forward. Gemmell booted the ball clear. As Moore tried to return it, Wallace blocked his clearance, steadied himself and fired a speculative strike from distance that cannoned back off the bar. But wait. The referee had given handball against the Celtic man. One last chance for England.

Moore. To Stiles. Back to Moore, just inside the England half. The captain took a touch to steady himself before launching a long, high, hopeful ball into the box in the direction of Jack Charlton. The Leeds man stretched, desperately trying to nod the ball into the path of Hurst or Greaves or anybody in white, but the ball was just beyond his reach. It travelled through to Gemmell on the six-yard line, who thumped it upfield and out of play close to the halfway line.

As the ball sailed across the touchline, Herr Schulenberg brought his whistle to his mouth and blew for full time.

'It's all over,' shouted Johns, his commentary barely audible over the tumultuous roar of the triumphant Tartan Army. 'The game is over. The world champions have been beaten here at Wembley by a fine, fighting Scottish side.'

England 2, Scotland 3.

Pandemonium ensued.

* * *

A LITTLE OVER 400 MILES NORTH OF WEMBLEY STADIUM, James and Georgina Brown were walking along the banks of the River Teith in the picturesque Stirlingshire town of Callander. James had been too anxious to travel to London to watch son Bobby take charge of his national team for the first time. Even listening to it on the wireless was more than his shot nerves could handle. So, to kill time, he went out for a walk.

A little after quarter to five, the tranquillity of the crisp spring evening was shattered by a sudden symphony of car horns, their shrill notes bending in the air.

There was no mistaking the meaning behind those triumphant toots. It was the news that Mr and Mrs Brown had been longing for.

Their boy had beaten Sir Alf at his own game.

Scotland had won.

TWENTY-FOUR

SOME PEOPLE ARE ON THE PITCH

BOBBY CHARLTON TOOK A DEEP BREATH and let out a huge sigh. Losing was one thing. But losing to Scotland? At Wembley? Less than a year after winning the World Cup? *At Wembley?* That was tough to take.

'My thoughts instantly turned to what the reaction would be of Denis Law and Paddy Crerand when I arrived back at Old Trafford,' he recalled, 'and how a reigning world champion would be told, in the briskest of terms, that he had lost his bragging rights.'

Touché.

Charlton's despair and that of his teammates was in stark contrast to the jubilant scenes amongst the Scots. Ronnie Simpson, the auld rookie of the team, looked up as the whistle blew to see his fellow debutant Jim McCalliog running towards him.

'He seemed absolutely thrilled by it all and hugged me as though he intended to burst my ribs,' said Simpson. 'The game to me had been all too short. It seemed to finish in no time, which meant that it was an enjoyable one.'

As the national anthem played, Simpson shook hands with his opposite number Banks.

'I didn't swap jerseys with him, though,' recalled the Scot. 'This was my first international jersey and, at my age, it could very well have been the last.'

Nobby Stiles sought out Scotland captain John Greig. 'Well done, John,' he told him. 'Scotland played much better than any of us thought you could play. That's why you beat us.'

That confirmed Greig's suspicion: that England had massively underrated them. He later said: 'On the surface, we had absolutely no reason to feel confident about our chances but we had a couple of points in our favour. Firstly, we had considered ourselves unfortunate not to qualify for the World Cup finals the previous year and we were desperate to make a point. Secondly, we got a huge lift from playing the world champions. But there was a third highly significant reason for Scotland's victory – the England players were far too bloody cocky.'

He added: 'I had positive vibes going into the game. I had a feeling that we were going to cause a real upset. I couldn't explain it. Captaining Scotland that day was the highlight of my international career. To have the honour to skipper a team containing players of the skills and craft of Baxter and Law was a big deal in its own right but to do so on an afternoon when history was made was extra special.'

In the dugouts, Ramsey went over to Brown and shook his hand. 'Well done,' he said grimly. 'You played very well today.' With that, he turned and disappeared up the tunnel and out of view, his poor personal run against Scotland extended.

Whilst the England boss was desperate to get away from the pitch, Scottish supporters were sprinting onto it.

'It was bedlam,' acknowledged Banks. 'Scottish supporters poured on to the pitch, many producing penknives to take a chunk of the Wembley pitch back home with them as a souvenir.

The turf was left pitted and scarred as dozens of ecstatic Scotsmen carved it to pieces.'

One supporter stuffed a bundle of notes and coins into Law's hands. 'Get the boys a drink tonight, Denis,' he told him. 'They've earned it.'

Another fan swept Willie Wallace, a standout performer in place of Jimmy Johnstone, clean off his feet. 'He shouted into my ear, "How are you, Wongo?"' recalled the Celt. 'That was my old nickname from school. As I cast a glance around at him, I realised it was Alex Kilpatrick, an old pal who had moved to London. He crushed me in a huge bear hug, dropped me to the ground, yelled, "Well done!" and disappeared away into the crowd.'

The scenes were of unbridled joy. Supporters danced, hugged, sang, screamed and generally acted with complete spontaneity. Finally, mounted police had to be called in more than half an hour after the full-time whistle had blown to move the jubilant masses along.

Safely back in their changing room, the Scots were free to start celebrating in earnest. This was more than a win. It was a triumph that lifted an entire nation, a victory that transcended sport. David had conquered Goliath before, but not when Goliath was standing at the top of Everest. This felt different. This *was* different.

Bobby Brown congratulated each of his players individually. Beaming SFA officials, led by Hugh Nelson, joined the festivities.

Law made a beeline for Brown. 'Congratulations boss,' he told him. 'You've got off to a great start.' Nobody knew it then, of course, but this was the first and last time these eleven Scottish heroes would play together.

The euphoria in the visitors' quarters was in stark contrast to the dejection that filled the English changing room. For Geoff Hurst, Martin Peters and Alan Ball, it was a first-ever defeat in an England shirt. For Jack Charlton, Nobby Stiles and George Cohen, it was a first-ever defeat at the hands of Scotland. Nine months earlier, they had taken the World Cup trophy back to this very space and passed it around, congratulating each other and revelling in the greatest day of their careers. How foreign those memories suddenly felt.

'The English dressing room was a sombre place after the game,' admitted Bobby Charlton. 'We'd done all we could, and despite the Scottish cries of jubilation, we still believed we were champions of the world. But nobody needed to tell us that some desperate months lay ahead. I remember thinking as I walked off the field, and the goalposts were disappearing beneath a Scottish swarm, "Oh my God, we are the world champions but now face a year of hell."'

Bobby Lennox witnessed the funeral scenes first-hand. 'After the final whistle, I approached Jimmy Greaves,' he explained. 'I was a great admirer of him and I asked him if I could swap shirts with him. He said that would be fine but we would have to do it inside, not out on the pitch. So, after a few celebrations with our players, I headed for the English dressing room and was greeted by absolute silence. Their players were sitting stunned, heads bowed and down.

'People can say what they like about the game mattering more to one side than the other but when Scotland and England collide, the ground rumbles. It's not a wee kiddie-on affair.'

Lennox and Greaves made their exchange and the Scot returned to the party next door.

Goalkeeper Banks recalled one particularly memorable scene as the despondent English players returned to their hotel.

'As the team coach left Wembley, our police motorcycle escort had to pull up at a crossroads. There was a pub on one corner and outside were hundreds of Scottish supporters toasting their team's victory. They saw our coach and, perhaps befuddled by copious amounts of alcohol, at first took us for the Scotland team. Glasses were raised and bonnets thrown into the air. There were cries of 'well done' and 'great performance'.

'Anyway, Alan Ball stood up to acknowledge their good wishes and suddenly it dawned on them who we were. I'd never seen Alan move so quickly. Pint glasses, pies and bottles crashed against the side of the coach. Our driver, throwing caution to the wind, put his foot down and shot across those crossroads with a bevy of tartan-clad supporters in hot pursuit.

'I was left trying not to think about what their reaction would have been if England had won.'

TWENTY-FIVE

THE OLD JOCK AND HAGGIS BIT

AFTER A QUICK CHANGE OF CLOTHES back at the team hotel, the Scots travelled into central London for a post-match reception at the Café Royal on Regent Street where they were joined by several members of the English side. It didn't take long for the celebrations – and the gloating – to begin.

'Any thoughts I had of the Scottish players being gracious in victory and appreciative of our efforts were immediately dispelled by Denis Law at the post-match buffet,' recalled Gordon Banks.

Jimmy Greaves takes up the story.

'Denis called Gordon over to where he was standing with Jim Baxter, Jim McCalliog, Billy Bremner and Ron McKinnon. "Gordon, we need your help," he said. "Can you answer a question that's stumped us?" Gordon said he'd try. "England are world champions," said Denis. "But we have just beaten you, so does that mean Scotland are the world champions now?" Needless to say, the Scots lads immediately fell about roaring with laughter.'

Banks, to his credit, saw the funny side, but only just. 'To the side of Denis was a large bowl of mayonnaise,' he said. 'I resisted the temptation.'

Another Scot, Tottenham Hotspur left-half Dave Mackay, showed up with some family and friends from Edinburgh who had been at the match. They covered their table with a large square of turf cut from the Wembley pitch.

As his players basked in their win and the drink started to flow – poor Bobby Lennox bleeding through his bandages and ruining his suit trousers – Brown tried to engage his opposite number Ramsey in conversation. Easier said than done. 'He was hard to warm to,' Brown later admitted. 'He didn't open up. It was as if it was costing him pounds each time he opened his mouth.'

Conceding defeat for the first and only time that day, the Scotland boss stepped outside for some fresh air. As he stood outside the doors of the hotel, a man was staggering towards him. The lop-sided tartan bunnet on his head gave away his allegiance and he was singing loudly to himself. He had evidently had a good day that he was almost certainly going to suffer for tomorrow.

As he shuffled past the well-dressed Brown, he gave him a sideways glance before stopping in his tracks, wheeling round, and jabbing a finger in the chest of the Scotland boss. 'See you,' he slurred. 'Scotland three, England two. We beat you easily today and don't you ever forget it!' With that, he wobbled away, oblivious to the fact he'd just met the mastermind of a day he'd struggle to remember.

Eager to keep the party going, the Scots players left the Café Royal and headed to a backstage theatre party in the West End where they rubbed shoulders with other big-name guests, such as comedian Frankie Howerd and singer Cilla Black.

They didn't stay long.

'Cilla, whom I never rated much as a singer, started to patronise us in that Scouse accent of hers,' said Baxter. 'It was the old "Jock" and "haggis" bit. She even had the nerve to suggest that Scotland had been lucky to win at Wembley that day.

'Well, that was too much for Billy Bremner. First, he compared her very unfavourably with Dusty Springfield. Then, he expressed astonishment that Cilla, with such a face, had ever managed to get into showbiz at all.'

More than fifty years after the fact, the encounter still makes Willie Wallace chuckle. 'Cilla took umbrage to those remarks,' he recalled, 'and we were all asked to leave.'

Unfazed, they moved on to the Astor Club where they met up with an old friend of the Scotland team, an Edinburgh businessman called Peter Williamson. He organised drinks for the players away from the bedlam that was steadily unfolding in the streets of the capital.

Wallace can't be sure but he thinks it was a good night.

'Aye,' he laughed, 'I'm afraid I don't remember much after the first hour.'

It's doubtful many of a Scottish persuasion could. Long into the night, fans laid jubilant siege to some of the capital's proudest landmarks, pouring out of underground stations at regular intervals, clanging bells and shaking rattles. Piccadilly Circus was ambushed by supporters chanting 'Sir Alf is on the dole!', 'England stole the cup!' and 'we all live in a tartan submarine'. The statue of Eros was fenced off for its own protection. The two fountains in Trafalgar Square were drained and their water supply turned off to prevent people from jumping in. At Euston Station, pieces of turf ripped from the Wembley pitch sold for several shillings a time. Even when the pubs shut at half past ten, the carnival atmosphere continued and carry-outs were shared.

From their Scotland Yard headquarters, the Metropolitan Police increased the number of officers on patrol that night out of an abundance of caution but they needn't have bothered. Reporting no major incidents, a spokesperson for the Met said: 'They're all too happy to cause any trouble.'

As the champagne flowed, reporters composed dispatches for their respective newspapers. To say the London-based media didn't take kindly to Scotland humbling their all-conquering, world champion hosts would be massively understating it.

Writing in the *Daily Telegraph*, Donald Saunders claimed that 'Scotland did not win a great victory, nor have they yet a great team. Spirit and individual skill allowed them to defeat players who had given too much of themselves last summer to be able to meet the less testing demands made on them nine months later.'

The *Daily Mail* went even further. 'The truth is this,' screamed the match report in its English edition. 'In two years, Scottish footballers have learned how to beat eight fit men, for in 1965 they could only draw against nine. Scotland have beaten England who are world champions, but the win does not give them the crown.'

Even the Manchester media corps struggled to muster much dignity in defeat. In his report for the *Daily Sketch* – the populist, Conservative-leaning tabloid which closed and merged with the *Daily Mail* in 1971 – Billy Liddell wrote: 'Keep the head. That's my message this morning to the football fans of Scotland who are still gloating.'

Others saw it differently. In *The People* newspaper, Joe Hulme savaged Alf Ramsey's team selection. 'A crippled and a creaking defence is never enough to pit against Scotland,' he lamented. 'That's the sad tale of Wembley. Jimmy Greaves made three fluffs in the first three minutes, and that was a start his temperament just couldn't handle.

'Poor Roger Hunt, the man deposed, must have wondered what is expected of him, for he has been in form, whereas Martin Peters, who kept his place, has not. That selection was a major blunder, for Peters was one of the weakest links in this fumbling England set-up.'

Hulme's colleague Maurice Smith described England's performance as 'pathetic by any standard', adding: 'Despite Sir Alf's excuses, I could never see England winning.'

The disposition leaping of the page of the Scottish newspapers was decidedly sunnier. The Glasgow-based *Evening Times* declared Bobby Brown's men 'GREAT SCOTS!' in its on-the-whistle, Saturday-evening edition. The following day, the *Sunday Mail* hailed the victory under the front-page headline 'SUPERMACS!' Hugh Taylor, the *Daily Record*'s long-standing and acclaimed football correspondent, urged supporters to salute the 'MASTERS OF WEMBLEY'.

'Scotland were magnificent,' he wrote, 'contemptuously humiliating the once-proud world champions. Their football was superb at times. And they had what England have never shown, even when they were winning the World Cup – real artistry, real ball workers, stars who can combine old-fashioned fantasy with relentless method. Even more important, Scotland revealed a style that will go a long way in helping us win the World Cup in 1970.'

In his match report for the *Aberdeen Evening Express*, Norman Macdonald wrote: 'This was Scotland's finest hour and a half. This was a team of whom all Scotland could justly be proud. The Scots were the more accomplished side, and they should have won by a more emphatic margin. What a blow it will be for England if, as reigning world champions, they fail to enter Europe.'

The *Sunday Post*'s Jack Harkness pulled no punches in his own assessment. 'Maybe this wasn't the greatest Scotland team ever to tread the Wembley turf,' he began. 'But it was certainly great enough to make chumps out of the World Cup champs. It can be said that England lost the services of Jackie Charlton who, after an absence of fifteen minutes, was a limping giant for most of the game. But this English team seemed to accept that as an excuse for defeat, instead of a reason to fight all the harder. The "champions of the world" label should have been backed by sterner stuff than we saw here.'

Harkness added that the Scots had 'an obvious will to win that England lacked' and demonstrated 'far more enterprise in their ranks'.

His *Sunday Post* colleague Ken Holmes offered an English perspective in the Scottish press. 'England were well beaten by a Scots side that came to Wembley very much the underdogs and caught the world champions in anything but champion mood,' he noted. 'For me, Scotland dominated almost the entire ninety minutes. Gone was the teamwork so vital to England's winning the World Cup. Instead of slick movements, the England attack was limited to bursts from individual players. Mostly Bobby Charlton, sometimes Alan Ball, occasionally Jimmy Greaves and Geoff Hurst. All famous names but reduced to a set of pretty punchless individuals by the quick tackling of the Scottish defence.'

Emotions ran high, fur flew and typewriters bore the brunt. The man with the coolest head? Scotland coach Bobby Brown.

'Things went exactly as I wanted them to,' he stated. 'I wanted the team to get control in the middle of the field, and we did that. I wanted them to play on their right back as much as possible, and they did that, too.

'The team co-operated magnificently. Everyone did a wonderful job. Everybody did exactly as he was told to and that pleases me just as much as the victory. I always felt that we could win and now we've done it.'

He added: 'The result is doubly important because by winning at Wembley we are in with a very good chance of qualifying for the later stages of the European Nations Cup. I've always felt that a place in the Nations Cup is vital in the build-up to the World Cup in Mexico in 1970. Perhaps the team slackened a little because they were so much in control, but that mistake won't be made again.

'We still have to achieve consistency to prove ourselves in the soccer land. But for the moment, London belongs to us.'

TWENTY-SIX

A CAT CALLED 'WEMBLEY'

THE SEISMIC PROPORTIONS OF SCOTLAND'S VICTORY – not to mention the celebrations – continued long into a new week.

The day after the game, for example, Celtic quartet Wallace, Gemmell, Lennox and Simpson flew home to Glasgow along with Bremner. Once word of their imminent arrival got out, excitement spread rapidly through the terminal and, as the players disembarked their plane, they found outgoing passengers, airport staff and others in the arrival hall lining balconies and corridors to cheer for them. It was a reception befitting of heroes.

After bidding farewell to his teammates, Lennox travelled back home to Saltcoats by train. 'I wandered up the road to my mum and dad's house with my bag over my shoulder and my boots under my arm,' he recalled. 'Unofficial world champions or not, normal life had to continue.' When he arrived, there was a surprise waiting for him. His fiancée Kathryn had been so convinced that Bobby and co. would win that she put £1 on Scotland to win – her first-ever bet. She used the winnings to go out and buy a little black kitten. 'It turned out lucky,' laughed Lennox. They called it 'Wembley'.

Gemmell's experience was somewhat different. From the airport, he limped straight to Parkhead for treatment on his spoils of war, an ankle injury sustained early in the game. He was lying, in fact, on the opposite side of the touchline, receiving attention from trainer Walter McCrae, when Law opened the scoring. 'It was the best injury of my life,' he grinned. Still, he had just cause for wanting to recover for the midweek visit of Aberdeen. Not only was it a vital match in determining the outcome of the league title, Gemmell was on a remarkable run of playing in over 130 consecutive matches for Celtic. It had been exactly two years – 17 April 1965 – since his name had been absent from the Hoops' teamsheet and he was in no mood for that streak to end. Bob Rooney, Celtic's physio, was put straight to work on the star full-back's niggle.

Wallace returned home to Abbotsinch, where his wife Olive and baby daughter Lynn were waiting for him, while Simpson discovered an enormous pile of telegrams waiting for him at his house in Glasgow.

John Greig and Ron McKinnon remained in London. Rangers were due to travel to Bulgaria on the Monday morning to play Slavia Sofia in the semis of the European Cup Winners' Cup, so they arranged to join up with their Ibrox teammates at Heathrow. That allowed Greig to accept an invitation to appear on the *Eamonn Andrews Show* the day after the game. Also on the show that night were crime writer Mickey Spillane and an up-and-coming Welsh singer called Tom Jones.

'The show was recorded in the afternoon and broadcast a few hours later,' recalled Greig. 'When I returned to the hotel where we were staying, the manager invited me to watch the recording in his office and treated me to a bottle of champagne on the house.' That, maybe unsurprisingly, wasn't the first drink he'd availed himself of that day. 'Shortly after a late breakfast, Denis Law and I had visited a nearby pub after Denis expressed a desire for a pint of shandy. He had a habit of wearing polo neck sweaters and, on this occasion, his maroon number made him look like a member of the Salvation Army. One thing was for sure: the barman didn't have a clue who we were.

'The pub was empty at that time on a Sunday and when the barman heard us speak and recognised our accents, he asked if we had been at the game. "Yes," I replied, "but that fellow Law is seriously overrated." The barman totally agreed with me. You should have seen his face when I pointed to Denis – now spluttering with indignation – and said, "Anyway, I'd like you to meet Denis Law."'

Praise rained down on the Scots from near and far. Former national team captain George Young, who had been at Wembley, called Bobby Brown's men 'as good a post-War team as has represented Scotland', adding: 'They were superior to anything England met in the World Cup last July.'

Brazilian officials, meanwhile, wasted no time in extending an invitation to the team to visit in the build-up to the 1970 World Cup in Mexico. The two countries had formed a deep bond following the South Americans' visit to Hampden in 1966, prompting Fred Pullen, Brazil's UK delegate, to send a telegram of congratulations to SFA secretary Willie Allan.

'Scotland's prestige is very high in Brazil,' added Pullen. 'The football fans in our country were thrilled to read about the Wembley triumph. With the next World Cup being played in Mexico, it would be a great chance for Scotland to warm up in a similar atmosphere. This could be arranged either next year or the following.'

The Scots' stock wasn't necessarily as high back in Blighty. Four supporters went before magistrates in Marylebone on the Monday after the game charged with causing bodily harm to a police officer. Two others were brought to Bow Street Court, one charged with theft, the other accused of assault.

As for the Wembley ground staff, they were faced with the mother of all clean-up operations. They returned to work to discover a pitch pock-marked with divots and a twelve-inch hole where the centre circle used to be. 'On Saturday, Wembley belonged to the Scots,' said a spokesperson. 'We just wish they hadn't tried to take it home with them.'

As the clean-up began, so too did an enquiry into how so many fans had been able to pour onto the pitch. That, apparently, was nothing to do with the fact that officials had mobilised only 600 police officers for the match – roughly one per every 165 supporters inside the ground – and was, instead, entirely the fault of the Scottish players for not taking a lap of honour.

'If they had given their supporters a chance to acclaim them, there would have been no trouble,' said a Wembley spokesperson. 'But they went straight off after the national anthem and their supporters had to find some way of letting off steam.' Translation: *Granted, this isn't much of a straw but excuse us whilst we clutch at it.*

Such shenanigans and bellyaching, of course, were none of Bobby Brown's concern. On the Monday after the game, he visited the SFA headquarters in Glasgow for a debrief, after which he and some of the officials went out for lunch. When it came time to settle the bill, the restaurant manager wandered over to the table open-handed. 'Mr Brown,' he insisted, 'you don't need to pay. This is on the house.'

SFA president Hugh Nelson issued a statement in which he lavished praise upon the new national coach. 'Bobby Brown,' he wrote, 'deserves the fullest recognition every Scot can give him. The Wembley win was his. He chose the team. He worked out the tactics. He put them over to the players. He kept us informed every step he took. He deserves all the credit he can get.'

Whilst sincere, nobody could have begrudged the SFA at least a little grandstanding. Their decision to give such a high-profile position to such a low-profile individual had been a risk. A calculated one, no doubt. But a risk all the same. As one reporter put it, 'The situation called for a Matt Busby or a Jock Stein to put us firmly on our feet. But we got Brown, an unsung, everyday boss from provincial St Johnstone, inexperienced in international football, except for his own games in goal years ago, and with little knowledge of Continental tactics, and world-class soccer.'

It was precisely because he was so apparently unqualified for the job that Brown was the most qualified candidate. He took to the position with no great aura, no particular track record to speak of and, crucially, no ego. There was enough of those on the pitch. Baxter, Bremner, Law, and the like. The last thing Scotland needed was another one in the dugout.

He hadn't tried to impose or impress his will upon the players. Instead, he imbued them with something that most of them hadn't been accustomed to on international duty: trust. The eleven men who tore up Wembley in a figurative sense – leaving the literal for their jubilant supporters – walked onto the pitch knowing that their manager had chosen them because he believed they were best placed to deliver the win. The tortuous interference of scheming committees, each member of whom had their own thoughts, ideas and agendas to pursue, had been consigned, at least for now, when it mattered the most, to the past. The responsibility, instead, passed to a man who quietly and meticulously studied every eligible player he could find in order to assemble a team capable of conquering their apparently invincible hosts.

In finding a way to not just accommodate but accentuate the abilities of both Baxter and Law in particular, Brown had solved a puzzle that had befuddled those who had gone before him. He proved that Scotland could – and should – indulge capricious, mesmeric talents, complementing genius and all its ancillary flaws with honest, rudimental industry elsewhere on the team sheet. For instance, nobody would ever have confused big Ron McKinnon or Eddie McCreadie for the most skilful players on the planet, but it was because their pragmatic, pugnacious 'yin' was capable of co-existing with Law and Baxter's more elegant, flamboyant 'yang' that Brown's side had a balance seldom before seen in navy blue.

He had resisted calls to sideline the Anglos in favour of home-based internationals, insisting: 'I would have picked eleven Anglos if I thought they were the best eleven players available to Scotland. I was guided by only two things – a player's birthplace and whether or not I considered him the best man for the job.'

He had gambled, too. Ronnie Simpson and Jim McCalliog were surprise inclusions in the starting XI. Calling up Willie Wallace at not so much the eleventh hour as a minute to midnight, then thrusting him straight into the team at the expense of travelling reserve Stevie Chalmers was another canny roll of the dice. To some onlookers, they were unnecessary risks. To the only man whose opinion mattered, they were all part of the plan. He made big calls, little calls, bold calls, brave calls, shock calls and more. And, in the end, his comprehensive diligence paid off handsomely. Doubters, be damned. Bobby Brown had out-Ramsey'd Ramsey and Scotland had won.

'We had a team that started well, went on to dominate the game, and never seemed to be in danger of losing,' he acknowledged. 'Baxter and Law fitted in wonderfully. It was one of my best moments when, at the end of the game, Law raced fifteen yards to say, "Well done, boss, a wonderful start." Every single player did his bit. Without doubt, it was the best managerial debut I could have been given.'

There was, however, space for some caution up on cloud nine.

'One win doesn't make us the greatest ever,' added Brown. 'That's why we didn't allow the players to do a lap of honour at the finish. Our aim now is to achieve consistency in winning.'

He was right, of course. Scotland had won nothing other than one ninety-minute match, a reductive way of describing it as that might be. There was a bigger prize at stake. At the midway point in qualifying for the European Nations Cup, Brown's men were perfectly poised to make it to Italy. They held their fate in their own hands. All they had to do was keep on winning.

Aye. Easier said than done.

TWENTY-SEVEN

GLORIOUS FAILURE

IT'S A TALE AS OLD AS TIME, pride coming before a fall. The history of Scottish sport is pockmarked with such chastenings. They have occurred with such startling regularity, in fact, that they have even been stitched into the fabric of the national football team and given a macabre, tragicomic identity.

Glorious failure.

Some insist this absurd affectation derives from the Scots' gallows interpretation of Rudyard Kipling's 19th-century advice to 'meet with triumph and disaster and treat those two impostors just the same'. Or is it Monty Python's 1980s guidance to 'always look on the bright side of life'? Perhaps it's true what they say, maybe it really is better to laugh than to cry?

Whatever the true genesis of this cultural phenomenon, Scottish football supporters have had countless opportunities to perfect their self-effacing schtick, starting, some say, with the sequence of events that followed the 3–2 win at Wembley.

Less than a month after that absorbing victory, Bobby Brown's men hosted the Soviet Union at Hampden Park in a friendly. It was the first-ever meeting between the two sides and most Scots were confident it would end well for their men. Sure, the Soviets had an abundance of star names within their ranks, not least their talismanic goalkeeper Lev Yashin, the so-called 'Black Spider'. There was, though, an intensifying sentiment that this particular Soviet side had peaked with victory in the inaugural European Nations Cup back in 1960. Since then, they'd lost in the quarters of the 1962 World Cup, been beaten in the final of the 1964 Euros and finished fourth in the 1966 World Cup, losing in the semis to West Germany before going down to Portugal in the consolation match. Okay, so they were a force but not the force they were. And Scotland? Scotland had just beaten the world champions. Humiliated them. Toyed with them. Could have put four, five or even six past them if they'd really wanted to. Even without the services of any of Rangers players – the Glasgow side taking John Greig and Ronnie McKinnon on a tour of Canada – what did they have to fear from the men from Moscow?

Pride.

With six minutes played, Tommy Gemmell misjudged a back-pass to the advancing Ronnie Simpson to gift the visitors the lead. Shortly before half-time, Ferenc Medved doubled the advantage, his curling effort from the edge of the penalty area bending beyond the reach of an outstretched Simpson and in off the underside of the bar. The match finished 2–0.

Fall.

A week later, Scotland embarked on an overseas tour that went some way to kick-starting the nation's feelgood factor. A 2–1 win over Israel – Alex Ferguson scoring the winner, no less – was followed by a hat-trick of victories over Australia, before a 7–2 thrashing of Canada brought the curtain down on a confidence-inspiring few months of globetrotting. Five wins. Fourteen goals scored. Four conceded. Good times. That Soviet result must just have been a fluke, eh?

Pride.

With the summer fun over, it was back to the serious business of the British Home Championship and, more specifically, European Championship qualifying.

The 3–2 victory over England in April had put Bobby Brown's men in a commanding position to qualify for the 1968 tournament in Italy. After the first round of matches, they had won two and drawn one, scoring six and conceding four. The five points they'd accrued put them top of the group, one clear of England, with Wales third and Northern Ireland propping up the standings. The latter, in fact, had managed only one goal in their three games courtesy of Jimmy Nicholson's early opener in the match with Scotland at Hampden in November 1966.

They got their second – and only other – goal of the qualifiers in their opening match of the 1967/68 British Home Championships in October 1967.

Guess who they scored it against . . .

With twenty minutes left in the match at Windsor Park in Belfast, Coventry City's Dave Clements pounced on a defensive blunder in the Scottish box to fire low past Simpson after characteristically brilliant build-up play by the imperious George Best. That defeat, combined with England's 3–0 thrashing of Wales in Cardiff, saw the actual world champions leapfrog Scotland into the top spot in the group.

The following month, Scotland returned to winning ways in the second round of matches, Ron McKinnon's late winner settling a five-goal thriller with Wales at Hampden. The same day, at Wembley, goals from Geoff Hurst and Bobby Charlton helped England to a 2–0 win over Northern Ireland. They maintained their one-point cushion at the top of the group and, with a vastly superior goal difference to the Scots, went into the final game at Hampden in February 1968 knowing they'd be Italy-bound that summer so long as they avoided defeat.

Their odds were improved by Scotland having to do without both Jim Baxter and Denis Law. Baxter had been beset by problems on and off the pitch since making a £100,000 move from Sunderland to Nottingham Forest the previous December. Law, meantime, was struggling with the same knee injury that had plagued him for most of 1967/68 season.

The Scots were dealt a further blow on the eve of the match when Arsenal defender Ian Ure withdrew injured, his place taken by Celtic captain Billy McNeill.

Not that Sir Alf Ramsey's men could boast a clean bill of health across the board. Jack Charlton was forced to miss the match because of neck and hip complaints that had kept him out of the Leeds United team for much of the previous month. His World Cup-winning teammate George Cohen was also out, whilst there were mounting concerns in some quarters over the indifferent form of inspirational captain Bobby Moore. Some commentators even called for him to be dropped in favour of Leeds United's in-form Norman Hunter.

As it turned out, fourteen of the twenty-two players who played in the Wembley fixture in 1967 took to a heavy Hampden pitch in February 1968, where a crowd of more than 134,000 braved freezing conditions and were treated to a diverse menu of pre-match entertainment. Cycle racing, short-distance running competitions, cheerleaders wearing tartan mini-skirts – it was a build-up befitting of a huge occasion that promised so much.

It turned out to be a damp squib.

After a Bobby Lennox goal had been disallowed in the opening minutes, West Ham United's Martin Peters silenced the home fans midway through the first half when he connected with a flick-on from debutant Mike Summerbee and lashed a half-volley high into the net past Simpson.

John Hughes equalised shortly before half-time, capitalising on a Gordon Banks slip to head home and give the hosts a glimmer of hope. However, despite some fantastic work by Chelsea's Charlie Cooke in the second half, the Scottish forwards spurned every chance that came their way. The game finished 1–1, giving England the point required. They finished European Nations Cup qualifying on nine points, one ahead of Scotland, to qualify for the Euros.

Fall.

The pens that had eulogised about the same side just ten months earlier were traded for swords as the media responded to the result in excoriating fashion.

Writing in the *Evening Times*, Gair Henderson lamented a '1–1 draw that was in reality a disastrous defeat'. 'That's it!' he groaned. 'That's Scottish international football in the cold store once again.'

He added: 'Woeful is the only word to describe our record in global football. Our last appearance as a nation with any relevance in the game was in Sweden in 1958 – and that finished in short and dismal World Cup failure.

'Scotland should now start a massive campaign to get our youngsters away from the television sets, the dance halls, and the nightclubs. Manager Brown should start at school level and encourage boys right through every grade to the very top. Every youngster should be taught the obvious – that the greatest honour in the game is to play for Scotland and play with everything they have got.'

Norman MacDonald was only marginally more kind in his report for *The Press & Journal*. 'The simple fact is that Scotland did not possess the attacking power to win the game,' he noted. 'Their front line cried out for a goal-getter of the Law type or a "heady" player in the [Alan] Gilzean mould.'

The 'official' verdict pulled just as few punches. Willie Allan, the secretary of the SFA, declared the draw 'more than we deserved', whilst selector Rankin Grimshaw admitted the Scots had 'many weaknesses' and that England were 'the better team by far'. Even the man in charge of UEFA, Hans Bangerter, thought that the English were 'a bit more consistent'.

Just as had been the case at Wembley ten months earlier, it was left to Sir Alf Ramsey to offer the most succinct – and, for Scots football fans, painful – summary of the match.

'I thought we outclassed them.'

And so it went that, as in 1966, Scotland's footballers and their supporters were left to watch from afar as the party went off without them. *Plus ça change, plus c'est la même chose*. Their only consolation was that England didn't win. Ramsey's men were drawn against Yugoslavia in the semi-finals and a tight, ill-tempered match at the Stadio Comunale in Florence was settled by a late goal from Dragan Džajić. Goals from Bobby Charlton and Geoff Hurst decided their third-place playoff with the Soviet Union as hosts Italy defeated Yugoslavia – albeit after a replay – to take the title.

As the English players were receiving their bronze medals in the Stadio Olimpico, the mood in Scotland was far from triumphant. On the contrary, football fans in the country had woken up that day – 8 June 1968 – to news that Matt Busby, the Scottish manager of Manchester United, was to be knighted. The Bellshill-born Busby had led the Red Devils to European Cup glory just under a fortnight prior courtesy of a 4–1 dismantling of Portuguese side Benfica at Wembley.

United were the second British side to win the trophy, following Celtic's triumph a year earlier. However, unlike Busby, the Glasgow side's manager Jock Stein had been overlooked for an honour. The apparent double-standard made front page news in Scotland as England prepared for their match with the Soviets. Politicians lined up to condemn the decision.

Winnie Ewing, the recently elected SNP MP for Hamilton, said: 'Many Scots will be disappointed that Celtic and Jock

Stein have been passed over when someone from an English club receives this outward symbol of recognition in similar circumstances.'

Glasgow councillor John Dunne was far less diplomatic. 'This is a slight on Glasgow and Scotland,' he blasted. 'I would be amazed if our Glasgow members of Parliament, the Lord Provost, councillors, and the Secretary of State for Scotland do not, without any promoting, demand "Why?"'

Tom Reid, the former president of the SFA, added: 'This is typical. Scotland's achievements never get the same recognition as those of England.'

Those frustrations intensified when Celtic reached the European Cup final once more in 1970. They lost on that occasion to Dutch side Feyenoord but, yet again, recognition for the achievement of Stein and his side was conspicuous by its absence. Scottish secretary Willie Ross lobbied hard for honours. In a letter to Prime Minister Harold Wilson, he wrote: 'There is, I find, a good deal of dissatisfaction, in Scotland over what is regarded as an undue proportion of honours for professional football going south of the border. Scottish teams are proving themselves fully the equal of English clubs.

'When England won the World Cup in 1966, there was a very natural group of awards, including Ramsey's knighthood. But when Glasgow Celtic became the first British club to win the European Cup in 1967, we failed to recognise this by an honour for Mr Stein to whom, as manager, a great deal of the credit was due.'

The mystery of Stein's snub was finally revealed in 2007 when a *Sunday Times* appeal to the Scottish Freedom of Information Commissioner prompted the declassification of government documents. They revealed that Stein had, in fact, been due to receive a knighthood in the 1968 New Year's honours but was removed following Celtic's bad-tempered Intercontinental Cup match with Argentine side Racing Club in the November of that year. An annual match contested by the reigning European Cup holders and the winners of the corresponding Copa Libertadores in South America, the two-legged affair finished 2–2 on aggregate, prompting a play-off at the 'neutral' ground of Estadio Centenario in Uruguay.

Aggrieved by their opponents' cynical fouling – a key feature of the previous two games – and the abject incompetence of Paraguayan referee Rodolfo Pérez Osorio, Celtic's players lost their composure and their discipline. Riot police had to intervene on several occasions as six players were shown red cards. Four of those were to Celtic players, including Bobby Lennox, who was escorted from the field by a sword-wielding police officer, and Bertie Auld, who refused to leave the pitch and played out the remainder of the game.

In the end, the result – a 1–0 win for Racing Club settled by a fifty-fifth minute winner from Juan Carlos Cárdenas – was almost incidental. The conduct of both teams drew widespread condemnation. Reuters described the match as 'a bar-room brawl with soccer skills abandoned for swinging fists, flying boots and blatant body checking'. French outlet *L'Équipe* called it a 'sad, lamentable spectacle', adding that whilst 'the Argentinians started the hostilities', Celtic 'made use of every opportunity to return the blows'.

Celtic's board of directors took an equally dim view. Chairman Robert Kelly fumed at what he branded 'an ugly, brutal match containing no football' and expressed his dismay that the Celtic players had 'descended to that level [of Racing Club] to defend themselves'. In the days that followed, every Celtic player was fined £250 for his role in what became known as 'The Battle of Montevideo'.

Stein, for his part, stood accused in certain quarters of having contributed to the shameful episode. In the build-up to the third match, he had promised his players 'would give as much as they are forced to take', adding that his side wanted to win the title 'to stop Racing from becoming world champions'.

That inflammatory language, it seems, cost him a knighthood. Harold Wilson was moved to ensure Stein's name was struck from the Honours List, lest the UK Government be perceived as condoning the shameful scenes in South America.

With those details unknown at the time, however, the perceived snub simply served to widen a growing chasm between the 'haves' from the south and the 'have nots' from the north. To those who felt the pain of the slight on Stein most acutely, it was blatant abasement, another example of shameless anti-Scottish sentiment that was suspected to course through the veins of 'The Establishment'. To others, the reaction was symptomatic of the Scots' ubiquitous and thoroughly exhausting inferiority complex, a position to which many of them were apparently much too willing to default.

The delirium of Jim McCalliog's winner at Wembley had long since faded to a residual echo in the deepest recesses of most supporters' minds.

Failure to qualify for the 1970 World Cup was compounded by a similar fate in the bid to make it to the 1972 European Championship. Even when the Scots did finally make it to World Cup – in West Germany in 1974 – they found a way to reinvent glorious failure for a new generation of wide-eyed, optimistic supporters.

Willie Ormond's side ended the tournament as the only unbeaten side in the competition but were eliminated at the group stage on goal difference. A 2–0 win over Zaire was followed by a 0–0 stalemate with defending champions Brazil and a 1–1 draw with Yugoslavia. With Brazil and Yugoslavia having also played out a draw, Group 2 was ultimately settled by which of the teams managed to beat Zaire by the biggest margin. Yugoslavia beat them 9–0 and Brazil 3–0, the upshot being that Brazil edged out Scotland by a single goal to advance to the knockout stages.

Typical. Even when we don't lose, we lose.

Three times, in fact, goal difference has cost Scotland a place in the World Cup knockout stages. It happened again in 1978, when the Netherlands progressed – and subsequently reached the final – and in 1982, when the Soviet Union went through at Scotland's expense. Subsequent trips to the finals in 1986, 1990 and 1998 ended at the group stage, as have the three European Championship finals in which Scotland have participated to date: 1992, 1996 and 2020 (played in 2021 due to the Covid-19 pandemic). Goal difference again cost them in 1996, when the Netherlands, once again, were the beneficiaries.

Win a major tournament? Scotland struggles just to get there and when they do, they don't last long. Successive generations of supporters have all suffered the same excruciating fate: death by hope. Hope that this time will be different. Hope that 'we might just cause an upset' or 'sneak a result'. Hope that 'our luck has to take a turn sometime'.

Hope.

The thread that binds us; the dream that blinds us.

TWENTY-EIGHT

STOP THE WORLD

WHILE THE SCOTTISH NATIONAL TEAM struggled to make meaningful progress in the months that followed their Wembley heroics, the Scottish National Party did – and how.

Encouraged by impressive performances in the local council elections of 1966 and, in particular, the Pollok by-election in March, the nationalists decided to contest the Hamilton by-election in November 1967. Despite the momentum they'd been gathering, it was still something of a surprise move. The seat was the strongest of Labour strongholds, a seemingly impenetrable fortress in one of the party's historic heartlands. Indeed, since the division of the Lanarkshire constituency created the seat in 1918, Labour had been its sole occupant. Fifteen consecutive trips to the polls – including one by-election in 1935 – had returned red MPs. The most recent of those, the 1966 general election, had seen Tom Fraser re-elected to a seat he had held since 1943. He secured an overwhelming 71.7% of the vote, up marginally from the 1964 general election, where he had polled 71.04%. All told, in general elections held from 1945 until 1966, Labour had taken over two-thirds of vote in Hamilton.

The idea of any other party claiming the seat seemed as remote as the Isle of Foula, an idea so far-fetched as to be beyond even the imagination of Robert Louis Stevenson. Hamilton was Labour's very own Treasure Island and they were not about to share it with anybody.

Even when Fraser surrendered the seat to take up a new post with the North of Scotland Hydro Electric Board, there was still total conviction amongst the Labour rank and file that the party would retain the seat.

The SNP had other ideas.

It was in June 1966, shortly before the World Cup kicked off in England, that the smell of blood first stung their nostrils. With the devaluation of the pound and an underperforming economy hitting the average Scottish Labour voter particularly hard, word got out that Fraser was planning to take a job with the South of Scotland Electricity Board and, as such, there would be a by-election to replace him. A huge public outcry called on him to reject the offer and remain *in situ*. He did but not without attracting the attention of the SNP. The party rallied quickly to prepare for the prospect of another job offer tempting Fraser away, and this time for good.

In July 1966, Winnie Ewing was selected as the party's by-election candidate. Born in Glasgow in 1929, Ewing became an active campaigner for Scottish independence during her time at the University of Glasgow where she combined studying for a degree in law with her membership of the Glasgow University Scottish Nationalist Association. Her Labour-supporting father was unimpressed.

A vivacious mother of three, Ewing was holidaying with her young family in Jersey in July 1967 when Fraser's anticipated departure was confirmed. Immediately, the campaign wheels began to turn. Party leader Arthur Donaldson backed her candidacy with gusto. So, too, world boxing champion Walter McGowan, TV personality Ludovic Kennedy, and even Sir Sean Connery. The latter lent his voice to campaign tapes that were played in cars stationed all over the constituency, whilst a slide-show setting out Scotland's case for independence was displayed on a lorry. It was a positive, front-footed campaign that energised a growing posse of nationalists.

Nonetheless, Labour remained confident of victory. On the eve of the election, their candidate, a former coal miner called Alex Wilson, described himself as 'more confident than ever, if that were possible' of victory and the bookies agreed. As the polls opened on a dreich November day, they had Labour at 1/10, with the SNP at 5/1 and the Conservatives rank outsiders at 33/1. Privately, and despite running a strong campaign, some of Ewing's own supporters seemed resigned to defeat, encouraging her to 'try to come a good second' to give some encouragement to the membership. Their pessimism was understandable. Whilst it was making up ground on the more established political parties, as proven by George Leslie's strong performance in Pollok earlier in the year, the 1966 general election had demonstrated just how far the SNP still had to go. It had taken only 5% of the vote across Scotland, despite standing candidates in twenty-three of the seventy-one seats. Sure, they were going places, but they weren't going there very fast. Ewing's candidacy in Hamilton would, by common consent, likely be another step in the right direction.

Instead, it was a leap.

In a stunning upset, Ewing polled more than 46% of the vote, defeating Wilson in a near 38% swing. Addressing her ecstatic supporters following the count, Ewing famously remarked: 'Stop the world! Scotland wants to get on!'

The result sent shockwaves across the land. The late political activist Oliver Brown said the result had made 'a shiver run along the Scottish Labour backbenches looking for a spine to run up'. Historian Tom Devine has since described it 'the most sensational by-election result in Scotland since 1945', with Isobel Lindsay branding it a 'watershed' moment in Scottish political history. It undoubtedly was. On 16 November 1967, as Ewing boarded the train taking her from Glasgow to be sworn in at Westminster, a locomotive affectionately dubbed the 'Tartan Express', there was a tangible feeling that the Scottish National Party had arrived.

Yes, it had sent an MP to the House of Commons once before, Robert McIntyre winning in Motherwell in 1945, but this was different. This was a statement. Not only had they stolen a Labour 'safe' seat but they had done so against all odds and in utterly emphatic fashion.

Ewing's seminal triumph, combined with that of Welsh nationalist Gwynfor Evans in the 1966 Carmarthen by-election, propelled the prospect of home rule from the fringes to the foreground. In April 1969, and in an attempt to satisfy the voters it was losing to increasingly trendy nationalist factions, Harold Wilson's Labour government agreed to establish a royal commission to examine the structures of the UK's constitution and, more significantly, to consider whether any changes should be made to them.

The so-called 'Kilbrandon Commission' examined various models of devolution, federalism and confederalism, as well as the possibility of dividing the UK into separate sovereign states. Chaired by the former editor of *The Economist* Geoffrey Crowther and, following his death in 1972, by Scottish law lord James Kilbrandon, the commission comprised sixteen other members, amongst them politicians, economists, Trade Unionists, religious leaders and academics.

A total of sixteen volumes of evidence and ten research papers were published by the group between 1969 and 1973 before the final report was delivered in October 1973 to Ted Heath's Tory government. Harold Wilson's attempts at appeasement didn't pass muster with the electorate who kicked him and his Labour counterparts to the curb in the general election of 1970.

Whilst the final report rejected the prospects of either independence or federalism for any of the constituent parts of the United Kingdom, it did recognise the value of devolved, directly elected Scottish and Welsh assemblies. In the case of Scotland specifically, eight members favoured a devolved legislature, whereby several significant areas of responsibility would be transferred to that assembly, including education, health, home affairs, legal matters, social services and the environment. It was suggested that the assembly should comprise 100 elected members, led by a head of the executive called the 'Scottish Premier'. In addition, the Westminster office of the Secretary of State for Scotland would be abolished and the number of MPs elected to the House of Commons from Scottish constituencies reduced from seventy-one to fifty-one. The report recommended that this should be one of seven 'regional' assemblies, with another in Wales and five in England.

Fast-forward five years and, after another change in government, a new Labour administration being ushered into power in September 1974, the Scotland Act was tabled in 1978. Intended to create a new Scottish Assembly but with very limited legislative powers, the provisions of the Act required the support of the electorate before they could come into force and so a referendum was held on 1 March 1979.

Crucially, an amendment to the Act, introduced by government backbencher George Cunningham, specified that it needed to have the support of 40% of the entire electorate. In other words, a strong turn-out was required for the Act to have any chance of succeeding.

As it so happened, that's where it fell short. Whilst a small majority of voters supported the introduction of a devolved executive – a total of 1,230,937 (51.6%) supporting it – they represented only 32.9% of the entire electorate. As a result, the referendum was lost and the Act was repealed.

Before the month was out, so too was the Labour government, the SNP, Liberals and Ulster Unionist Party all backing a Conservative-led motion of 'no confidence' in the administration on 28 March 1979. A subsequent general election in the May of that year saw the Tories, led by the country's first-ever female Prime Minister Margaret Thatcher, beginning a sequence of eighteen years of Conservative rule.

By this time, the SNP had established itself as a reputable force within Westminster. Whilst Winnie Ewing lost Hamilton at the 1970 general election, Donald Stewart won the party's first-ever seat at a general election when he ended Malcolm McMillan and Labour's thirty-five-year stranglehold on the Western Isles. Stewart was joined by ten other SNP MPs at the September 1974 election, the nationalists securing a party-record 839,617 votes. A disappointing performance in the 1979 election saw their Commons representation slashed to two and appeared to vindicate the taunts of ousted Prime Minister Jim Callaghan. He described the SNP as 'the turkeys who voted for Christmas' after they backed Thatcher's no confidence motion.

Throughout the 1980s, the party was undermined by factional divisions and infighting. Everybody agreed that the objective was to protect Scotland's interests by establishing the country's independence. They just had radically differing views on how best to achieve that. On one side, there was the ultra-nationalist Siol nan Gaidheal. On the other, was the left-wing 79 Group, which railed against the party's established leadership. Caught in the crossfire were a group of 'traditionalists', who centred around Winnie Ewing, by now serving as a Member of the European Parliament in Strasbourg where she was affectionately known as *Madame Écosse*.

A decade of discontent and rancour was resolved in the early 1990s after Alex Salmond, elected as an MP for Banff and Buchan in 1987, seized control of the party following the resignation of Gordon Wilson. Around this time, resentment over the controversial 'poll tax'– where Scots were, to all intents and purposes, used as lab rats by Thatcher for her new flat-rate, per-capita tax system – fostered anti-Westminster sentiment amongst large chunks of the electorate. However, it took until the 1997 general election for them to fully capitalise. A landslide Labour victory grabbed all the headlines but a best performance in almost a quarter of a century by the SNP reignited the home rule flame.

Contained within the Labour Party manifesto was a commitment to hold a second devolution referendum in Scotland. Unlike in 1979, the executive would have a broader remit and, if the electorate agreed, would have tax-varying powers, too. The logic was simple: give Scots more control over Scottish affairs and that will surely sate their appetite for independence at the expense of the Union.

The referendum, held on 11 September 1997, was and remains unique in the United Kingdom in that it was the only major referendum where voters were asked two questions in the same plebiscite. The first ballot paper asked if there should be a Scottish Parliament; the second, if it should have tax-varying powers.

Both were endorsed. A whopping 74.3% of all voters backed the proposed parliament, with 63.5% endorsing its right to vary taxes. And with a huge 60% turnout, nobody could argue with the legitimacy of the outcome.

Reacting to the result, Prime Minister Tony Blair claimed that 'the era of big, centralised government is over'.

On 19 November 1998, just five months after a global TV audience of more than one billion watched Craig Brown's Scotland open the World Cup in France with a narrow 2–1 defeat at the hands of holders Brazil, the Scotland Act 1998 received royal assent. The following May, elections to the first sitting Scottish Parliament in almost 300 years took place, the Labour Party comfortably defeating the SNP. Amongst those to win a seat at Holyrood that year was Winnie Ewing, who was elected to represent her beloved Highlands and Islands.

As the oldest qualified member, it was left to her to preside over the opening of the new executive on 12 May 1999.

'The Scottish Parliament,' she said, 'adjourned on the 25th day of March in the year 1707, is hereby reconvened.'

Three weeks later, the Scottish national team recorded one of the worst results in the country's history, a 1–1 draw against the Faroe Islands and their part-time team made up of fisherman and tradesmen. That result ultimately reduced Scotland to needing to win a two-legged playoff to qualify for the European Championships taking place in Belgium and the Netherlands in the summer of 2000.

Standing in their way?

England.

Kevin Keegan's star-studded side won the first leg at Hampden thanks to two goals from Manchester United's Paul Scholes. The return leg at Wembley four days later finished 1–0 to the Scots courtesy of a Don Hutchison goal shortly before half-time. England progressed to Euro 2000, winning the tie 2–1 on aggregate.

Scotland had to make do with beating them on their own patch.

Glorious failure once more.

* * *

IN MAY 2007, voters went to the polls in the third election to the devolved Scottish Parliament. Labour, led by First Minister

Jack McConnell, entered it with a small overall majority of five seats via a coalition with the Liberal Democrats. However, against a backdrop of council tax reform, controversy over the Trident nuclear programme and, increasingly, question marks over the Union, the SNP swept to power. Its forty-seven seats were one more than Labour could muster and thirty more than the Scottish Conservatives. Led by Alex Salmond, the SNP did something that no party had done in Scotland for over half a century: they'd beaten Labour.

'Scotland has changed for ever and for good,' declared Salmond. 'There may be Labour governments and first ministers in decades still to come but never again will the Labour Party think it has a divine right to government.'

It was a result that penetrated the established heart of UK politics, never mind Scotland. Prime Minister Tony Blair was days away from announcing his much-anticipated resignation after a decade in 10 Downing Street, with Scotland's Gordon Brown, the then Chancellor of the Exchequer, heavily fancied to replace him. Meanwhile, the Conservative Party, under the leadership of David Cameron, was gaining ground rapidly.

In short, the United Kingdom was in a state of political flux bordering on chaos. By the time the next Scottish parliamentary election took place in 2011, the UK was being governed by a coalition formed by the Conservatives and the Liberal Democrats. It was the fifth time in eight general elections that Scotland got a government it hadn't voted for and, with disillusionment spreading, the SNP took full advantage.

On 5 May 2011, and despite an electoral system designed to prevent such an outcome, the party won an overall majority at Holyrood, taking sixty-nine of the 129 seats available. They gained a remarkable thirty-two constituencies: twenty-two from Scottish Labour, nine from the Scottish Liberal Democrats and one from the Scottish Conservatives.

It was Labour's worst election defeat in Scotland since 1931. The Liberal Democrats managed only 5% of the vote, losing twenty-five deposits in the process. The Scottish Conservatives suffered a net loss of five seats. The result prompted the Scottish leaders of all three parties to stand down almost immediately. Much more significantly, it provided the SNP with a clear mandate to hold an independence referendum.

Eighteen months later, on 15 October 2012, a deal setting out terms for the historic vote was signed by Prime Minister David Cameron and First Minister Alex Salmond. The Edinburgh Agreement, as it was called, paved the way for a vote in the autumn of 2014 with a single Yes/No question on whether Scotland should leave the UK to become a fully independent nation. Salmond called it the 'right decision for Scotland' and 'a major step forward in Scotland's home rule journey'. Cameron, by contrast, said: 'I passionately believe Scotland will be better off in the United Kingdom but also, crucially, the United Kingdom will be better off with Scotland.'

It was on 21 March 2013 that the Scottish Government announced that a referendum on Scottish independence would be held on 18 September 2014. It didn't go unnoticed that 2014 marked the 700th anniversary of the Battle of Bannockburn. Salmond himself acknowledged that it was 'a good year to hold a referendum'.

According to the UK Government, if a simple majority of the votes were cast in favour of independence, then Scotland would become an independent country once more. If the majority was opposed, it would continue to be a part of the United Kingdom but with further powers devolved to the Scottish Parliament as a result of the Scotland Act 2012. In the event of a majority 'yes' vote, the Scottish Government proposed an independence date of 24 March 2016.

Two separate campaigns launched almost immediately. On one

side was Yes Scotland, fronted by former broadcasting executive Blair Jenkins and supported by the SNP, the Scottish Green Party and the Scottish Socialist Party. On the other was Better Together. It was led by Alistair Darling, the former Chancellor of the Exchequer, and had support from the Conservative Party, Labour Party and Liberal Democrats.

For eighteen months, the case for independence was made and challenged, made, and challenged, made and challenged. Agriculture, border controls and immigration, childcare, citizenship, currency, defence spending, the economy, nuclear weapons, NATO, North Sea oil, education, healthcare, welfare, the monarchy, and the EU – all were debated, dissected and disputed in forensic, exhaustive detail. The cases for and against independence were made time and again in town halls, universities, pubs, the streets of every town from Lerwick to Langholm, and, of course, on TV and radio. Unionists dismissed nationalists as idealistic separatists; nationalists rebranded the Better Together campaign 'Project Fear'. It was a schismatic, chaotic, compelling time.

Finally, the country went to the polls, as planned, on 18 September 2014. A YouGov opinion poll on the eve of the referendum suggested that the result was very much in the balance, with 45% intending to vote 'Yes', 49% planning to vote 'No' and 6% still undecided.

The following morning, at 6.08 a.m., the result was made official. A total of 2,001,926 votes had been cast for 'No' as compared to 1,617,989 for 'Yes'. With a majority of 55%, Scotland had voted to remain part of the United Kingdom. The result led to the resignation of Alex Salmond as SNP leader and was welcomed by David Cameron who said: 'There can be no disputes, no re-runs; we have heard the will of the Scottish people.' Controversially, he also claimed that the Queen – required by the constitution to be politically neutral – had 'purred down the line' when he phoned to tell her the outcome of the vote.

Whilst unionists celebrated in the streets, pro-independence campaigners were left anguished by the outcome. The end of the matter? Hardly.

In the weeks following the referendum, thousands of people joined the three main parties who had campaigned for independence. By 2 October 2014, the SNP membership had tripled from 25,000 to 75,000, overtaking the Liberal Democrats as the third-largest political party in the UK. Not even the delivery of further devolved powers to the Scottish Government – as had been promised by Westminster – could halt the nationalists' momentum, with the SNP establishing a clear and significant lead over the other parties in Scottish opinion polls.

In the 2015 general election, held just 231 days after the referendum, the SNP received 1,454,436 votes, exactly half of the Scottish vote, and won fifty-six of the fifty-nine Scottish seats contested. Having overtaken the Lib Dems as the third-biggest political party in the UK, the nationalists also replaced them as the third-largest party in the House of Commons.

Demands for a second vote on independence intensified following the UK Government's decision to allow a referendum on the country's membership of the European Union in 2016. Uncertainty over an independent Scotland's ability to join the EU were used by the 'No' campaign as a reason to remain part of the UK. Indeed, it was widely assumed that the people of Scotland favoured being part of the European single market, a suspicion that was confirmed when 62% of the electorate voted for 'Remain' in the so-called Brexit referendum. However, 51.9% of the total UK vote went in favour of 'Leave'. Having been persuaded of the benefits of EU membership, Scotland suddenly found itself pulled from the union against its will. Pro-independence campaigners were incensed.

Subsequent trips to the polls, in 2017 and 2019, saw the SNP maintain its position as the third-biggest party in Westminster, whilst at Holyrood the party has continued to govern, winning the Scottish parliamentary elections in both 2016 and 2021. According to then First Minister Nicola Sturgeon, the most recent of those provided a mandate for a second independence referendum.

'There is simply no democratic justification whatsoever . . . to block the right of the people of Scotland to choose our future,' she insisted. 'For any Westminster politician who tries to stand in the way of that I would say two things. Firstly, you are not picking a fight with the SNP; you are picking a fight with the democratic wishes of the Scottish people. And secondly, you will not succeed.

'The only people who can decide the future of Scotland are the Scottish people and no Westminster politician can or should stand in the way of that.'

Stand in the way of that, they did. In July 2022, in response to the First Minister announcing plans for a second independence referendum in October 2023, the soon-to-be-ousted PM Boris Johnson rejected the request. 'As our country faces unprecedented challenges at home and abroad,' he said, 'I cannot agree that now is the time to return to a question, which was clearly answered by the people of Scotland in 2014.'

The Supreme Court supported Westminster's position in October 2022, leaving the SNP to appoint the next UK general election – expected in 2024 – as a 'de facto referendum' on independence.

More than fifty years after the Hamilton by-election, Scotland is, depending on your politics, either still trying to stop the world, or insisting that it bend to one small nation's tartan will.

* * *

EXACTLY TWO MONTHS TO THE DAY after the 2014 independence referendum, Scotland hosted England in a friendly at Celtic Park. It was the 112th meeting of the two sides and was England's first visit north of the border since 1999.

The timing of the match, so soon after the most seismic political event in more than three hundred years, provoked much debate. Welcoming a country from which the hosts had just attempted to divorce themselves and combining the occasion with football and all its caustic, toxic unpredictability, seemed like a recipe for unnecessary disaster.

Many Scottish football fans had responded angrily to the referendum result, with some lobbying for the national team to drop 'Flower of Scotland' as the national anthem. How, they reasoned, could any Scot bring themselves to sing the line 'For we can still rise now, and be a nation again' when the population had allowed that very opportunity to pass them by? The SFA resisted. 'The Scotland fans have shown a fondness for "Flower of Scotland" in football, rugby and other sports,' they said, 'and it is the established national anthem.'

In front of a capacity crowd of 60,000 – including, in his last act as First Minister, Alex Salmond – England ran out convincing 3–1 winners. Manchester United's Wayne Rooney helped himself to a double, with Alex Oxlade-Chamberlain grabbing the other. Andy Robertson's late consolation for the hosts was, in reality, anything but. By the time the Swedish referee Jonas Eriksson blew for fulltime, the stadium was mostly empty, save for a jubilant band of 5,000 English supporters.

In his match report for the *Daily Mail*, Neil Ashton described a scene of stubborn Scottish resistance. 'There was a boo for everything,' he wrote. 'England flag transported across the pitch. Boo. Fraser Forster's name read out. Boo. Nathaniel Clyne. Boo. Luke Shaw. Boo. And so it went on. It was old school, blood and thunder and a reminder of the days when these two slugged it out for pride and honour at the end of every season on a churned-up pitch at Wembley or Hampden Park.'

Despite being outnumbered twelve to one, the English supporters gleefully seized the opportunity to taunt their hosts over the referendum result. Refrains of 'You're British 'Til You Die', 'We All Voted Yes', 'Rule Britannia' and 'God Save the Queen' echoed around the stadium throughout the ninety minutes. On the way into the ground, some England fans spotted half-and-half scarves being sold by street vendors and suggested they really ought to have been 55–45.

Extra police were deployed to the streets of Glasgow in anticipation of trouble. UEFA applied its highest security risk rating to the match. Chief Superintendent Andy Bates, the local policing commander for Glasgow, said: 'There will not be many of my officers wanting to take the day off. This is as big as it gets. This is what we joined for, to be involved in events like this.'

Ahead of kick-off, each set of fans booed the other's national anthem. Some Scottish supporters unfurled a 'No Surrender' flag in the stands. Saltires belonging to Tartan Army battalions from Alloa, Arran, Aberdeen, Castlemilk, Prestwick, Larbert and Sunderland were draped over advertising hoardings. St George's Cross flags bearing the names of Bethnal Green, Stoke, Doncaster, Barnsley, Carlisle, Birmingham, Sheffield, Wolverhampton, Norwich, Macclesfield and more billowed in the away end. The official Football Association band performed tune after tune until an FA representative had to ask them to stop when their songs were hijacked by anti-IRA chanting.

Friendly? Rarely has so kind and innocent a word been so egregiously misappropriated.

As Scotland defender Charlie Mulgrew put it, 'There's never a friendly between Scotland and England.'

TWENTY-NINE

WHERE THE GREEN GRASS GROWS

THERE IS A GARDEN IN CASTLE DOUGLAS – a small town around forty miles inside Scotland's border with England – where a large chunk of turf stolen from Wembley in 1967 hides in plain sight. John Low knows exactly where it is. He ought to. He put it there.

Now seventy-seven, Low – 'Ludo' to his friends – is one of the best-known members of Scotland's Tartan Army, not to mention one of the most travelled. For the last fifty-plus years, he has followed the national team all around the globe. There's no mistaking him in a crowd. He's the kilted pensioner with the Scottie dog tea cosy on his head. More than likely, he'll be tooting on a bugle, too. Inconspicuous, he ain't.

A lifelong passion for football was ignited when he was taken to nearby Palmerston Park to watch Queen of the South. His grandfather was the Doonhamers' first-ever club secretary and, naturally, Low's father and uncle fell in love with the game, too. The latter, indeed, even had a short stint as a player for Aston Villa.

In 1962, he attended his first Scotland international at Hampden, a 2–0 victory over England. Since then, he has barely missed a match, his commitment to the cause rewarded with more passport stamps than Kenny Dalglish has caps.

Name a country – any country – and there's a good chance he's been. Estonia? Of course, loves it. Faroe Islands? Multiple times. Iceland? Yes, with his daughter. San Marino? Lichtenstein? Spain? Italy? France? Germany? All yes.

He went to Mexico with his son for the 1986 World Cup. He was in Japan in 2006 when Scotland won the Kirin Cup. He drove to Germany in a blue Simca for the 1974 World Cup. He's played football on the beaches of Bondi and Acapulco.

In the summer of 2008, when the Scotland rugby side toured Argentina, Low followed them out there. By coincidence, it coincided with the thirtieth anniversary of Archie Gemmill's unforgettable solo goal against the Netherlands during the 1978 World Cup. You know the one. The Nottingham Forest midfielder pounced on a loose ball on the edge of the Dutch box, his first touch taking him past future Celtic manager Wim Jansen. He then skipped past Ruud Krol and Jan Poortvliet before clipping a wonderful finish over onrushing goalkeeper Jan Jongbloed. Magnificent. It's a long story but the short version is that the BBC engineered an opportunity for Low to visit the Estadio Ciudad de Mendoza and attempt to recreate Gemmill's moment of magic on the very same pitch. 'Aye, that was good fun,' he laughs.

On 4 September 2016, Low was in the Ta'Qali National Stadium as Scotland beat Malta 5–1 in the opening match of qualifying for the 2018 World Cup in Russia. It was the 100th away match he'd attended with the national team. The first? England at Wembley on 15 April 1967.

At the time, Low was twenty-one and an apprentice mechanic. Having managed to secure gold-dust tickets through local amateur team Threave Rovers, he and three friends decided to make the trip to London for the big game. Beating England was always important but, with the Auld Enemy having won the World Cup nine months earlier, and the media seizing every opportunity to remind people across the land of that fact, the game took on extra significance.

'To this day, I can't stand to even mention the number "sixty-six",' says Low. 'If I need to make a mention of it, I'll say "sixty-seven minus one" instead.' He's not kidding.

Under normal circumstances, he and his pals would have been able to hitch a ride to the game on one of the buses laid on by the Rovers. Not on this occasion. With every seat taken, they had to get the train instead.

'If I'm remembering it correctly, we got one of the extra services that had been put on for the game. It left Glasgow Central about eleven o'clock on the Friday night and stopped at Kilmarnock before arriving at Dumfries gone midnight. By the time we got on, there were no seats. It was one of those old-fashioned carriages with a passageway down the outside, and all the cabins were jam-packed. Every single one. You'd open a door and get shouted at. In the end, we had to make do with bunking down on the hard floor in the guard's van.

'The train got in about six in the morning and we were left thinking, "What are we going to do now?" We remembered that some boys we knew from Dalbeattie were staying near Victoria, so we went and met up with them and sneaked into their hotel to freshen up. After that, it was off to Trafalgar Square for the usual pre-match carry-on – boys jumping in fountains and so on – before we all marched to the stadium.'

Like most others, Low remembers the game being low on quality and high on tension. 'Even when we went 3–1 up, I was still nervous and when they scored their second, I thought "Oh no, here we go again." It was a long two minutes until the referee blew for fulltime.'

Sitting quite near the front and to the side of one of the goals, he and his friends were perfectly placed to invade the pitch but, initially, resisted the urge.

'We knew we'd get into bother if we did. But I remember looking up the touchline and there were three other supporters running towards where we were. They had rolled a scarf up into a ball and were kicking it down the pitch and just jumping around celebrating. It wasn't until they got a bit closer that I realised it was "Touchy" Smith, Chris Rudd and Dick Shaw – three Threave Rovers players! Well, that was it. That was all the encouragement I needed. I skipped past a policeman and made my dash.'

Whilst most fans ran aimlessly in reckless, euphoric abandon, Low was a man on a mission. A huge fan of Denis Law, he had taken a mental note of the approximate spot from which the talismanic forward had scored the opening goal. He bolted straight for it, dug his fingers and nails into the ground and heaved out a chunk of the pitch as a souvenir. 'It came away just fine actually,' he laughs.

Beyond stuffing his pockets with sod, there was hardly any time to celebrate what was a famous victory; the train shuttling Low and his friends back to Scotland left only a few hours later.

'This time, we managed to get a carriage. We got in about four or five in the morning and I went straight to my mum and dad's to plant the grass I'd taken. It's funny, I remember quite a big fuss was made afterwards about the damage that was done to the pitch. The way I see it, Wembley used turf that was grown in Solway, so it was ours to begin with! We were only taking back what was rightfully ours.'

On 15 April 2017, Low returned to Wembley to mark the fiftieth anniversary of Scotland's win. On a wet morning in the Big Smoke, he posed for photographs underneath a statue of the late Sir Bobby Moore. He was wearing a Scotland replica shirt and his trademark tea cosy, a Saltire hanging out of one trouser pocket, and a Lion Rampant dangling from the other. He held his bugle in one hand and a chunk of turf in the other.

'It wasn't long before a security guard appeared, wondering what I was up to,' he smiles. 'I told them I'd brought some good Scottish turf to replace what I'd taken in 1967. It was all good fun and, you know, that's what supporting the team for me has always been about. Sometimes it's hard, especially when things aren't going well, but it's a good thing in life to have hope. Something to believe in, you know? I mean, what's the alternative?

'Aye. I'll never stop supporting them.'

THIRTY

WHAT HAPPENED NEXT?

Jim Baxter
'Slim' played only twice more for Scotland after that wonderful win at Wembley. The first, the following month in an abject 2–0 defeat at home to the USSR. The second, a 3–2 victory over Wales, also at home, in November 1967.

A month after that, he was on the move, swapping Sunderland for Nottingham Forest in a £100,000 deal. Forest had finished runners-up in the English top flight in 1966/67 and, with the arrival of Baxter, a man described by club chairman Tony Wood as 'one of the best footballers in the world', they believed they had acquired somebody capable of helping them to the title. It didn't work out. With Baxter a shadow of his former self, Forest laboured to eleventh.

The following season, and for reasons known only to him, Forest manager John Carey decided to redeploy Baxter as a striker. The experiment went about as well as expected. Baxter was dropped in October and, weeks later, was transfer-listed and suspended by the club for a 'breach of training rules and players' instructions'.

Carey was sacked before the year was out and although his replacement, Matt Gillies, gave Baxter another chance, he was allowed to leave on a free at the end of the season.

'While I'm one of those who love to watch and sometimes purr over a player of Baxter's ability, I have to be realistic,' said Gillies. 'The days of a ball-juggling inside forward have gone. Ball artistry does not matter if it doesn't fit in with modern conditions.'

Former club Rangers swooped to bring the prodigal son back to Ibrox but, again, off-field issues and flamboyances continued to get in the way of the Fifer's undoubted gift. He made only fourteen appearances for the Light Blues – the last of which came in a 3–2 win away to Aberdeen in December of 1969 – before being released the following April, whereupon he announced his retirement from football at the age of thirty.

After hanging up his boots, Baxter bought a pub on Paisley Road West in Glasgow and, in 1994, needed two liver transplants just four days apart. In February 2001, he was diagnosed with pancreatic cancer and he passed away at his home in Glasgow's south side two months later with his partner Norma and sons Alan and Steven at his bedside. His ashes were buried at Ibrox.

In the weeks and months following his passing, the high regard and affection in which Baxter was held was clear for all to see in the tributes that were paid to him.

Former Manchester United manager Sir Alex Ferguson described him as 'arguably the best player to play in Scottish football'. 'He had touch, balance, vision and this wonderful aura that indicated you were in the presence of someone touched by football genius,' added Ferguson. 'You could go on all day about his lifestyle but what a player. I don't know if we will ever see his like again.'

The late, great George Best – no angel, himself – included Baxter amongst the best eleven players he had played with or against. 'He was even more of a showman than me which is saying something,' said the former Manchester United man. 'That's perhaps why I got on with him so well. He was so skilful, a real genius. Whenever we played against each other we would try to outdo one another.'

Ronnie MacKinnon branded him a 'magician'. Kenny Dalglish insisted 'he had a swagger and an arrogance about him on the pitch that only truly great players have'.

Pelé? Pelé thought he should have been born a Brazilian.

However, perhaps the most compelling – not to mention poignant – tribute was paid during the 2001 Scottish Cup semi-finals, just days after Baxter's passing. It took the form of a banner, unfurled in the stands, which read: 'Slim Jim. Simply The Best.'

It came from the Celtic end.

In 2002, Baxter was one of the inaugural inductees to the Scottish Sporting Hall of Fame. Two years later, he was added to the Scottish Football Hall of Fame. In between time, a bronze statue of him was erected in his birthplace, Hill of Beath.

As cursed as he was blessed, Baxter reckoned that he gambled away more than half a million pounds. Later in life, when he was asked if earning the huge amounts of money earned by modern footballers would have made any material difference to his life, he famously remarked: 'Aye, I would have gambled £50,000 a week on the horses instead of £100.'

He was a one-off – and he knew it.

'Everything I did on the pitch was off-the-cuff,' he insisted. 'Sheer instinct. If I'd been a good boy, maybe the swashbuckling stuff would have got stifled. Perhaps I did enjoy myself too much, but what's too much? Moderation, as far as I'm concerned, is for moderate people.'

Denis Law

Following his Wembley heroics, Law played only eighteen more times for Scotland, his final appearance coming in the 2–0 defeat of Zaire in the opening match of the 1974 World Cup. It was the only time the Aberdonian – then thirty-four – ever played in the finals of the tournament and, by his own admission, he was past his best.

Still, his best was better than most. According to Sir Alex Ferguson, Law was 'the finest player Scotland ever produced' and 'one of the greatest the world has ever seen'. In 2022, football magazine *FourFourTwo* published a ranking of the best Scottish players of all time, with Law second behind Kenny Dalglish, the man with whom he shares the country's all-time goalscoring record. Each found the net thirty times. Law, though, did it in almost half the number of games. He finished his career with fifty-five Scotland caps, compared with 102 for Dalglish.

He played on with Manchester United until the summer of 1973, forming one-third of the club's iconic 'Holy Trinity' frontline alongside Sir Bobby Charlton and the late George Best. A knee injury forced him to miss the Old Trafford club's 1968 European Cup victory over Benfica – something he later described as the 'greatest disappointment of my career' – and he continued to be blighted by knee issues for the rest of his career.

By the time he left United, he had scored 237 goals in 404 appearances. To date, he is third on the club's list of all-time top goalscorers. His time at Old Trafford yielded two league titles and an FA Cup winner's medal.

He spent the 1973/74 season at Manchester City and played just two games early the following season before formally retiring from football on 26 August 1974.

In November 2003, the SFA named Law the country's 'Most

Outstanding Player' of the past fifty years and, the following year, he was inducted into the Scottish Football Hall of Fame.

Extraordinarily talented, Law was also a pugnacious, combative player. Former teammate Best once told of an incident during training at Manchester United when the club's strapping centre-half Bill Foulkes knocked the Scot to the ground. 'Bill had been working down the mines and only quit at the age of twenty, when he broke through in football,' recalled the late forward. 'He was an authentic tough guy. What happened next? Denis got up and punched him. Bill hit him back and the next thing everyone was piling in. Denis gave as good as he got.'

He added: 'He was a showman on the pitch and there was never a dull moment on or off the field with Law around but beneath all the joking, Denis was a deadly serious footballer. Above all he wanted to win.'

John Greig, who captained Law several times on international duty, once said: 'When it comes to strikers, there was none braver or more aggressive than Denis Law. He may have looked puny, but he had the heart of a lion and would have fought with his shadow. When I met him for the first time, he made an instant impression; he had an almost magical aura because of his personality.'

Former Celtic captain Billy McNeill praised his 'wonderful sense of anticipation', whilst the late Sir Bobby Robson called him a 'real will o' the wisp player, as sharp as a needle and lightning fast in his movements, with a brain to match.'

The greatest tribute of all came from Portuguese great Eusébio. 'I admired Denis as a player because he was exceptional and very different from a lot of British players from his era,' he said. 'Then British football was characterised by stamina and determination of the players, who had excellent physical fitness. This is true, too of other European countries – including the Germans, who are superbly prepared physically. But the British and the

Germans, generally, both lacked technique. I played against Denis Law quite a few times and also played with him for FIFA and UEFA representative teams. He was a very fine footballer and thoroughly deserved the European Footballer of the Year award he gained in 1964. He was a good team man with fine individual skills.'

It has been suggested that Netherlands icon Dennis Bergkamp was named after him, the extra 'n' only being added at the insistence of Dutch authorities who refused to recognise it otherwise.

Nicknamed 'The King', Law's story came full circle in 2017 when he received the freedom of his home city, Aberdeen. From Woodside to Wembley and all points in between, the boy with the squint grew up to be a giant among men.

Ronnie Simpson

The victory over England was the first of five caps won by the veteran shot-stopper. Weeks after the win at Wembley, Simpson was part of the Celtic side that defeated Internazionale in Lisbon to become the first British team to win the European Cup. In all, he won four league championships, three Scottish League Cups and one Scottish Cup with the Glasgow club. A dislocated shoulder, sustained in 1969, forced him to miss Celtic's 1970 European Cup final with Feyenoord and, ultimately, led to his retirement from the game later the same year. After a brief spell as manager of Hamilton Academical, he served on the Pools Panel and was also a Progressives Councillor on Edinburgh City Council in the 1970s. In 2002, Simpson was included in Celtic's 'Greatest Ever Team', ahead of John Thompson and Pat Bonner. He died of a heart attack in April 2004. Seven years later, he was posthumously inducted into the Scottish Football Hall of Fame.

Eddie McCreadie

Left-back McCreadie went on to make a further thirteen appearances for Scotland after the victory over England, the last of those coming in an 8–0 win over Cyprus at Hampden in May 1969. The Glasgow man won the FA Cup with Chelsea in 1970, playing a role in the build-up to David Webb's winner over Leeds United at Old Trafford. Chelsea went on to win the European Cup Winners' Cup the following season, but McCreadie missed the final against Real Madrid in Athens through injury. He stayed with Chelsea for the remainder of his career and, by the time he retired as a player in 1973, he had made more than 400 appearances for the Stamford Bridge outfit. In 1975, he was appointed manager of the Londoners and helped rebuild them following their relegation to the old Second Division. However, he left the club in 1977 after a bizarre disagreement over a club car with chairman Brian Mears. McCreadie subsequently emigrated to the United States in the late 1970s where he was appointed manager of the Memphis Rogues in the NASL and later the indoor Cleveland Force. He finally retired from football in 1985.

Ronnie McKinnon

Just a few months after helping take down the world champions at Wembley, centre-half McKinnon scored his first and only goal for Scotland in a 3–2 win over Wales. All in, he made twenty-eight appearances for his country and more than 300 for Rangers, where he won two Scottish league championships, four Scottish Cups and three League Cups. He made his final appearance for Rangers in the second round of the 1971/72 European Cup Winners' Cup away to Sporting Lisbon where he suffered a broken leg. Rangers went on to win the competition that season, but McKinnon missed an entire year due to complications stemming from the injury. He subsequently moved to South

Africa, where he played for local side Durban United for a season. He later returned to Scotland, settling on the Isle of Lewis in the Outer Hebrides, where his mother had been born.

John Greig
The win at Wembley was the only victory defender Greig managed in eight matches against England. He went on to play for another eleven years and, although he never made it to the finals of any international competition, he enjoyed huge success at club level. A one-club man, Greig made 755 appearances in all competitions for Rangers, winning five Scottish First Division titles, six Scottish Cups and four Scottish League Cups. He also captained the side to victory in the European Cup Winners' Cup final in Barcelona in 1972. After retiring, he was appointed Rangers manager, succeeding Jock Wallace. His time at the helm yielded two Scottish Cup titles and a further two League Cups but, crucially, no league titles. He resigned in October 1983 before later returning to the Ibrox club as part of the public relations team, youth development coach and, finally, a member of the board of directors. More recently, he was named the club's honorary president. In 1999, he was voted 'The Greatest Ever Ranger' in a poll of club supporters, with a statue of him unveiled outside the club's ground as part of the 1971 Ibrox disaster memorial two years later.

Jim McCalliog
The Wembley match-winner played only nine more times for his country, his tenth and final appearance coming in 1971 in a 2–0 defeat away to Portugal. By then, he was playing for Wolverhampton Wanderers, moving there in 1969 in a £70,000 deal after almost four years at Sheffield Wednesday.

He was a virtual ever-present in his three years at Molineux, scoring thirty-four goals for the Midlanders. One of those was a vital away goal against Juventus in Wolves' run to the 1972 UEFA Cup Final. He was on target again in the final, a two-legged affair against fellow English outfit Tottenham, but he ended up with a runners-up medal.

Injuries curtailed his appearances in 1973/74 and, days after he missed out on a starting berth in the League Cup Final against Manchester City, he joined Manchester United for £60,000 where he was reunited with his former Chelsea boss Tommy Docherty. The Red Devils were relegated to Division Two at the end of McCalliog's first season at Old Trafford and he was sold to Southampton the following year. He came back to haunt United in the 1976 FA Cup Final, when he set-up Bobby Stokes to score Southampton's winning goal. That gave him the first (and only) winners' medal of his career.

Brief stints followed at Chicago Sting in the USA, Norwegian side SFK Lyn, and Lincoln City before he finished his career as player-manager at non-league Runcorn. He then managed Halifax Town for eighteen months between March 1990 and October 1991. That was his last job in football.

After leaving the game, he spent several years as a publican before returning to Scotland in 2010, where he and his wife Debbie now run a bed and breakfast in the quiet Ayrshire village of Fenwick.

Tommy Gemmell
Another of the Lisbon Lions who won the European Cup with Celtic a matter of weeks after the Wembley win. It was Gemmell, in fact, who equalised for the Glasgow giants with a second-half strike after Sandro Mazzola had given Internazionale an early lead. The Motherwell man scored again in Celtic's 1970 European Cup final defeat at the hands of Feyenoord, making him, to date, one of only three British footballers to score in two different European Cup finals (Phil Neal of Liverpool

and Gareth Bale of Real Madrid being the others). After a trophy-laden decade with Celtic, during which he made 418 appearances and scored 63 goals, Gemmell moved south to join Nottingham Forest in December 1971 as cover for Northern Ireland's Liam O'Kane. Forest were relegated from the top flight at the end of that season. A short stint in the NASL followed with the Miami Toros before Gemmell returned to Scotland in 1973 with Dundee. He captained the Dens Park side to victory in the 1973 Scottish League Cup final – ironically at the expense of Celtic – before retiring in 1977. He did so having made eighteen appearances for Scotland and scoring one goal, from the penalty spot against Cyprus in a 1970 World Cup qualifier. Gemmell went on to manage Dundee from 1977 until 1980, during which time he signed his former Celtic teammate, Jimmy Johnstone. Two stints in charge of Albion Rovers were to follow. He passed away in March 2017 after a long illness.

Willie Wallace
Former Heart of Midlothian forward Wallace attained Scottish footballing immortality as part of Celtic's 'Lisbon Lions' that won the European Cup in May 1967 and had four-and-a-half trophy-laden seasons at Parkhead. He won four league championships, three Scottish Cups and two League Cups, racking up an impressive 140 goals in 239 games. In October 1971, he and teammate John Hughes were sold to Crystal Palace for a combined fee of £30,000. However, he found success in England hard to come by and, less than a year later, was back in Scotland playing for Dumbarton. In the twilight of his career, he moved to Australia where he won two league titles with APIA Leichhardt before returning to Scotland with Partick Thistle. A week after signing for the Jags, he moved north to Ross County where he played out the remainder of the 1976/77 season as player-coach. A spell on the Dundee coaching staff followed

before he returned to APIA, eventually settling in Sydney and opening his own sports shop.

Bobby Lennox

Like Wallace, Simpson and Gemmell, Lennox played in Celtic's European Cup victory in May 1967. A prolific outside-left, he remains the Glasgow side's second-highest scorer of all time, having notched 301 goals across two spells with the club. In 1967/68, he even finished third in the race for the European Golden Boot. All told, he won eleven league championship titles as well as eight Scottish Cups and five League Cups with the Glasgow side. An extremely pacy forward, Lennox was nicknamed 'Lemon' by some supporters because he had a habit of making opposition defenders look like 'suckers'. He was also greatly admired by some of the game's biggest stars. Bobby Charlton, whom he faced at Wembley in 1967, once said: 'If I had Lennox in my team, I could have played forever. He was one of the best strikers I have ever seen.' Real Madrid icon Alfredo di Stefano added: 'The Scotsman who gave me the most trouble was Bobby Lennox. My testimonial at the Bernabeu was against Celtic as, of course, they were the champions of Europe in 1967, and although I remember the stadium rising to Jimmy Johnstone, I admired Lennox greatly.' The 1967 win over England was just Lennox's second appearance for Scotland. He scored on his debut against Northern Ireland in November 1966 and again at Wembley but, despite being tipped to have a long and successful international career, he played only eight more times, a goal in a 1968 friendly with Denmark the only other time he found the net for his country. A brief stint at Houston Hurricane in the NASL punctuated his career with Celtic and he ultimately joined the club's coaching staff in 1980 when he retired – the last of the Lisbon Lions to call time on his career. He was inducted into the Scottish Football Hall of Fame in November 2005 and, in 2002, Celtic supporters voted him into the club's all-time greatest XI.

Bobby Brown
The architect of Scotland's Wembley victory continued as Scotland manager until 1971 but cut an increasingly frustrated figure as player call-offs, injuries and club demands undermined his position and made it hard for him to field his strongest side on a consistent basis. He won nine of the twenty-eight games for which he was at the helm but, to his disappointment, was unable to steer his country to either the 1968 European Championship or the 1970 World Cup. The Scotland job proved to be Brown's last in football, after which he switched his focus to his other business interests. He and wife Ruth settled in Helensburgh, to the west of Glasgow, where they ran a gift and coffee shop. Sadly, Ruth passed away from blood cancer in 1983 at the age of fifty-nine. Brown was also involved in property development and was an outdoors enthusiast who enjoyed climbing Munros with his church rambling group. He was also a passionate Rotarian who raised huge sums for charity. In 2015, he was inducted into the Scottish Football Hall of Fame. Two years later, Rangers FC bestowed the same honour upon him. He passed away in January 2020 at the age of ninety-six.

Sir Alf Ramsey
Ramsey continued to manage England until May 1974 when he was unceremoniously, and surprisingly, sacked. Following the World Cup victory in 1966, he led the Three Lions to third place at the 1968 European Championship in Italy and the quarter-finals of the 1970 World Cup in Mexico. Despite leading West Germany 2–0 with twenty minutes remaining, England succumbed to a 3–2 defeat. Ramsey's decision to substitute Bobby Charlton and Martin Peters – supposedly

to rest them for the semi-final – was subsequently widely condemned.

West Germany again defeated England in qualifying for the 1972 European Championship. Hugh McIlvanney described the football they played in a 3–1 defeat at Wembley and a stalemate in Berlin as 'joyless', prompting many to wonder if the Ramsey era had run its course. The murmurings of dissent transformed into a full-blown crescendo in 1974 when England failed to qualify for the World Cup for the first time in their history. A month after an ultimately decisive draw with Poland, Ramsey was sacked by the Football Association.

'It was the most devastating half-hour of my life,' he would later remark. 'I stood in a room almost full of staring committee men. It was just like I was on trial. I thought I was going to be hanged.'

Many suspected Ramsey's sacking to have been an act of open malevolence and the settling of a personal grudge by FA chief Sir Harold Thompson. Leo McKinstry, Ramsey's biographer, maintains that Thompson harboured an intense, class-driven animosity towards the World Cup-winning manager. 'Though Sir Alf spoke in the clipped manner of an army officer, he was from a deprived Dagenham background,' said McKinstry. 'But Thompson was obsessed with public school and university pedigree.' It didn't go unnoticed, either. 'He always referred to me, even to my face, as Ramsey, which I found insulting,' Sir Alf once said.

The manner of his sacking sent shockwaves through the game. Alan Ball, one of his World Cup-winning team, described it as 'the most incredible thing that ever happened in English football'. Even more incredible was his meagre pay-off. At the time of his dismissal, Ramsey's salary was reported to be just £7,200 – less than that of some Third Division managers. His redundancy payment came to just £8,000 whilst his FA pension amounted to a paltry £25 per week. Lacking financial security, Ramsey returned to management with Birmingham City in 1977 followed by a brief stint in Greece with Panathinaikos.

After retiring from football management, Ramsey lived a somewhat reclusive life in his beloved Ipswich, spending his days playing golf and watching westerns.

On the eve of the 1998 World Cup – having been diagnosed with Alzheimer's disease and prostate cancer – he suffered a stroke and spent three months in hospital. He died less than a year later, on 28 April 1999, in a nursing home following a heart attack. He was seventy-nine years old.

Three years later, Ramsey was made an inaugural inductee of the English Football Hall of Fame. In 2010, he became the first person to be inducted twice, when he was included for his achievements as a player in addition to those as a manager.

Portman's Walk, a street that runs along the north side of Ipswich's Portman Road stadium, was renamed Sir Alf Ramsey Way shortly after his death and, in 2012, the club's South Stand was renamed the Sir Alf Ramsey Stand.

A statue of him was unveiled in the players' tunnel at Wembley in 2009, which, according to World Cup-winning full-back George Cohen, would 'remind every player to give their best out on the pitch'.

Widely regarded as one of the greatest football managers of all-time, with an iron will to match, Ramsey's style might not have been universally popular, but it was unquestionably effective.

'He was in a class of his own,' said goalkeeper Gordon Banks. 'Some managers are tactically aware. Some excel at coaching. Others are good at motivation and man-management. Alf was superb at everything. That is what made him so special.'

In twelve senior international matches in which he managed England against Scotland, Ramsey won six, drew three and lost three.

EPILOGUE

FOR MANY YEARS, there was a bar in Anstruther, a small seaside town in the East Neuk of Fife, called the Craw's Nest. It occupied part of a beautiful white building that had, at one time, been the local manse.

Sir Bobby Charlton visited it regularly. A fanatical golfer, he travelled to the area every autumn for several years to play in the Alfred Dunhill Links pro-am at nearby St Andrews. Soon, the Craw's Nest become one of his favourite watering holes. He couldn't, though, help noticing one thing about it.

'The proprietor Sandy Bowman proudly displayed a single malt whisky labelled "Wembley, 1967",' he recalled. 'You may not be surprised to learn that there was no companion bottle marked "Wembley, 1961".

'On my visits, I always pointed out that a similar commemoration of the 1961 match, when things went less well for Scotland, might provide a little historical balance. My suggestion was never taken up but, each year, I checked, mostly in a spirit of supreme optimism.'

Charlton could always console himself with having had the last laugh. There was no bottle of whisky to trump his World Cup winner's medal. He knew it. Everybody knew it. Losing at Wembley in 1967, whilst immediately painful, amounted to little more than a tiny ink blot on England's copybook. If Scotland wanted to call themselves world champions, so be it. Fact was, they weren't.

Writing in his autobiography years later, Charlton observed how Scotland had defeated themselves in their pursuit of the 'extremely practical goal' of qualifying for the 1968 European Championships at England's expense, an isolated result that snowballed into a prolonged pattern of tartan pratfalls.

'For so long, it seemed that, if England had lost many competitive values, if they were finding it increasingly hard to make any kind of impact on the major tournaments, Scotland might actually have lost its football soul.

'While England still manage to produce, spasmodically admittedly, players of potentially world-class talent, such as Michael Owen, Paul Scholes, David Beckham, Steven Gerrard and Wayne Rooney, where were the new Laws and Baxters, St Johns and Gemmills?'

In Charlton's mind, the cause was clear. 'The old supply line from the boys clubs seemed to have been cut, a disaster magnified, for followers of the national team, by the ability of clubs to invest a sudden gush of television money on European players, many of them of questionable quality.'

If those in charge of Scottish football could have bottled that kind of thinking and foresight with the efficiency and gusto with which they bottled whisky, things could have worked out very differently.

Along with Charlton, Sir Geoff Hurst is the sole survivor of the England team that Brown's boys beat at Wembley in 1967. He played Scotland four more times after that, avoiding defeat on each occasion. By the time he retired from playing in the late 1970s, he had represented his country forty-nine times, scoring twenty-four goals in the process, good enough to remain one of England's twenty most prolific goalscorers of all time.

'Every Scotsman I meet, the most asked question I get is, "Did I play in 1967?",' he admitted. 'So, yes, I get reminded of it fairly regularly. Of course, there was disappointment that we got beat but, as we know in life, in football you can't win them all.'

As for Denis Law, he later reflected on how Scotland reacted to that win with something approaching embarrassment. 'We paid too much attention those England games,' he conceded. 'Treating that April 1967 game as an unofficial World Cup final was unprofessional. I know how important it is for Scotland to beat the English but I often think that if our approach had been a bit more disciplined, we could have done a lot better than we did in competition football.'

It's hard to argue. To this day, that Wembley win is eulogised and celebrated in Scotland with giddy abandon. Younger members of the Tartan Army actively seek out their elder foot soldiers to hear what it was like to be there. Mementoes from the day invite huge curiosity and change hands for huge sums. Recently, indeed, the shirt reportedly worn by Jim Baxter at Wembley in 1967 was brought to auction in Glasgow. The company handling the sale anticipated that it would fetch up to £60,000, such is the scarcity of memorabilia from the game and the enduring fascination the match engenders.

As it turned out, the auction was scrapped at the eleventh hour when two notices of dispute were lodged against the shirt's authenticity. Two businessmen from Falkirk and a musician from East Lothian each claimed they had Baxter's actual No.6 jersey. At the time of writing, the dispute remained unresolved but there have been suggestions that many people were handed signed shirts by Baxter for charity fundraisers and the like, each accompanied by earnest assurances that it was indeed that which was on his back when he performed his keepie-uppies. Slim Jim: the loveable rogue's loveable rogue.

Still, the fact the match is regarded by many as the apogee of more than 150 years of the Scottish national team is, as far as some are concerned, both revealing and risible. Cabinet-makers tend not to build display cases for moral victories and bragging rights. In almost every sport, silverware is the ultimate benchmark of success and that's something that is conspicuously absent from the Hampden Park trophy room.

There are others, however, who contend that success, much like beauty, exists in the eye of the beholder. Should trophies and medals be its sole unit of measurement? Consider, for example, San Marino. A microstate enclaved by Italy, it has the smallest population of any UEFA country. Since they made their international debut against Canada in 1988, the Sammarinese have played more than 200 competitive matches without recording a single win and scoring only twenty goals. For context, Argentina scored fifteen at the 2022 World Cup finals. Are we really to believe that there would be less justification in San Marino celebrating an end to that sequence simply because there's no trophy at stake? Or what about the 134 countries who have never qualified for the World Cup? Luxembourg, for example, or Finland, India, Venezuela and the like. Should they not rejoice in finally getting there because for bigger, better-resourced nations, qualification is only the means and not the end? The case for success being entirely open to interpretation, defined according to a pliable set of parameters, is compelling.

For all that, there remains a nagging feeling that Scotland should be better than that. Victory over England in 1967 was akin to running a world record time for the 100m but doing so in the first leg of a 400m race in which they finished second. Impressive but, ultimately, unavailing.

EPILOGUE

Even the SFA seems unsure about how best to commemorate the win. In June 2017, just a matter of weeks after the fiftieth anniversary of the match, Scotland hosted England at Hampden in a qualifier for the 2018 World Cup. In the build-up to the match, goalkeeper Craig Gordon called on his teammates to summon the spirit of the Class of '67. 'If we can replicate that,' he said, 'it'd be a nice way to finish the season.'

SFA president Alan McRae, however, invited only two of the players who featured at Wembley to take in the game as a guest of the association, Jim McCalliog and Willie Wallace. It appeared that the blazers simply forgot all about it. McCalliog received his invite eight days before the game, meaning that the pre-match programme could not be altered with UEFA, limiting his involvement in the match to the hospitality suites.

Bobby Lennox was also given a last-minute invite but was left bewildered when the SFA said it would struggle to accommodate his request for a ticket for his wife, too. Every other surviving player – Denis Law, John Greig, Ron McKinnon and Eddie McCreadie – was snubbed. So, too, was the architect of it all, Bobby Brown.

At the time, one anonymous former player blasted the move, saying: 'A team's a team. We should all have been invited or none at all. The organisation is very poor but, sadly, it's what we've come to expect from the SFA.'

Perhaps. Or perhaps that's as it should be. Perhaps the unofficial World Cup final is best memorialised in an appropriately unofficial way; by botched celebrations, by contested auctions, by banter that is easily defeated and by commemorative bottles of whisky.

Wha's like us? Damn few, indeed.

APPENDIX A

1966/67 BRITISH HOME CHAMPIONSHIP RESULTS IN FULL

October 22, 1966

Wales   1–1   **Scotland**
Davies (77)   Law (86)

Wales: Sprake, Hennessey, Williams, England (c), Rodrigues, Hole, Reece, Jarvis, Jones, W. Davies, R. Davies.

Scotland: Ferguson, Gemmell, McKinnon, Bremner, Greig (c), Clark, Johnstone, Baxter, Henderson, Law, McBride.

Ninian Park, Cardiff
Attendance: 33,269
Referee: Ken Dagnall (England)

APPENDIX A

N. Ireland 0–2 England
Hunt (40)
Peters (60)

N. Ireland: Jennings, Harvey, Todd, Parke, Elder (c), McCullough, Best, Irvine, Dougan, Ferguson, Crossan.

England: Banks, J. Charlton, Cohen, Moore (c), Wilson, Ball, Peters, Stiles, B. Charlton, Hunt, Hurst.

Windsor Park, Belfast
Attendance: 47,897
Referee: Robert Holley Davidson (Scotland)

November 16, 1966

Scotland 2–1 N. Ireland
Murdoch (14)   Nicholson (9)
Lennox (35)

Scotland: Ferguson, Gemmell, Greig (c), McKinnon, Bremner, Clark, Henderson, Murdoch, McBride, Chalmers, Lennox.

N. Ireland: Jennings, Harvey, Neill, Parke, Elder (c), Clements, Nicholson, Irvine, Dougan, Wilson, Crossan.

Hampden Park, Glasgow
Attendance: 45,281
Referee: John Keith Taylor (England)

England   5–1   Wales
Hurst (30, 34)   W. Davies (36)
B. Charlton (43)
Hennessey (65, og)
J. Charlton (84)

England: Banks, Cohen, Wilson, Stiles, J. Charlton, Moore (c), Ball, Hurst, B. Charlton, Hunt, Peters.

Wales: Millington, Green, Williams, Hennessey, England (c), Hole, Rees, W. Davies, R. Davies, Jones, Jarvis.

Wembley Stadium, London
Attendance: 75,380
Referee: Thomas Wharton (Scotland)

April 12, 1967

N. Ireland   0–0   Wales

N. Ireland: McKenzie, Craig, Neill, Elder, Bruce, Clements, Nicholson, Stewart, Welsh, Dougan, Trainor.

Wales: Millington, James, Thomas, Williams, Durban, Hole, Jarvis, Rees, Davies, Vernon, Pring.

Windsor Park, Belfast
Attendance: 17,643
Referee: Kevin Howley (England)

April 15, 1967

England 2–3 Scotland
J. Charlton (84)   Law (27)
Hurst (88)   Lennox (78)
   McCalliog (87)

England: Banks, J. Charlton, Cohen, Moore (c), Wilson, Ball, Peters, Stiles, B. Charlton, Greaves, Hurst.

Scotland: Simpson, Gemmell, Greig (c), McKinnon, McCreadie, Baxter, Bremner, McCalliog, Law, Lennox, Wallace.

Wembley Stadium, London
Attendance: 99,063
Referee: Gerhard Schulenburg (West Germany)

APPENDIX B

INTERNATIONAL CAREERS OF THE SCOTLAND XI AT A GLANCE

Ronnie Simpson
Position: Goalkeeper
Caps: 5
Goals: 0
First match: England 2–3 Scotland, 15 April 1967
Last match: Scotland 2–1 Austria, 6 November 1968

Tommy Gemmell
Position: Full-back
Caps: 18
Goals: 1
First match: Scotland 3–4 England, 2 April 1966
Last match: Belgium 3–0 Scotland, 3 February 1971

John Greig
Position: Defender
Caps: 44
Goals: 3
First match: Scotland 1–0 England, 11 April 1964
Last match: Scotland 3–1 Denmark, 29 October 1975

Ron McKinnon
Position: Defender
Caps: 28
Goals: 1
First match: Scotland 1–0 Italy, 9 November 1965
Last match: USSR 1–0 Scotland, 14 June 1971

Eddie McCreadie
Position: Full-back
Caps: 23
Goals: 0
First match: England 2–2 Scotland, 10 April 1965
Last match: Scotland 8–0 Cyprus, 17 May 1969

Jim Baxter
Position: Left-half
Caps: 34
Goals: 3
First match: Scotland 5–2 Northern Ireland, 9 November 1960
Last match: Scotland 3–2 Wales, 22 November 1967

Billy Bremner
Position: Midfielder
Caps: 54
Goals: 3
First match: Scotland 0–0 Spain, 8 May 1965
Last match: Denmark 0–1 Scotland, 3 September 1975

Jim McCalliog
Position: Midfielder
Caps: 10
Goals: 1
First match: England 2–3 Scotland, 15 April 1967
Last match: Portugal 2–0 Scotland, 21 April 1971

Denis Law
Position: Centre-forward
Caps: 55
Goals: 30
First match: Wales 0–3 Scotland, 18 October 1958
Last match: Zaire 0–2 Scotland, 14 June 1974

Bobby Lennox
Position: Outside-left
Caps: 10
Goals: 3
First match: Scotland 2–1 Northern Ireland, 16 November 1966
Last match: Scotland 0–0 Wales, 22 April 1970

Willie Wallace
Position: Inside-forward
Caps: 7
Goals: 0
First match: Scotland 3–2 Northern Ireland, 25 November 1964
Last match: England 4–1 Scotland, 10 May 1969

APPENDIX C

COMPLETE LIST OF RESULTS OF MATCHES BETWEEN ENGLAND AND SCOTLAND: 1872–2022

30/11/1872	Scotland	0–0	England	Hamilton Crescent, Glasgow
08/03/1873	England	4–2	Scotland	The Oval, London
07/03/1874	Scotland	2–1	England	Hamilton Crescent, Glasgow
06/03/1875	England	2–2	Scotland	The Oval, London
04/03/1876	Scotland	3–0	England	Hamilton Crescent, Glasgow
03/03/1877	England	1–3	Scotland	The Oval, London
02/03/1878	Scotland	7–2	England	Hampden Park, Glasgow
05/04/1879	England	5–4	Scotland	The Oval, London
13/03/1880	Scotland	5–4	England	Hampden Park, Glasgow
12/03/1881	England	1–6	Scotland	The Oval, London
11/03/1882	Scotland	5–1	England	Hampden Park, Glasgow
10/03/1883	England	2–3	Scotland	Bramall Lane, Sheffield
15/03/1884	Scotland	1–0	England	Cathkin Park, Glasgow
21/03/1885	England	1–1	Scotland	The Oval, London
27/03/1886	Scotland	1–1	England	Hampden Park, Glasgow
19/03/1887	England	2–3	Scotland	Leamington Road, Blackburn
17/03/1888	Scotland	0–5	England	Hampden Park, Glasgow
13/04/1889	England	2–3	Scotland	The Oval, London
05/04/1890	Scotland	1–1	England	Hampden Park, Glasgow

04/04/1891	England	2–1	Scotland	Ewood Park, Blackburn
02/04/1892	Scotland	1–4	England	Ibrox Park, Glasgow
01/04/1893	England	5–2	Scotland	Athletic Ground, Richmond
07/04/1894	Scotland	2–2	England	Celtic Park, Glasgow
06/04/1895	England	3–0	Scotland	Goodison Park, Liverpool
04/04/1896	Scotland	2–1	England	Celtic Park, Glasgow
03/04/1897	England	1–2	Scotland	Crystal Palace, London
02/04/1898	Scotland	1–3	England	Celtic Park, Glasgow
08/04/1899	England	2–1	Scotland	Villa Park Birmingham
07/04/1900	Scotland	4–1	England	Celtic Park, Glasgow
30/03/1901	England	2–2	Scotland	Crystal Palace, London
03/05/1902	England	2–2	Scotland	Villa Park, Birmingham
04/04/1903	England	1–2	Scotland	Bramall Lane, Sheffield
09/04/1904	Scotland	0–1	England	Celtic Park, Glasgow
01/04/1905	England	1–0	Scotland	Crystal Palace, London
07/04/1906	Scotland	2–1	England	Hampden Park, Glasgow
06/04/1907	England	1–1	Scotland	St James' Park, Newcastle
04/04/1908	Scotland	1–1	England	Hampden Park, Glasgow
03/04/1909	England	2–0	Scotland	Crystal Palace, London
02/04/1910	Scotland	2–0	England	Hampden Park, Glasgow
01/04/1911	England	1–1	Scotland	Goodison Park, Liverpool
23/03/1912	Scotland	1–1	England	Hampden Park, Glasgow
05/04/1913	England	1–0	Scotland	Stamford Bridge, London
04/04/1914	Scotland	3–1	England	Hampden Park, Glasgow
10/04/1920	England	5–4	Scotland	Hillsborough Stadium, Sheffield
09/04/1921	Scotland	3–0	England	Hampden Park, Glasgow
08/04/1922	England	0–1	Scotland	Villa Park, Birmingham
14/04/1923	Scotland	2–2	England	Hampden Park, Glasgow
12/04/1924	England	1–1	Scotland	Wembley Stadium, London
04/04/1925	Scotland	2–0	England	Hampden Park, Glasgow
17/04/1926	England	0–1	Scotland	Old Trafford, Manchester
02/04/1927	Scotland	1–2	England	Hampden Park, Glasgow
31/03/1928	England	1–5	Scotland	Wembley Stadium, London

APPENDIX C

13/04/1929	Scotland	1–0	England	Hampden Park, Glasgow
05/04/1930	England	5–2	Scotland	Wembley Stadium, London
28/03/1931	Scotland	2–0	England	Hampden Park, Glasgow
09/04/1932	England	3–0	Scotland	Wembley Stadium, London
01/04/1933	Scotland	2–1	England	Hampden Park, Glasgow
14/04/1934	England	3–0	Scotland	Wembley Stadium, London
06/04/1935	Scotland	2–0	England	Hampden Park, Glasgow
04/04/1936	England	1–1	Scotland	Wembley Stadium, London
17/04/1937	Scotland	3–1	England	Hampden Park, Glasgow
09/04/1938	England	0–1	Scotland	Wembley Stadium, London
15/04/1939	Scotland	1–2	England	Hampden Park, Glasgow
12/04/1947	England	1–1	Scotland	Wembley Stadium, London
10/04/1948	Scotland	0–2	England	Hampden Park, Glasgow
09/04/1949	England	1–3	Scotland	Wembley Stadium, London
15/04/1950	Scotland	0–1	England	Hampden Park, Glasgow
14/04/1951	England	2–3	Scotland	Wembley Stadium, London
05/04/1952	Scotland	1–2	England	Hampden Park, Glasgow
18/04/1953	England	2–2	Scotland	Wembley Stadium, London
03/04/1954	Scotland	2–4	England	Hampden Park, Glasgow
02/04/1955	England	7–2	Scotland	Wembley Stadium, London
14/04/1956	Scotland	1–1	England	Hampden Park, Glasgow
06/04/1957	England	2–1	Scotland	Wembley Stadium, London
19/04/1958	Scotland	0–4	England	Hampden Park, Glasgow
11/04/1959	England	1–0	Scotland	Wembley Stadium, London
09/04/1960	Scotland	1–1	England	Hampden Park, Glasgow
15/04/1961	England	9–3	Scotland	Wembley Stadium, London
14/04/1962	Scotland	2–0	England	Hampden Park, Glasgow
06/04/1963	England	1–2	Scotland	Wembley Stadium, London
11/04/1964	Scotland	1–0	England	Hampden Park, Glasgow
10/04/1965	England	2–2	Scotland	Wembley Stadium, London
02/04/1966	Scotland	3–4	England	Hampden Park, Glasgow
15/04/1967	England	2–3	Scotland	Wembley Stadium, London
24/02/1968	Scotland	1–1	England	Hampden Park, Glasgow

10/05/1969	England	4–1	Scotland	Wembley Stadium, London
25/04/1970	Scotland	0–0	England	Hampden Park, Glasgow
22/05/1971	England	3–1	Scotland	Wembley Stadium, London
27/05/1972	Scotland	0–1	England	Hampden Park, Glasgow
14/02/1973	Scotland	0–5	England	Hampden Park, Glasgow
19/05/1973	England	1–0	Scotland	Wembley Stadium, London
18/05/1974	Scotland	2–0	England	Hampden Park, Glasgow
24/05/1975	England	5–1	Scotland	Wembley Stadium, London
15/05/1976	Scotland	2–1	England	Hampden Park, Glasgow
04/06/1977	England	2–1	Scotland	Wembley Stadium, London
20/05/1978	Scotland	0–1	England	Hampden Park, Glasgow
26/05/1979	England	3–1	Scotland	Wembley Stadium, London
24/05/1980	Scotland	0–2	England	Hampden Park, Glasgow
23/05/1981	England	0–1	Scotland	Wembley Stadium, London
29/05/1982	Scotland	0–1	England	Hampden Park, Glasgow
01/06/1983	England	2–0	Scotland	Wembley Stadium, London
26/05/1984	Scotland	1–1	England	Hampden Park, Glasgow
25/05/1985	Scotland	1–0	England	Hampden Park, Glasgow
23/04/1986	England	2–1	Scotland	Wembley Stadium, London
23/05/1987	Scotland	0–0	England	Hampden Park, Glasgow
21/05/1988	England	1–0	Scotland	Wembley Stadium, London
27/05/1989	Scotland	0–2	England	Hampden Park, Glasgow
15/06/1996	England	2–0	Scotland	Wembley Stadium, London
13/11/1999	Scotland	0–2	England	Hampden Park, Glasgow
17/11/1999	England	0–1	Scotland	Wembley Stadium, London
14/08/2013	England	3–2	Scotland	Wembley Stadium, London
18/11/2014	Scotland	1–3	England	Celtic Park, Glasgow
11/11/2016	England	3–0	Scotland	Wembley Stadium, London
10/06/2017	Scotland	2–2	England	Hampden Park, Glasgow
18/06/2021	England	0–0	Scotland	Wembley Stadium, London

NOTES

THIS BOOK IS predominantly the result of interviews conducted with surviving players who played in the England-Scotland fixture of April 1967, reporters, and supporters of both sides, as well as a huge number of contemporaneous newspaper accounts of the match and the build-up to it. These interviews were conducted between December 2021 and January 2023.

Sadly, many of the players who played in the match have since passed away but, happily, they documented their experiences of it in various autobiographies, biographies and other newspaper and television interviews. Where contextually appropriate, I have woven in some of their quotes and reflections to this book. For those wishing to find out more about any individual player, I'd warmly refer you to the bibliography where you will find details of them and a great many other points of reference.

A recurring thought dominated my research into this story: the value of journalism. The global media landscape has transformed spectacularly over the last couple of decades to satisfy the needs of an increasingly on-the-go, impatient audience. Consequently, two things have happened: one, vastly reduced word counts have squeezed critical detail into the margins; two, smaller operating budgets have ransacked the space previously occupied by specialism and authority, claiming it in the name of generalists and versatility.

Ken Gallacher wasn't a generalist. Neither was Gair Henderson, nor Sam Leitch, nor Allan Herron, nor Shearer Borthwick, nor Norman MacDonald. It is precisely because they were so assiduously devoted to their fields – and because they were given the latitude to operate that way – that writing this book was possible. Without them and their peers, our window into the past would be fitted with frosted glass. For their diligent commitment to comprehensive coverage, I am immensely grateful.

SELECTED BIBLIOGRAPHY

Billy Bremner: The Real King Billy – The Complete Biography. Richard Sutcliffe. (Great Northern Books Ltd, 2011)

Bobby Brown: A Life in Football, From Goals to the Dugout. Jack Davidson. (Pitch Publishing, 2017)

Scotland in the Sixties: The Definitive Account of the Scottish Football Team 1960–69. Ronnie McDevitt. (Pitch Publishing, 2016)

Sir Bobby Charlton: My Manchester United Years. Sir Bobby Charlton with James Lawton. (Headline, 2007)

Sir Bobby Charlton: My England Years. Sir Bobby Charlton with James Lawton. (Headline, 2008)

Slim Jim: Simply the Best. Isobel Murray & Tom Miller. (Black & White Publishing, 2014)

Slim Jim Baxter: The Definitive Biography. Ken Gallacher. (Virgin Books, 2002)

Sport And National Identity in The Post-War World. Adrian Smith & Dilwyn Porter. (Routledge, 2004)

Stone Voices: The Search for Scotland. Neil Ascherson. (Granta Books, 2002)

Stop The World: The Autobiography of Winnie Ewing. Winnie Ewing & Michael Russell. (Birlinn Ltd, 2004)

Sure It's a Grand Old Team to Play For. Ronnie Simpson. (Souvenir Press, 1967)

The Association Game: A History of British Football. Matthew Taylor. (Pearson Education Limited, 2008)

The King: My Autobiography. Denis Law with Bob Harris. (Bantam Press, 2003)

Hail Cesar: The Autobiography. Billy McNeill. (Headline, 2004)

Thirty Miles From Paradise. Bobby Lennox with Graham McColl (Headline, 2007)

The Winning Touch: My Autobiography. Stevie Chalmers with Graham McColl (Hachette, 2012)

John Greig: My Story. John Greig with Jim Black (Headline, 2005)

Banksy: The Autobiography. Gordon Banks (Penguin Books, 2003)

SELECTED BIBLIOGRAPHY

Greavsie: The Autobiography. Jimmy Greaves (Time Warner Books, 2003)

Jack Charlton: The Autobiography. Jack Charlton with Peter Byrne (Partridge Press, 1996)

Sir Alf: A Major Reappraisal of the Life and Times of England's Greatest Football Manager. Leo McKinstry (Harper Sport, 2010)

If Only: An Alternative History of the Beautiful Game. Simon Turner (Pitch Publishing, 2017)

ADDITIONAL SOURCES

BBC, *Daily Express, Daily Mirror, Daily Record, Daily Sketch, Daily Telegraph, Evening Express, Evening Times, Liverpool Echo, Manchester Guardian, Nutmeg, Sunday Post, The Courier, The Guardian, The Herald, The Press & Journal, The Scotsman, The Times.*

ACKNOWLEDGEMENTS

IT WOULD NOT have been possible for me to write this book without the support of many wonderful people. To each and every one, I am deeply and sincerely grateful.

To Jim and Debbie McCalliog, who welcomed me into their home and gave me the opportunity to not just hear what it was like to score the winning goal in a match of such significance but to *see* it, too. Jim's memories of the game and the emotions it continues to visibly stir in him are genuinely humbling. I hope that today's top footballers, who are lavishly rewarded irrespective of success or failure, share of that same passion.

To Willie and Olive Wallace, who spoke to me from their home in Australia. Willie told me it was nice to know he 'hadn't been forgotten'. In addition to being part of the Scotland side that beat England at Wembley in 1967, he also won the European Cup with Celtic, five league titles, three Scottish Cups and two League Cups. We'll all be long gone before there is even the slightest risk that he'll be forgotten. Thanks, also, to Kevin McQuillan and all at Celtic Football Club for their assistance.

ACKNOWLEDGEMENTS

To John 'Ludo' Low, a gregarious force of nature. The Tartan Army has a reputation for being one of the best, most loyal and most friendly fanbases of any team, in any sport, anywhere in the world. John is the embodiment of all those qualities; an absolutely terrific man.

There are many more people that I spoke to anecdotally or formally interviewed for this book. My apologies if I don't name you all. Hopefully, you know who you are and your contributions are greatly appreciated.

To the brilliant staff at the Mitchell Library in Glasgow, the National Library of Scotland in Edinburgh, and various other institutions where I spent entirely too much time. Thank you for being so patient and accommodating with daft request, upon daft request, upon daft request . . . To the misguided local authorities that would shut down such invaluable resources, don't.

To the relentlessly brilliant Peter Burns and all at Polaris Publishing. This is the third book that Pete and I have worked on and I sincerely hope there will be many more. You make this entire process an absolute joy and it is always a pleasure to work with you.

To Lorne Gardner, for casting an assiduous eye over this project and for doing such a sterling job of editing. Thanks for letting me borrow your keen eyes and sharp storytelling instincts.

To my colleagues in the 'day job' at DC Thomson, huge thanks as always for supporting my latest piece of shameless moonlighting. Particular thanks to Bryce Ritchie, who as well as being a boss, is a great friend with an uncanny knack for keeping me honest.

To my oldest pal, Michael Hoare, for continually challenging me, being an outrageously good sounding board for ideas and opinions, and for being always being there with a cold pint when I needed a break from the laptop.

To my family. My father-in-law, Michael, passed away around the time I started work on this book and I've missed him terribly:

for his enthusiasm, his interest, his questions, his counsel and just, well, *him*. He was a proud Scot and a huge football fan, so I hope he would have got a real kick out this. To my mother-in-law, Christine, and my own parents, George and Madeline, thank you for all of your support.

To my wife Juliet and our daughter Sadie. Yet again, you allowed me to disappear into my own little bubble – often at the expense of get-togethers, parties and so on – while I worked on this latest indulgence. Not once did either of you complain. Instead, you brought me a limitless supply of coffee, biscuits, drawings, notes, hugs, encouragement, love and support. I couldn't do any of this without either of you, nor would I ever wish to.

And finally, to you – thank you for reading. Somebody (I forget who) once said that storytelling is the art of sharing happiness. Well, I've enjoyed it. I sincerely hope you have, too.

ABOUT THE AUTHOR

Michael McEwan is a sportswriter based in Glasgow, Scotland.

He is currently the deputy editor of *bunkered*, one of the UK's leading golf media brands, and is a former winner of both the RBS Young Sportswriter of the Year and *Evening Times* Young Football Journalist of the Year awards.

Gallus is his third published book.

His first, *Running The Smoke: 26 First-Hand Accounts of Tackling the London Marathon*, was an Amazon.co.uk No.1 bestseller and was published in 2016.

His follow-up, *The Ghosts of Cathkin Park: The Inside Story of Third Lanark's Demise*, was also an Amazon.co.uk No.1 bestseller and was published in 2021.

INDEX

A
Aberdeen *Evening Express*, xix, 6, 92, 237
Aberdeen FC, 36, 80, 89, 93, 100, 121, 122, 124, 145
Aberdeen Journal, 15
Aberfan disaster (October 1966), 33 5, 42
AC Milan, 66, 74
Afghanistan, King and Queen of, 171
Airdrie FC, 46
Aitken, Jimmy, 121
Albion Rovers, 126, 286
Alcock, Charles, 12 13, 14
Alexander Brothers, 131
Allan, Willie, 5, 89, 196, 242, 251
Amancio (Real Madrid outside-right), 41
Andersen, Hans Christian, 65
Anderson, Alexander, 113
Anderson, Jimmy, 64, 66
Andrade, José Leandro, 20
anglophobia, xiii
APIA Leichhardt, 286, 287
Arbroath FC, 2
Archer, Ian, xv
Ardeer Recreation FC, 47
Argentina, 19, 67 9, 294
Argentina, Scottish rugby in (2008), 273
Arispe, Pedro, 20
Aristotle, 125
Armfield, Jimmy, 78 9, 117
Arsenal, 51, 57, 58, 121, 122 3, 131, 198
Ascherson, Neal, xv
Ashton, Neil, 270
Associated TV, 199
The Association Game (Taylor, M.), xii
Aston Villa, 40, 272
Athens Intercalated Games (1906), 18
Athletic Ground in Richmond, 17
Athletic News, 172
Augusto, José, xxi, 134
Auld, Bertie, 124, 254
'Auld Alliance' with France, 105 6
Australia, 248
Austria, 23, 28, 54
Automobile Association, 197
Ayr United, 74
Ayresome Park in Middlesbrough, 92 3
Aytoun, Professor William, 111

B
Badger, Len, 93, 97
Baird, Sammy, 25

Bale, Gareth, 286
Ball, Alan, 44, 118 19, 189, 209, 211, 231, 232, 238, 289
   England-Scotland (15th April 1967) participation, 213, 218, 221, 224
Balliol, John, King of Scots, 105 6
Balunas, Matt, 147
Bangerter, Hans, 252
Banks, Gordon, xxii, 78, 97, 120, 165, 190, 229 30, 250 51, 290
   England-Scotland (15th April 1967) participation, 214, 215, 216, 217, 220 22, 223, 224, 225
   'last line of defence,' 116
   post-Wembley memories for (1967), 231 2
   'Scotland as World Champions' query for, 233 4
   shinpads on Denis Law, sign of battle ahead for (Wembley 1967), 210
Bannerman, John, 112
Bannockburn, Battle of (1314), xiii, xiv, 266
Barassi, Ottorino, 29
FC Barcelona, xv
Barr, John (Leeds United Glasgow scout), 159
Barry Bridges, 162
Bates, Chief Superintendent Andy, 271
Bates, Ted, 60
Baugé, Battle of (1421), 106
Baxter, Agnes, 126
Baxter, Jim, 40, 49, 101, 124, 185, 233, 292
   Alex Ferguson on skills of, 278
   birth and early years, 126
   Brown's faith in unpredictable talents of, 140 41, 244 5
   Cilla Black and, 'Jock' and 'haggis' bit, 235
   class of, comparison with Ramsey's men, 7, 8
   coal mining, attitude to, 126 7
   Cowdenbeath Palais, bird pulling trials at, 129
   death of, 278
   dream-like abandon of, 125 6
   England-Scotland (15th April 1967), matchday prelims, 206 7, 208, 209 10, 211
   England-Scotland (15th April 1967) participation, 216, 219 20, 221, 222 3, 224
   English players, relationships with, 201
   form dip, run ours of wild ways and dropping for (December 1962), 130 31
   George Best on skills of, 278 9
   immense, indisputable talent of, 135 6
   international career of, 301
   Kenny Dalglish on skills of, 279
   Law and, Brown's solution to balance between, 244 5
   lifestyle legend, 133 4
   Malky Macdonald's dropping of Baxter against Northern

316

INDEX

Ireland (1966), 50
marriage to Jean Ferguson, 133 4
National Service in Black Watch, 129 30
Newcastle 0-3 defeat by Sunderland, Barry Robson on mesmerising Baxter in, 135
Paisley Road West pub proprietor (1994), 278
Pelé on skills of, 279
Raith Rovers years, 127 8
Rangers new deal for (August 1963), 132
Rangers signing for record transfer fee (1960), 128 9
Rest of the World v England, surprise selection for (October 1963), 132
Ronnie McKinnon on skills of, 279
Scotland win at Wembley with (April 1963), 131
Scotland without, injury problems for (1967/68), 250
Scottish Sporting Hall of Fame inductee, 279
shirt worn at Wembley 1967 by, attempted auction of, 293 4
skills and craft of, big deal for Scotland, 229
Skocik tackle in Austria, injury and aftermath, 132 3
'Slim Jim,' Simply the Best,' 279
St Enoch Hotel, favourite haunt of, 134
struggles, continuation of (1963/64 season), 132
Sunderland, move to, 133 4
transfer list experiences for, 131 2
what happened next for, 277 9
World Cup qualification, near-misses in, 26
Baxter, Robert, 126
Baxter, Stanley, 126
Bayeux Tapestry, 125
BBC Sports, 199
Beattie, Andy, 6, 24, 37 9
Beattie, Archie, 37
Beckenbauer, Franz, 118
Beckham, David, 292
Becontree Heath School, 56
Bell, Jack, 218
Bell, Willie, 8, 122
Bell's Life and Sporting Chronicle, 16
Benburb Juniors, 138 9
Bentley, Roy, 23
Bergkamp, Dennis, 282
Bert Murray, 162
Berwick Rangers, 148
Best, George, 9, 43, 45, 51 2, 81 2, 123 4, 125, 249, 278 9, 280, 281
Betts, Monty, 14
Birmingham City, 60, 192
Bishop, Sid, 171
Black, Cilla, 234 5
Blackburn Rovers, 120
Blacklaw, Adam, 121, 146
Blackpool FC, 63, 78, 118
Blair, Tony, 263, 265
Blantyre Celtic, 143
Blantyre Victoria, 126
Bobby Tambling, 162
Bolton Wanderers, 96
Bonetti, Peter, 97, 100, 120
Bonner, Pat, 282
Bonsor, Alexander, 16
Borthwick, Shearer, 95
Bowen, Dave, 42
Bowen, David, 54
Bowman, Sandy, 291

Bozsik, József, 63
Bradshaw, Tom ('Tiny') ('Wembley Wizard 1928'), 169, 172 3, 174
Bramall Lane in Sheffield, 17
Brand, Ralph, 129
Brazil, 3, 19, 50, 52, 66, 67, 122, 123, 141, 242
Scotland-Brazil in World Cup 1974 (West Germany), 255 6
Bremner, Billy, 7, 8, 10, 50, 53, 159, 233, 235, 240, 244
Baxter and, partnership between, 141, 143
Don Revie on determination of, 103
England-Scotland (15th April 1967), matchday prelims, 209, 210, 211
England-Scotland (15th April 1967) participation, 213 14, 215, 216, 217, 218, 219, 220, 221, 222, 223, 224 5
English players, relationships with, 201
international career of, 301
pre-match odds on scoring (Wembley 1967), 202
pugnatious, tenacious and fearless, 139 40
Scotland's Nobby Stiles, 123
Shankly and Docherty on skills of, 179, 181
Brent Bridge Hotel in Hendon, 191, 203 4
Brentford FC, 58
Brexit referendum (2016), 268
Bridgeton by-election (1961), 114 15
Brightman, Mr Justice, 43
British Home Championship, xiv, 2, 3, 189 90, 218
debut season (1884), 17
England-Scotland at Wembley (9-3 victory for England 1961), 73 82, 120
establishment of (1882), xii
season 1928, 169
season 1949/50, 23
season 1950/51, 62
season 1953/54, 23
season 1957/58, 46
season 1958/59, 39
season 1963/64, 31, 40, 132
season 1966/67, 4, 10, 31, 34 5, 41, 50 54, 249
results in full, 296 9
season 1967/68, 31, 249 51
British Railways, 'Soccer Specials' for Wembley (1967), 197 8
Britishness, xii
Brown, Alan, 144, 155 6, 164 5
Brown, Bill, 146
Brown, Bobby, 103, 122 4, 247 8, 249, 251, 295
architect of Scotland's Wembley victory (1967), 288
Baxter and Law, solution to balance between, 244 5
Belgium, first Scotland cap against (1946), 87
birth and early years, 84
choice of players to beat England on April 10, 1967 at Hampden, 137 44
death at 96 (2020), 288
engagement with Sir Alf, problem for, 234
England-Scotland (15th April 1967) game, comments on, 214, 222, 223, 224, 227
England-Scotland (15th April 1967) game, congratulations from Ramsey, 229
England-Scotland (15th April 1967) game, individual players, thanks and congratulations for, 230
England-Scotland (15th April 1967) game, praise for Scots players (and management), 242, 243 4, 244 6
England-Scotland (15th April 1967) game, press euphoria

317

     on, 237, 238 9
experience and drive of, Scotland's need for, 83 4
faith in unpredictable talents of Baxter, 140 41, 244 5
Falkirk, impressive performances at, 85, 88
Falkirk return, retirement and management calling, 88
Fleet Air Arm, 86 7
gambling on Baxter, considerations about, 135 6
Inter-League matches, comments on, 99 101
Larbert Village School, football at, 84 5
masterminding upset, 116
plotting and scheming, diligence in, 120 21
Portsmouth College and wartime football, 86 7
preparations for Wembley, Johnstone and Wallace, 187 9
preparations for Wembley, Saturday at last, 203, 204, 205, 206, 208 9
preparations for Wembley, site visit, 200 201
preparations for Wembley, so far so good, 182 6
Queen's Park, 85, 87
Rangers, success at, 87
Rangers career (and winning record), 87
Scotland management, clear vision and strategy for, 89 90
Scotland Under-23 matches for (press criticism and subsequent praise), 91 6
Shankly and Docherty on Scotland's prospects under, 178, 181
St Johnstone, management at, 88 9
what happened next for, 288
Brown, Craig, 85, 263 4
Brown, Gordon, 265
Brown, Hugh (PE teacher), 85
Brown, James and Georgina (parents of Bobby), 84, 226 7
Brown, Oliver, 259 60
Brown, Ruth (wife of Bobby), 88, 89, 288
Buckard, Bill, 127
Buckingham, John, 120
Buckley, Paddy, 36, 37
Burgess, Ron, 62, 63
Burnden Park in Bolton, xviii
Burnley FC, 51, 52, 61, 65, 93, 121
Bury FC, 17, 122
Busby, Sir Matt, xiii, xx xxi, 6, 9, 25, 39, 62, 102 3, 147, 244, 252
 Brown and, concerns over fitness of Law, 182 3, 184
 transfer-listing of Denis Law by, xix
Byrne, Gerry, 117
Byrne, Johnny, 138

C

Café Royal on Regent Street, 233, 234
Caldow, Eric, 74, 92
Callaghan, Ian, 97, 100
Callaghan, Jim, 262
Callaghan, Willie, 122
Cameron, David, 265, 266, 267
Canada, 248
Cann, Sydney, 59
Cantona, Eric, 125
Cárdenas, Juan Carlos, 254
Cardiff, 'city of silence and mourning,' 34 5
Carey, John, 277 8, 278
Carmichael, James, 127
Castle Douglas, 272
Cathkin Park, 157
Catterick, Harry, 165
Cea, Pedro, 20

Celtic, 121, 124, 134, 145, 148 50, 183, 187, 188, 189, 190
 Bobby Lennox signing for (and drama of time at), 47 9
 Brown's Old Firm choices for Scotland, 99 100, 122
 European Cup final (1970), defeat by Feyenoord in, 253
 European Cup quarter-final against Vojvodina, 93
 European Cup triumph (1967), 252, 253
 International Cup against Racing Club of Argentina (1968), 253 4
 locomotive-like start to 1966/67 season, 45 6
 Rangers and, bitter rivalry between, 45, 48
Celtic Park, 17, 96, 97
Central European International Cup, 28
Chalmers, Stevie, 46, 47, 52, 100, 122, 144, 150, 190 91, 245
 England-Scotland (15th April 1967), matchday prelims, 206 7, 208
Charles, John, 97
Charlton, Bobby (later Sir Bobby), xiii, xiv, 9, 43, 45 6, 54, 67, 70, 74, 77, 189
 Anstruther in Fife, regular visits to, 291 2
 on Bobby Lennox, best striker for, 287, 288
 despair in defeat (in contrast with jubilation of Scots), 228
 England-Scotland (15th April 1967) participation, 215, 216, 217, 218, 220, 223 4, 225
 English dressing room after Wembley game (1967) for, 231
 'Holy Trinity' frontline at Manchester United, 280
 on Ramsey's determination to win over Scots, 193, 209
 World Cup experience for, xxi xxii
 World Cup final (1966), participation in, 119 20
 World Cup final (1966), pre-match activities, xx xxi, xxii
Charlton, Jack, xiii, xxiii, 54, 70, 117 18, 183 4, 189, 201 2, 210, 231, 237 8, 250
 England-Scotland (15th April 1967) participation, 213, 214 15, 216, 217, 218 19, 220, 221, 224, 226
Charlton Athletic, 59, 121
Chelsea FC, 8, 23, 74, 86, 94, 120, 122, 139, 153, 161 4, 175 6
Chenery, Charles, 16
Chester FC, 86
Chevalier Casino in Glasgow, 134
Chicago Sting, 285
Christie, Norman, 147
Churchill, Winston, 169
Clark, Bobby, 93, 94, 121, 146
Clark, John, 50 51, 99, 146
Clarke, Allan, 93, 98, 100
Clegg, Sir J.C., 56
Clements, David, 51, 249
Clitheroe, Jimmy, 209
Clyde FC, 2, 87, 130, 142, 145
Clyne, Nathaniel, 270
Coates, Ralph, 93
Cocker, Les, 68
Cohen, George, xxi, 142, 178, 231, 250, 290
 England-Scotland (15th April 1967) participation, 219, 220, 223
Coleman, David, 73
Collins, Bobby, 160
Common Wealth Party, 113
Communist Party, 113
Company of Scotland Trading to Africa, 107
Confederación Sudamericana de Fútbol (CONMEBOL), 27, 28
Connery, Sir Sean, 259

INDEX

Connors, Joe, 47
Conservative Party, 104, 113, 115, 167, 236, 259, 260 61, 262, 265 6
Cooke, Charlie, 122, 251
Copa America, 19, 28
Copa Libertadores, 254
Corinthians FC in Brazil, 60 61
Cormack, Peter, 93, 94, 99, 100, 123
Coventry City, 1, 51
Craig, Tully, 85
Crawford, Ray, 65
Craw's Nest in Anstruther, 291
Crerand, Paddy, 9, 26, 45, 156, 157, 228
Crossan, Johnny, 51
Crossgates Primrose, 127
Crowther, Geoffrey, 260
Crystal Palace FC, 14, 16, 286
Culloden, Battle of (1746), 109 10
Cumberland, Duke of, 109 10
Cunningham, George, 261
Cunningham, Willie, 10 11
Cunninghame Graham, Robert Bontine, 112
Currie, Dan, 92
Czechoslovakia, 26, 28, 29, 30, 54, 67, 80, 81

D

Dagnall, Ken, 42
Daily Express, 120, 131
    'Community Singing' at Wembley arranged by, 207
Daily Herald, 212
Daily Mail, 236, 270 71
Daily Mirror, 70 71, 120
    ENGLAND FLOP - NO EXCUSES PLEASE! (1955), 95
Daily Record, 7, 102, 103, 161, 170, 175, 196, 237
Daily Sketch, 236
Daily Telegraph, 236
Dalglish, Kenny, 273, 279, 280
Dalyell, Tam, 115, 199
Danish League XI, 97
Darién scheme, 106 8
Darling, Alistair, 267
Davenport, Kenny, 96
Davidson, Bobby, 44
Davidson, Jack, 88
Davies, Ron, 42
Davies, Wyn, 54
Davis, Harold, 133
Dawson, Jerry, 150
Day, Eric, 60
Dean, Dixie, 169, 173
Debrett's Peerage & Baronetage, 72
Delaunay, Henri, 10, 28, 29
Delaunay, Pierre, 29, 30
Derby County, 96
Devine, Tom, 260
Di Stefano, Alfredo, 40, 132, 157, 287
Dienst, Gottfried, xxiii
Ditchburn, Ted, 61, 63
Divine, Bill, 196
Docherty, Tommy, 8 9, 24, 25, 139, 153 5, 161 4, 166 7, 285
    'We Can Do It' interview with Ken Gallacher (1967), 175 6, 177, 178 9, 180, 181
Dodd, Joseph, 169
Dodgin, Bill, 59 60, 61

Donaldson, Arthur, 259
Dougan, Derek, 43, 51
Douglas, Bryan, 75
Douglas, Dick, 104
Duke of Cornwall's Light Infantry, 57
Dukla Prague, 145, 151, 183, 187 8, 190, 191
Dumbarton FC, 2, 286
Duncan, Scott, 64
Dundee Courier, 92
Dundee FC, 11, 47, 51, 102, 121, 189, 286 7
Dundee United, 10, 93
Dunfermline Athletic, 11, 100, 121, 122
Dunipace Juniors, 138 9
Dunn, James ('Wembley Wizard 1928'), 170
Dunne, John, 253
Durno, Bill, 37
Dutton, Bill, 168
Džajić, Dragan, 252

E

Eakins, Brigadier General Ted, 1 2, 3
Eamonn Andrews Show (ABC TV), 241 2
East India Company, 107
East Stirlingshire, 139
The Economist, 260
Edinburgh City Council, 282
Edinburgh University, 111
Edwards, Alex, 93
Eglinton, Earl of, 111
Eintracht Frankfurt, 157 8
Elder, Alex, 51
Queen Elizabeth II, 34, 69, 80, 267 8
Ellerington, Bill, 59 60, 61
England, 7, 10, 11, 60, 132, 143, 273
    British Home Championship, winners (1949/50), 23
    British Home Championship 1928, 169 74
    Brown and Scotland Under-23 matches against, 91, 92 3, 92 5
    Inter-League matches between Scotland and, 96 101, 102 3
    'Magical Magyars' at Wembley, 3-6 defeat for, 63
    pride (at times) but also sad failures against, 249 52
    Ramsey takeover from Winterbottom as manager, 66 72
    Scotland, 3-4 defeat at Hampden by (April 1966), 138
    Scotland, 9-3 victory at Wembley over (1961), 73, 74 6, 102
    Scotland-England, first formal match between (1872), xii, 12, 13 16
    Scotland-England fixtures, effects of early success of, 16 17
    Scotland's biggest rivals, 26
    World Cup 1958 in Sweden, 25
    World Cup holders on a roll, 42 4, 53 4
    see also British Home Championship results (1966/67)
England, Mike, 41 2
English Football League, 96, 98 9, 103, 121, 169, 189
    season 1946/47, 59
    season 1947/48, 60
    season 1949/50, 61 2
    season 1950/53, 62 3
L'Équipe, 21, 254
Eriksson, Jonas, 270
Estadio Centenario in Uruguay, 254
Estadio Ciudad de Mendoza, 273
Estonia, 273

European Champion Clubs' Cup, 28
European Championship, 218, 249
   Scottish failure to qualify for (1972), 255
   season 1968, 10, 30 31, 44, 292
   season 2000, 264
European Cup, xviii, 31, 66, 93, 128, 132 3, 134, 142, 183, 187 9
   final at Hampden (1960), 157 8
European Cup Winners' Cup, 40, 48, 93, 121, 123, 149, 241
European Nations Cup, 28, 53 4, 67, 135, 177, 192, 246, 248
   season 1960, 29 30
   season 1964, 30
European Parliament, 262
Eusébio, xviii, xxii, 40, 132, 134
   praise for Denis Law from, 281 2
Euston Station, 235
Evening News, 101
Evening Times, 34 5, 83, 92, 95, 237, 251
Everton, 17, 94, 117, 118, 153, 169
Ewing, Winnie, 252 3, 258 60, 262, 264
Ewood Park in Blackburn, 17

F
FA Cup, 14, 40, 119, 121, 147 8, 176
   season 1953, 63
Facchetti, Giacinto, 49
Fairbrother, Jack, 147
Fairey Swordfish ('Stringbag'), 86
Falkirk FC, 2, 11, 84, 85
Falkirk Muir, Battle of (1746), 109
Falkirk Violet, 85
Fallon, John, 148 9
Fallon, Sean, 48, 148
Faroe Islands, 273
Fergus, Tom, 205
Ferguson, Alex (later Sir Alex), 88, 100, 101, 118, 122, 201, 248, 278, 280
Ferguson, Billy (Linfield winger), 43 4
Ferguson, Bobby, 42, 50, 52, 99, 121, 143, 144, 146
Ferguson, Jean, 134 5
Fernie, Willie, 157
Ferrier, George, 127
Feyenoord, 253
The Field, 15
FIFA, 19, 21, 22, 23, 27, 28, 68
   mid-match personnel changes, rules on, 215
Finland, 48, 294
Finnigan, John, 199
Fiorentina, 40
Fitzalan-Howard, Bernard, 16th Duke of Norfolk, 210
Five Elms FC, 57
Fleet Air Arm, 86 7
Foinavon, Grand national winner (1967), 116, 120
Fontaine, Just, 25
Football Association (FA), 12, 19, 22, 66, 68, 132, 194 5, 199
   Wembley pre-match entertainment arrangements, 207
Football in the Sun and Shadow, 19 20
Forbes, Charlie, 121
Forbes, James, 6 7, 92
Ford, David, 94, 199
Ford Dagenham automobile factory, 56
Fordell Colliery, 126
Foresta Hotel in Stockholm, 29
Forster, Fraser, 270
Fort George in Inverness, 109

Forthbank, 84 5
Foula, Isle of, 258
Foulkes, Bill, 281
FourFourTwo magazine, 280
France, 20, 25, 29, 67, 273
   French Football Federation, 10, 28
Fraser MP, Tom, 255 8
Fulham FC, 74, 93, 142

G
Galbraith, Walter, 148
Galeano, Eduardo, 19 20
Gallacher, Hughie ('Wembley Wizard 1928'), 170, 171, 174
Gallacher, Ken, 103, 161
   'We Can Do It' interview with Bill Shankly and Tommy Docherty (1967), 175, 176 81
Gardes Écossaises, 106
Gardner, Robert, 14, 16
Garrow, Alex, 104
Gascoigne, Paul, 125
Gemmell, Tommy, 50 51, 99, 100, 122, 139, 143, 210, 240, 241, 248
   England-Scotland (15th April 1967) participation, 213, 214, 216, 218, 220, 221, 222, 226
   international career of, 300
   what happened next for, 285 6
Gemmill, Archie, 273
Gemmill, Bobby, 292
George Graham, 162
SC Germania (now Hamburger SV), 18
Germany, 273
   see also West Germany
Gerrard, Steven, 292
Gibb, Andrew Dewar, 112
Gibb, William, 16
Gillies, Matt, 278
Gilzean, Alan, 102, 138, 251
Gimnasia FC in Argentina, 18
FC Girondins de Bordeaux, 18
Glanville, Brian, 23, 71
Glasgow Academical Rugby Club at Burnbank, 14
Glasgow and District League, 85
Glasgow Citizens' Theatre, 126
Glasgow Cup, 45, 87, 145
Glasgow Herald, 172
Glasgow Schools League, 85 6
Glasgow University Scottish Nationalist Association (GUSNA), 111, 112, 258
Go Ahead of Holland, 149
Golby, Arthur (Wembley catering manager), 195
Goodall, Roy, 170
Goodison Park inverpool, 17
Gordon, Craig, 295
Graça, Jaime, 134
Graham, George, 124
Grandstand (BBC TV), 73
Gray, Eddie, 93, 140, 159
Greaves, Jimmy, 67, 69, 71, 98, 120, 176, 189, 192, 231, 233, 236, 238
   devastating form in 9-3 demolition of Scotland (1960), 74 5, 79 80
   England-Scotland (15th April 1967) participation, 214, 215, 217, 219, 221, 224, 226
   on Haffey performance (and rest of Scots), 78
Green, Geoffrey, 204

INDEX

Greenwood, Ron, 178
Gregg, Harry, 119
Greig, John, 50 51, 99, 101, 122, 138, 139, 229, 241 2, 248, 281, 295
   England-Scotland (15th April 1967), matchday prelims, 210, 211
   England-Scotland (15th April 1967) participation, 213, 215, 217, 218, 219, 220, 222, 224
   'Greatest Ever Ranger' (1999), 284
   international career of, 300
   praise for Denis Law from, 281
   what happened next for, 284
Grimshaw, Rankin, 251 2
The Guardian, 17

H

Haarlemse FC in Netherlands, 18
Hackett, Desmond, 120
Haddock, Harry, 157
Haffey, Frank, 75, 76 9, 81 2
   'almost ten past' - 'HAPLESS HAFFEY,' 77
Haffey, Ronnie, 77
Halbeath Juniors, 127
Halifax Town, 285
Hamilton, George, 36
Hamilton, Gordon, 86
Hamilton, J.H., 113
Hamilton, Robert, 17
Hampden Park, 14 15, 17, 45 6, 53, 86, 97, 157, 188, 193
   Brazil-Scotland at, 122, 123
   England at, qualifying match for 2018 World Cup at, 295
   England at, Scotland's 2-0 victory over (1962), 273
   Scottish Football Museum at, 23
   Soviet Union-Scotland at, 247 8
   trophy room at, lack of recognition of Wembley victory (1967) in, 294
Hamrin, Kurt, 40
Hanot, Gabrliet, 21
Hardaker, Alan, 98
Harkness, Jack ('Wembley Wizard 1928'), 171, 174
Harkness, Jack (journalist), 92, 237 8
Harris, Ron ('Chopper'), 154, 180
Harrow Chequers, 14
Harvey, Colin, xviii, 94
Harvey, Martin, 51
Haynes, Johnny, 74 5, 76, 78, 81
Heart of Midlothian, 2, 10, 189, 190
Heath, Ted, 260 61
Held, Siggi, xxiii
Henderson, Gair, 34 5, 83 4, 92, 98, 251
Henderson, Tommy, 159
Henderson, Willie, 8, 50 51, 53, 100, 122, 157, 188
Hendon Amateurs, 188
Hendon Hall, 192
Hendon House Hotel, xx xxi
Hennessey, Terry, 41, 54
Henry V of England, 106
The Herald, xv, 34
Herd, Davie, 216
Herd, George, 92
Herdsman, Bert, 127 8
Heritable Jurisdictions Act (1747), 110
Hewie, John, 25 6
Hibernian, 48, 93, 99, 138, 147 8, 151, 185
Hidegkuti, Nándor, 63

Highbury Stadium, 193
Highland Clearances, 110 11
Hill, Jimmy, 1
Hillsborough, Earl Alexander of, 86
Hodges, Cyril, 58
Hogan, John (businessman friend of Denis Law), xvii xviii, xix xx, xxiii xxiv
Hollins, John, 94, 97, 100
Holmes, Ken, 238
Holt, Richard, 102
Hooman, Thomas, 14
Hope, Bobby, 93
Houston Hurricane, 287
Howerd, Frankie, 234 5
Huddersfield Town, 37 9, 51, 117, 170
Hufton, Ted, 171
Hughes, John, 250 51, 286
Hulme, Joe, 236
Hungary, 28
   'Magical Magyars,' 63
Hunt, Roger, 43, 67, 120, 138, 176, 236
Hunter, Norman, 250
Hurst, Charlie, 119
Hurst, Geoff (later Sir Geoff), xxii, 54, 69, 97 8, 100, 119, 180, 211, 238, 249, 252, 292 3
   England-Scotland (15th April 1967) participation, 213, 215, 225, 226
   post-match dejection in dressing room (Wembley 1967), 230 31
Hutchison, Don, 264

I

Ibrox Park, 17, 97, 121
Iceland, 273
Independence for Scotland, referendum on, xi
India, 294
Inland Revenue, 43
Inter Milan, 40, 41, 132
Inter-Cities Fairs Cup, 121, 176
International Cup, 253 4
International Football Association Board (IFAB), 22
Inverclyde Sports Centre, 184
Ireland, 23, 29
   British Home Championship 1928, 169
   Irish League XI, 97
   see also Republic of Ireland
Irvine, Willie, 51, 52
Israel, 248
Italian League Select, 46
Italian League XI, 97
Italy, 6, 26, 28, 29, 48 9, 49, 252, 273
   Italian FA, 29

J

Jackson, Alex ('Wembley Wizard 1928'), 170, 171, 173 4
Jackson, Fred (Wembley box office manager), 194
Jacobite Rebellion, 109 10
Jacobs, Raymond, 34
Jairzinho, 122
James, Alex ('Wembley Wizard 1928'), 170, 171, 172, 174
James, Brian, 120
Jansen, Wim, 273
Japan, 273
Jarvie, Grant, 102
Jenkins, Blair, 267

Jennings, Pat, 43, 51, 52, 53
Joan of Arc, 106
John Hollins, 162
Johns, Hugh, England-Scotland (15th April 1967) commentary, 212 13, 214 15, 217, 218, 219, 220, 222
Johnson, Boris, 269
Johnson, Mick, 127
Johnston, Willie, 49
Johnstone, Jimmy ('Jinky'), 42, 46, 50, 100, 122, 181, 230, 286, 287
   maverick 'Lord of the Wing;, 142 3
   preparations for Wembley, injury worries for, 187 8, 191, 203
Jones, Cliff, 42
Jones, Ken, 71
Jones, Mick, 93
Jones, Tom, 241
Jongbloed, Jan, 273
Jordanhill College, 86 7
Jules Rimet Trophy, xv, 42 3, 67, 99, 118

K

Keegan, Kevin, 264
Keith, Sir Henry, 112
Kelly, Bernie, 127
Kelly, Bob, 170, 172
Kelly, Robert, 254
Ken Shellito, 162
Kennedy, Ludovik, 259
Kenyon-Slaney, William, 16
Kernohan. Robert, 104
Kerr, Jerry, 10
Kilbrandon, Lord Charles James (and 'Kilbrandon Commission'), 260 61
Kilmarnock FC, 11, 45, 46, 93, 99, 121, 122, 143, 185
Kilpatrick, Alex, 230
Kilsyth Rangers, 189
Kinnaird, Arthur, 14
Kipling, Rudyard, 247
Kirin Cup, 273
Kirkcaldy FC, 189
Kjøbenhavns Boldklubb in Denmark, 18
Knowles, Cyril, 93
Kopa, Raymond, 25
Kreitlein, Rudolf, 69
Krol, Ruud, 273

L

Labone, Brian, 97
Labour Party, 113, 260 63, 267
   see also Labour Party in Scotland
Lambie, William, 218
Lamond, Alex, 89
Lauder, Harry, 76, 216
Law, Denis, xiii, xiv, 7 10, 26, 49, 50 52, 250, 275, 292 3, 295
   Aberdeen and football for, 36 7
   attacking lead for Scotland under Brown, 141 2
   Ayresome Park goal against England (Under-23 team against England 1961), 92 3
   Ballon d'Or winner (1964), xviii, 41
   Baxter and, Brown's solution to balance between, 244 5
   Bill Durno, influence on, 37
   Billy McNeill, praise from, 281
   birth and early file, 35 6

   critical to fortunes of Scotland, 102 3, 121 2
   England-Scotland (15th April 1967), matchday prelims, 210, 211
   England-Scotland (15th April 1967) participation, 212, 214, 215, 216, 217, 220, 221, 222, 223, 224, 225
   English players, relationships with, 201
   Eusébio, praise from, 281 2
   fitness double for Wembley 1967, 182 4
   Footballer of the Year (1964), 282
   form and fortunes, dip in (1965/66), xviii xix
   golf as diversion tactic for World Cup 1966 final (and failure of), xvii xviii, xix xx, xxiii xxiv
   good to go for Wembley 1967, 184, 186, 187
   Haffey in Australia, query on safety at home?, 81 2
   'Holy Trinity' frontline at Manchester United, 280
   Huddersfiled Town, professional football at, 37 9
   immediate post-match for (Wembley 1967), 228, 229, 230
   international career of, 302
   John Greig, praise from, 281
   Ninian Park, controversial equaliser at, 41 2
   pre-match odds on scoring (Wembley 1967), 202
   pub post-match repartee with Greig, 242
   Scotland as 'World Champions' for, 233 4
   Scotland's 9-3 hammering by England, 'blackest day' for, 75 6, 79 80
   Scotland's 'Most Outstanding Player' (SFA 2003), 280 81
   Shankly and Docherty on skills of, 179, 181
   shinpads on, sign of battle ahead for Banks (Wembley 1967), 210
   Sir Bobby Robson, praise from, 281
   Torino and Italian League select, 46 7, 97
   transfer-listed in comeuppance by Matt Busby, xix
   what happened next for, 280 82
Lawler, Chris, 93, 94
Lawlor, James, 198 9
Lawrence family, 11
Leadbetter, Jimmy, 65
League of Ireland, 97
'Lean Years' in Scotland (17th century), 108
Leckie, Robert, 15
Leeds United, 7, 42, 93, 103, 117, 122, 123, 131, 140, 183 4
Leggatt, Graham, 39, 92
Leicester City, 40, 43, 51, 116, 171
Leigh, Andy, 127
Leitch, Sam, 71, 73, 74
Lennon, John, 199
Lennox, Bobby, 8, 52 3, 122, 150, 201, 231, 234, 250, 254, 295
   Alfredo di Stefano, praise from, 287
   birth and early years, 46 7
   cat called 'Wembley' for girlfriend, 240 41
   Celtic signing for, 47 8
   Celtic's 'Greatest Ever Team,' inclusion in, 288
   England-Scotland (15th April 1967), matchday prelims, 205, 206, 209, 210
   England-Scotland (15th April 1967) participation, 214 15, 217, 218, 221 2, 224 5
   home to Salcoats after win, Kathryn and a cat called 'Wembley,' 240 41
   international career of, 302
   pace and skill to trouble Cohen, 142
   pre-match odds on scoring (Wembley 1967), 202
   Prentice, Macdonald and, overlooked by Scotland by

INDEX

both, 49 50
recall to Scotland at last for (November 1966), 50 51
Scotland call-up for, 48 9
Scottish Football Hall of Fame inductee, 287 8
Stein a huge fan, 48
what happened next for, 287 8
Leslie, George, 104, 259
Leslie, Jeanette (Lawrie's wife), 79
Leslie, Lawrie, 74, 75, 79
Liberal Democrat Party, 265 6, 267, 268
Lichtenstein, 273
Liddell, Billy, 236
Liddell, Ned, 57
Lincoln City, 285
Lindsay, Isobel, 260
Linfield, 43 4
Liverpool Daily Post, 98
Liverpool FC, 9, 61, 93, 94, 120, 180 81
London County Council (LCC), 56
Lorenzo, Juan Carlos, 68
Lorimer, Peter, 159
Low, John ('Ludo'), 272 6
return to Wembley (2017) for 50th anniversary of 'World Cup' win, 275 6
Wembley 1967 experiences, 273 5
Lunsden, Jimmy, 159
Luton Town, 61
Luxembourg, 294

M

MacCormick, John, 111 12
Macdonald, Ian, 114
Macdonald, Malky, 11, 41, 45, 50 51, 185
MacDonald, Norman, 95, 237, 251
Mackay, Dave, 25, 75, 78, 81, 92, 123, 234
Manchester City, xviii xix, 40, 51, 59, 81, 151
Manchester Guardian, 16
Manchester United, xviii, xx xxi, 45, 62, 102, 119, 132, 141, 155, 179, 182 3
'Busby Babes' at, 39
Denis Law's signing for, 40 41
Ferguson's 'Class of 92' at, 162
'Holy Trinity' frontline at, 280
Machiavellian maestro George Best at, 43, 51
Munich air disaster (1958), 40
victory over Benfica (European Cup 1968), 280
Mannion, Wilf, 97
Mansour, Mustafa, 86
Maradona, Diego, 125
Marsh, Rodney, 71
Martin, Bill, 207
Martin, Fred, 80
Marvin Hinton, 162
Masopust, Josef, 145
Matthews, Sir Stanley, 56, 96 7, 143
Ballon d'Or winner (1956), xviii
Mazzola, Sandro, 285
Mbappé, Kylian, 119
McBrearty, Richard, 24 5
McBride, Joe, 41 2, 46, 51, 52, 53, 121 2, 142, 189
McCalliog, Debbie (wife of Jim), 285
McCalliog, Jim, 93, 94, 122, 176, 182, 202, 228, 233, 245, 255, 295
birth and early years, 156
Chelsea, ups and downs at, 162 4

Docherty and, 153 6
England-Scotland (15th April 1967), matchday prelims, 205, 208
England-Scotland (15th April 1967) participation, 218, 219, 221, 222, 224, 225
European Cup, Hampden 1960, catalyst for, 157 8
European Cup final at Hampden (1960), effect on, 157 8
FA Cup final against Everton for (1966), 165
family life in Gorbals Glasgow, 156
football daft, 157
football daft, typical Gorbals kid, 157
injuries, toll on, 285
international call-up, talk of, 165 6
international career of, 301
Irish FA calling, 166
Leeds United come calling, 158 61
perfect man for the job, Brown's view on, 143 4
schoolboy caps for Scotland, 158
Scotland eligibility and Dad's advice for, 166 7
Scotland schoolboys cap for, 158
Sheffield Wednesday, move to, 164 5
what happened next for, 284 5
World Cup 1966, holiday in Marbella for, 165
McCalliog, Mary (Jim's mother), 153, 156, 159, 161, 199 200
McCann, Bert, 81
McCann, Johnny, 74
McCartney, Paul, 199
McColl, Ian, 6, 74 5, 78, 80, 185
McColl, Robert Smyth, 171
McConnell, Jack, 265
McCrae, Walter, 49, 184, 185, 186, 208, 241
McCreadie, Eddie, 8, 122, 139, 162, 201, 245, 295
England-Scotland (15th April 1967), matchday prelims, 210, 211
England-Scotland (15th April 1967) participation, 216, 219, 220, 222
international career of, 301
what happened next for, 283
McDowall, Les, 81
McDowell, John Kevan, 112
McFaul, Willie, 43
McGhee, Frank, 95
McGowan, Walter, 259
McGrory, Jimmy, 47 8, 169
McIlvanney, Hugh, xiii, 76, 142, 289
McIntyre, Robert, 113, 260
McKinnon, Ron, 50, 122 3, 133, 141, 233, 241, 245, 248, 249, 279, 295
defensive reliability, unflappable and uncompromising, 138 9
England-Scotland (15th April 1967), matchday prelims, 207
England-Scotland (15th April 1967) participation, 214, 217, 219, 222
international career of, 301
what happened next for, 283 4
McKinstry, Leo, 62, 289
McLean, Tommy, 93, 94 5, 122, 188
McLeod, John, 74
McLintock, Frank, 122 3, 144, 190 91
McMillan, Ian, 157
McMillan, Malcolm, 262
McMillan, Sam, 74
McMillan, Tommy, 93, 94
McMullen, Jimmy ('Wembley Wizard 1928'), 169, 170, 172

McNaught, Willie, 127, 128
McNeil, Mick, 74
McNeill, Billy, 74, 79, 81, 99, 101, 122, 135 6, 139, 146, 250, 281
   praise for Denis Law from, 281
McNeill, Malcolm, 114
McNiven, Tom, 184, 185 6, 208
McPhail, Bob, 169
McRae, Alan, 295
McStay, Willie, 169
Mears, Brian, 283
Medved, Ferenc, 248
Meiklejohn, Davie, 169
Meisl, Hugo, 28
Metropolitan Police, 235 6
Mexico, 67, 120, 273
Middlesborough FC, 124
Milburn brothers, 117
Miller, Tom, 133
Mitchell, John, 93
Mitropa Cup, 28 9
Montgomery, Jimmy, 93, 94
Mooney, Harry, 147
Moore, Bobby (later Sir Bobby), 42 3, 55, 66 7, 69 70, 71, 97, 117 18, 209, 210, 211, 250, 273
   England-Scotland (15th April 1967) participation, 216, 218, 221, 225, 226
Moorhouse, Bob, xii xiii
Mora, Bruno, 49
Morten, Alec, 14
Morton, Alan ('Wembley Wizard 1928'), 170, 171 2
Motherwell, by-election at (1945), 112 13
Motherwell FC, 74, 121
Mudie, Jack, 63
Muirton Park, Perth, 88
Mulgrew, Charlie, 271
Munich air disaster (1958), 25, 40, 119
Murdoch, Bobby, 50 51, 52, 124

N
FC Nantes, 142
FC Napoli, 40
Nasazzi, José, 20
National Association for the Vindication of Scottish Rights (1853), 110 11
national identity, rivalry as bedrock of, xiii xiv
National Party of Scotland (NPS), 112
Neal, Phil, 285
Neill, Terry, 51, 53
Nelson, Hugh, 89 90, 230, 243
Nelson, James ('Wembley Wizard 1928'), 171
Netherlands, 3, 20, 29, 50, 92, 124
New York FC, 11
Newcastle United, 60, 94, 147, 151, 170
Newport County, 59
News Chronicle, 212
Newton, Keith, 97, 100, 120
Nicholson, Bill, 61, 62
Nicholson, Jimmy, 249
Nicholson, Johnny, 51, 52
Nine Years' War, 108
'Ninety Minute Patriots: Scottish Sport in the Making of the Nation' (Jarvie, G. and Walker, G.), 102
Ninian Park, 41, 50
Niven, George, 87

North American Soccer League (NASL), 1 2, 3, 283, 285, 287
North of Scotland Hydro Electric Board, 258
Northern Ireland, 22, 30, 31, 39, 42 3, 50, 51 3, 130, 132, 142, 249
   see also British Home Championship results (1966/67)
Nottingham Forest, 94, 132, 277
Notts County, 39

O
O'Kane, Liam, 286
Old Carthusians, 17
Olympic Games, 18 22
   Antwerp Olympics (1920), 19, 22
   London Olympics (1908), 18 19, 21 2
   London Olympics (1948), 147
   Los Angeles Olympics (1932), 22
   Paris Olympics (1900), 18
   Paris Olympics (1924), 19 20
   St Louis Olympics (1904), 18
   Stockholm Olympics (1912), 19, 22
Ormond, Willie, 255 6
Osorio, Rodolfo Pérez, 254
O'Sullivan, Peter ('Voice of Racing'), 168 9
Ottaway, Cuthbert, 15
The Oval, 12, 16
Overath, Wolfgang, xxiii
Owen, Michael, 292
Oxford University, 15
Oxlade-Chamberlain, Alex, 270

P
Paine, Terry, 138
Palmerston Park, 272
Paraguay, 19, 25
Parke, John, 51
Partick Thistle, 45, 93, 130, 286
Partizan Belgrade, xviii
Pascutti, Ezio, 49
Paterson, William, 106 8
Peacock, Bertie, 43, 50, 51, 52
Pelé, 118, 123, 141, 206, 279
Penman, Andy, 189
The People, 236
Peter Bonetti, 162
Peters, Martin, 43, 119, 231, 236 7, 250, 288
   England-Scotland (15th April 1967) participation, 216, 220, 221
Petrone, Pedro ('Peruchito'), 20 21
Philip IV of France, 106
Phillips, Ted, 65
Piccadilly Circus, 235
Pittodrie Stadium, 36
Plaid Cymru, 114, 115
Plymouth Argyle, 59, 86
Poland, 48, 122
Polland, Willie, 127
Pollok by-election in Glasgow, 103 4, 257, 259
Ponedelnik, Viktor, 29
Poortvliet, Jan, 273
Porter, Dilwyn, xii
Portsmouth FC, 57, 86
Portugal, xviii, 3, 50, 69, 117, 120, 134
Possilpark YMCA, 198
Prentice, John, 1 2, 3, 4 7, 10, 11, 31, 49, 89, 189 90, 197
The Press & Journal, 95, 201, 251

INDEX

Preston North End, 65, 172
Proscription, Act of (1746), 110
Pullen, Fred, 242
Puskás, Ferenc, 63, 132, 157

Q

Qatar World Cup, 294
Queen of the South, 272
Queens Club in Glasgow, 134
Queen's Hotel in Largs, 184
Queen's Park, 13, 14, 86, 87, 100, 144, 147
  Recreation Ground at Crosshill, 14
Quinn, Pat, 74 5

R

Racing Club of Argentina, 254
Racing Post, 126
Raith Rovers, 73, 125, 127, 189, 190
Ramsey, Albert, 56
Ramsey, Sir Alf, xviii, xx, 2, 10, 32, 180, 184, 189, 245, 250, 252
  antecedents and early life, 56 7
  Brazil, Southampton tour to, 60 61
  Brown, failure of attempt to engage with, 234
  Brown, grim post-match hand-shake for, 229
  captain of England against Wales and Yugoslavia (1950), 62
  Dagenham Co-op and, 57, 59
  death of (1999), 290
  England debut against Switzerland (1948), 61
  England manager, appointment as, 66 7
  England squad in Switzerland and Italy, personal milestone for, 60
  England-Scotland (15th April 1967) game, comments on, 214, 216, 219, 223, 227
  English Football Hall of Fame inductee, 290
  enigmatic nature of, 71 2
  final (of 32) England appearances, Hungary (1952), 63
  football 'Svengali,' 70
  'The General' nickname for, 62
  'greatest football manager of all time,' 290
  Ipswich Town, management at, 64 5
  juggernaught of, invincibility of, 165
  knighthood for, 55 6, 70 71
  life beyond football, retirement and planning for, 63 4
  magnanimous in defeat, 95
  Moore named as England captain by, 66 7
  Palestine deployment, 59
  'player who thinks football, talks football and lives football,' 60
  press savagery after Wembley loss for, 236 7
  sacking of, shockwaves from, 289
  selection problems for (March 1967), 97 101
  selection problems for Under-23 side (1961), 93 4
  SFA, effect of Ramsey's World Cup win on, 3, 7 8
  shrewd and meticulous management by, 53 4
  'SOCCER MIRACLE' at Ipswich for, 65 6
  Southampton and pro football, 58 61
  Southampton and pro football for, 58 60, 72
  Southern Rhodesia, coaching in, 64
  starting XI selection April 1967, fierce and formidable, 116 17
  straightforwardness of, 72
  Tottenham Hotspur, transfer to (and success at), 61 3
  Villa Park blunder for (FA Cup semi-final1953), 63

  wartime experience, 57 8
  Wembley win, personal reason for wanting, 192 3
  what happened next for, 288 90
  Windsor Park, first hurrah as world champion for, 42 4
  World Cup 1966, focus on, 67
  World Cup 1966, reality of challenge in, 67 70
Rangers, 11, 121, 124, 128, 130, 134, 138, 139, 158, 188
  Bobby Brown at, 87 8
  Brown's Old Firm choices for Scotland, 99 100, 122
  Celtic and, bitter rivalry between, 45, 48
  European Cup Winners' Cip tie against Real Zaragoza, 93
  European Cup Winners' Cup final, Fiorentina in, 130
  Haffey, Rangers supporters on, 77
  Jim Baxter's transfer to, 125
  season 1962-63, imperious start for, 130 31
  treble winning campaign (1948/49), 87
Rapid Vienna, 132 3
Raploch Hearts, 85
Rattín, Antonio, 69
Real Madrid, 25, 41, 134, 157 8
Real Zaragoza, 93
Reaney, Paul, 93, 94
Red Star Bratislava, 128
Reformation, 106
Regent Palace Hotel in London, 170
Reid, Tom, 4, 6, 42, 196, 253
Renny-Tailyour, Henry, 14, 16
Republic of Ireland, 30, 51, 63, 80
Revie, Don, 7, 10, 103, 131, 158 62, 161 2, 184
Reynolds, Harry, 161
Richards, Sir Joseph, 56
Rimet, Jules, 21
Ring, Tommy, 157
Ritchie, Billy, 204
Ritchie, Sergeant Bob, 129 30
Robertson, Andy, 270
Robertson, Archie, 25, 157
Robson, Barry, 135
Robson, Bryan, 94
Robson, Sir Bobby, 74 5, 78, 80, 281
  praise for Denis Law from, 281
Rodger, Jim, 161
Ron Harris, 162
Rooney, Bob, 187, 241
Rooney, Wayne, 270, 292
Ross, Willie, 253
Ross County, 286
Rous, Sir Stanley, 56
Rowe, Arthur, 61 2, 64
Royal Antwerp FC, 18
Royal Engineers, 14
Rudd, Chris (Threave Rovers player), 273
Rvans, Gwynfor, 260

S

Sadler, David, 94
Salmond, Alex, 263, 265, 266, 267, 270
San Marino, 273, 294
Santos, Beniamino, 40
Saunders, Donald, 236
Saurez, Luis, 40, 41
Schiaffino, Juan Alberto, 24
Schmeichel, Peter, 78
Scholes, Paul, 264, 292
Schulenburg, Gerhard, 209

England-Scotland (15th April 1967) referee, 213, 218, 221, 226
Scotland, 22, 29, 31 2, 48 9, 52 3, 91 2, 92 5, 117, 130, 132, 134, 193
  'Auld Enemy' (England), importance for Scots of victory against, xiv
  British Home Championship 1928, 169 74
  defeat of England (6-1), Kenniongton Oval (1881), 172
  England, 3-4 defeat at Hampden by (April 1966), 138
  England defeat 3-9 at Wembley (1961), 74 82, 102
  England-Scotland, first formal match between (1872), xii, 12, 13 16
  England-Scotland, World Cup qualifying at Hampden (2018), 295
  England-Scotland fixtures, effects of early success of, 16 17
  England-Scotland matches, results 1872-2021, 303 6
  European Championship finals, failures in group stages at, 256
  hope for, binding and blinding nature of, 256
  Inter-League matches between England and, 96 101, 102 3
  Labour Perty in, 104, 114 15, 199, 257 60, 262, 264 5
  management of, bickering about, 1 11
  Scotland-England friendly? (Celtic Park 2014), 270 71
  Sweden, 1958 World Cup in, 25 6
  wartime internationals, 87
  World Cup finals, failures in group stages at, 256
  World Cup qualification, issue for, 23 5
  World Cup qualification, near misses for (1962 and 1966), 26
  see also British Home Championship results (1966/67)
Scotland Act (2012), 266
Scotland Act (1978), Scottish Parliament and, 261 2, 264
Scotland Yard, 235 6
Scots Independent, 111
Scots National League (SNL), 111, 112
Scots National Movement, 112
The Scotsman, 13
Scottish Command, 130
Scottish Cup, 2, 48, 100, 142
Scottish *Daily Express*, 161
Scottish Football Association (SFA), 2, 34, 154, 191, 196 7, 230, 253, 295
  Bobby Brown, appointment as manager by, 83, 89 90
  Bobby Brown, recognition from, 243 4
  Denis Law voted Scotland's 'Most Outstanding Player' by (2003), 280 81
  Inter-Leage matches, beginnings of, 96
  international selection, refusal to include those playing outside Scotland, 101
  John Prentice and, 4 5, 31 2
  professional management, problem for, 9 11
  Ramsey's World Cup win, effect on, 3, 7 8
  SFA Council, 196
  winter game and beginnings of, 12 17
  World Cup qualification, issue for, 21 2, 23 5
Scottish Freedom of Information Commissioner, 253 4
Scottish Home Rule Association, 112
Scottish League, 196
  season 1964/65, 48
Scottish League Cup, 45, 46, 48, 138, 145, 149
Scottish League Management Committee, 98, 196
Scottish League Select XI, 46, 189
Scottish National Party (SNP), 104, 112 13, 115, 252 3, 257

  8, 258 9, 260, 262 3
  '55 Group' within, 113 14
  Holyrood majority for (2011), 265 6
  membership boost following referendum defeat, 268
  success at Westminster and Holyrood, continuation of (2017-21), 269
Scottish Nationalism, 104, 105 15
Scottish Office, establishment of (1885), 111
Scottish Parliamentary election 2007, 264 5
Scottish Parliamentary election 2011, 265 6
Scottish referendum (2014), 266 8, 270
Scottishness, xi xii, xv
Seamill Hydro, 145, 190
Sebes, Gustáv, 29
Settle, Jimmy (Bury player), 17
Shankly, Bill, 9 10, 39, 117
  'We Can Do It' interview with Ken Gallacher (1967), 175, 176 7, 178, 179 80, 180 81
Sharpe, Ivan, 172
Shaw, Dick (Threave Rovers player), 273
Shaw, Luke, 270
Shaw, Sandie, 207
Shawfield Park, 92
Shearer, Bobby, 74
Sheffield United, 93
Sheffield Wednesday, 51, 61, 65, 94, 121, 122, 143, 144, 153, 155, 182
Shepherdson, Harold, 68, 193, 214
Shilton, Peter, 116
Simon, Jacques, 68
Simpson, Jimmy (Ronnie's dad), 146, 151 2
Simpson, Ronnie, 87, 121, 143, 191, 202, 240, 245, 248, 249, 250
  Celtic's 'Greatest Ever Team,' inclusion in, 282
  England-Scotland (15th April 1967), matchday prelims, 204, 206 7
  England-Scotland (15th April 1967), post match for auld rookie, 228 9
  England-Scotland (15th April 1967) participation, 217, 219, 221, 224, 225
  footballing life, 145 51
  international career of, 300
  Jimmy Simpson, influence on, 151 2
  'Lisbon Lion,' 282
  Scottish Football Hall of Fame inductee, 282
  what happened next for, 282
Simpson's Bar in Govan, 151
Sinatra, Frank, 131
Sinn Féin, 111
Siol nan Gaidheal, 262
Skocik, Walter, 132 3
Slavia Sofia, 241
Smith, Adrian, xii
Smith, Billy, 170, 171
Smith, Bobby, 75
Smith, Davie, 100
Smith, Gilbert, 17
Smith, Jack (Wembley 'maister'), 195
Smith, James, 14
Smith, Jim, 93, 94 5
Smith, Maurice, 237
Smith, Robert, 14
Smith, Tommy, 94
Smith, 'Touchy' (Threave Rovers player), 273
Smith Dave, 124

INDEX

Smollett, Patrick, 104
South of Scotland Electricity Board, 258
Southampton FC, 63
Southend Standard, 212
Soviet Union, 28, 29 30, 247 8, 252, 277
Spain, 30, 123, 273
Spence, Ian, 148
Spence, Lewis, 112
Spillane, Mickey, 241
Sport and National Identity (Smith, A. and Porter, D.), xii
Sporting Life, 208
Sprake, Gary, 41 2
Springett, Ron, 116, 165
Springfield, Dusty, 235
St Gallen FC in Netherlands, 18
St James' Park in Newcastle, 11, 91, 121, 143
St John, Ian, 26, 39, 77 8, 292
St Johnstone, 84, 89, 124, 244
St Mirren, 11
Stadio Comunale in Florence, 252
Stanton, Pat, 93, 122, 186
Staroscik, Felix ('Starry'), 147
Stein, Jock, 2, 42, 148, 150, 185, 187, 190, 244
    Bobby Brown, best wishes for, 90
    Bobby Moore, 'should be a law against,' 118
    Celtic management, success in, 48, 49, 142, 145
    knighthood for, debacle on refusal of, 252 3, 254 5
    pits of Lanarkshire, football beginnings in, 126
    Scotland management, poisoned chalice for, 6
Stenhousemuir FC, 189, 190
Stevenson, Billy, 49
Stevenson, Robert Louis, 258
Stevenson, Sir Daniel, 112
Stewart, Donald, 262
Stewart, William Ian, 115
Stiles, Nobby, 9, 45, 68 70, 118, 123, 189, 190, 210, 229, 231
    England-Scotland (15th April 1967) participation, 216, 217, 220, 223, 225, 226
    superstition of, knitwear and, xx
Stirling Albion (formerly King's Park), 84 5, 121
Stoke City, 116, 132
Stokes, Bobby, 285
Stone Voices: The Search for Scotland (Ascherson, N.), xv
Stonehouse Violet, 185
Storey-Moore, Ian, 94
Štrunc, Stanislav, 145
Struth, Bill, 87
Stuart, Charles Edward, 109 10
Sturgeon, Nicola, 269
STV, 198
Summerbee, Mike, 250
Sunday Mail, 5, 198 9, 237
Sunday Mirror, 73
Sunday People, 65, 212
Sunday Post, 197, 237 8
Sunday Times, 253 4
Sunderland FC, 5, 51, 93, 133, 134 5, 277
Supreme Court, ruling on independence referendum (2022), 269
Surrey and Hants News, 212
Swan, Peter, 74
Swansea City, 63
Switzerland, 28
Symon, Scot, 11, 128, 129 30, 196
    Jim Baxter's lifestyle choices and, 133 4

T

Talking Football (Ramsey, A.E.), 57
Ta'Qali National Stadium, 273
Tartan Army, 272 3
    armchair regiment, 198 9
    Bow Street Court for members of, 242 3
    Rolls Royce workers from East Kilbride, 198
    'Walking to Wembley' (1967), 197
    'Wembley Wizards' detachment (1928), 170 71
Taylor, Hugh, 237
Taylor, Jack, 53
Taylor, John, 114
Taylor, Matthew, xii
Temple, Derek, 199
Terry Venables, 162
Thatcher, Margaret, 262, 263
Third Lanark, 11, 147, 157, 185
Thompson, John, 282
Thompson, Peter, 97, 100
Thompson, Sir Harold, 289
Thyne, Bob, 121
The Times, 16, 17, 77, 204
Tinney, Hugh, 93, 122
Tipperary Tim, Grand national winner (1928), 168 9
Tom McClurg Anderson's Scottish School of Physiotherapy, 185
FC Torino, 40, 46
Torquay United, 59
Tottenham Hotspur, 43, 51, 61 3, 65, 93, 102, 120, 121, 132, 192, 234
    FA Cup semi-final v Blackpool FC (1953), 63
    League and Cup double winners (1961), 123
    League champions (1951), 62
Townsend, Jim, 124
Townsend, Len, 58
Trafalgar Square, 235
Tranmere Rovers, 179
Trebilcock, Mike, 199
Turnbull, Eddie, 2, 185
Turner, Simon, 22

U

UEFA Champions League, 28
UEFA European Championship, 28
Union, Treaty of (1707), 105 6, 109
Union des Associations Européennes de Football (UEFA), 27 8, 29, 31, 91, 97, 252, 294, 295
United Crossroads Boys Club, 138
United States, 4, 20, 283
Ure, Ian, 122 3, 250
Uruguay, 19 20, 21, 24, 67, 117

V

Vancouver FC, 3, 4, 11
Venezuela, 294
Villa Park in Birmingham, 17
Vojvodina in Yugoslavia, 93

W

Waddell, Willie, 2
Wales, 10 11, 22 3, 29 31, 34, 39, 41 2, 50, 53 4, 93, 143, 249, 277
    British Home Championship 1928, 169
    see also British Home Championship results (1966/67)
Walker, Dawson, 25
Walker, Graham, 102

Walker, James, 113
Walker, Tommy, 10, 151, 173
Wall, Sir Frederick, 56
Wallace, Jock, 284
Wallace, Olive (wife) and Lynn (baby daughter), 190, 241
Wallace, William ('Willie'), 84, 90, 122, 235, 240, 241, 245, 295
   England-Scotland (15th April 1967), matchday prelims, 203, 205 6, 210 11
   England-Scotland (15th April 1967) participation, 215, 216, 217, 220, 221, 222, 225, 226
   'Hammer of Dukla,' 188 91
   international career of, 302
   'Lisbon Lion,' 286
   pre-match odds on scoring (Wenbley 1967), 202
   standout performance, swept clean of feet by fan for, 230
   what happened next for, 286 7
Walters, Sonny, 61
The Wanderers, 14, 16
Wartime League, 86
Webb, David, 283
Weekly News, 170
Weir, Andrew, 39
Welch, Reginald, 14
Wembley Stadium, 54, 171 2, 190, 193
   Argentina v England at (1951), 200
   'British Empire Exhibition Stadium,' 200
   capacity of, 200
   centrepiece for World Cup final (1966), 201
   FA Cup Final at (1923), 200
Wembley Stadium, England-Scotland (15th April 1967), xiv
   aftermath, 228 32
   Brown's pre-match address to players, 208 9
   celebrations, 233 9
   emergence of teams, 209 11
   English dressing room, post-match mood, 231 2
   ground staff at, aftermath for, 243
   John 'Ludo' Low, Scottish superfan at, 273 5
   kick off, 212 13
   limbering up for, 208
   match in detail, 212 27
   pre-match activities, 203 11
   pre-match entertainment, 207
   pre-match odds on result, 202
   preparations for, 194 202
   Scotland's victory, seismic proportions of, 240 46
   team coach to Stadium, experiences of those on, 204 6
   victory for Scotland, seismic proportions of, 240 46
'Wembley Wizards' (1928), xiv, 101, 111 12, 168 74
   birth of, 171 2
   'Cult of Wembley,' spread of, 173
West Bromwich Albion, 5
West Germany, 29, 43, 69 70, 117, 119
West Ham United, 57, 66 7, 81, 118, 119, 178, 180
West Kilbride Golf Club, 145, 150
West of Scotland Cricket Club, 12, 13 14
West of Scotland Cup, 47
White, Desmond, 196
White Heart Lane, 192
Whyte, Jim, 93, 94
Wick Academy Football Club, 198
Williams, Graham, 42
Williamson, Peter, 235
Wills, Ron, 70 71
Wilson, Alex, 259

Wilson, Davy, 75 6, 157
Wilson, Gordon, 263
Wilson, Harold, 104, 115, 253, 255, 260 61
Wilson, Jimmy, 100, 122
Wilson, Ray, xxi, xxii, 67, 117
   England-Scotland (15th April 1967) participation, 215, 216, 217, 220
Wilson, Sammy, 51, 52
Wilson, Thomas, 170
Wilson Davie, 134
Windsor Park, Belfast, 42 3, 173, 249
Winterbottom, Walter, 66, 73
Wolfe, William, 114 15
Wolstenholme, Kenneth, xxiii, 34, 212
Wolverhampton Wanderers, 213
Wood, Tony, 277
World Cup, 10
World Cup (1930), 21, 22
World Cup (1950), 23, 31
World Cup (1954), 23, 63
World Cup (1958), 25, 39
World Cup (1962), 26, 30, 66, 79, 80, 116, 117
World Cup (1966), xv, xviii, 3, 6, 10, 26, 31, 117 21, 193, 248, 253, 258
   England's route to final, optimism and, xxii
   England's win, brushing aside all comers, 165, 189
   final day, Bobby Charlton's pre-match activities (and thoughts), xx xxi, xxii, xxiii
   final day, Denis Law and, xvii xviii, xix xx
   final day, excitement on emergence of players, xxiii
   Ramsey's focus on, 67
   Scotland's failure to qualify for, 48 9
   Wolstenholme's commentary on final, 212 13
World Cup (1970), 4, 9, 239, 242
   Scottish failure to quality for, 255
World Cup (1974), 273
   Scottish reinvention of glorious failure in, 255 6
World Cup (1978), 273
World Cup (1986), 273
World Cup (1998), 263 4
World Cup (2018), 273
Wright, Billy, 23
   England-Scotland (15th April 1967) commentary, 213, 214, 216 17, 222, 225 6
Wright, Esmond, 104
Wright, Wright, 64

Y

Yashin, Lev ('Black Spider'), 40, 132, 146, 248
Yates, Horace, 98
Yorston, Henry, 36, 37
Young, Alex, 39, 92
Young, Andy, 127
Young, George, 11, 242
Yugoslavia, 20, 25, 28, 29 30, 252, 255 6

Z

Zaire, 255
FC Zürich, 45